53-

THE VOLATILITY EDGE
IN OPTIONS TRADING

THE VOLATILITY EDGE IN OPTIONS TRADING

NEW TECHNICAL STRATEGIES FOR INVESTING IN UNSTABLE MARKETS

Jeff Augen

Vice President, Publisher: Tim Moore
Associate Publisher and Director of Marketing: Amy Neidlinger
Executive Editor: Jim Boyd
Editorial Assistant: Pamela Boland
Digital Marketing Manager: Julie Phifer
Marketing Coordinator: Megan Colvin
Cover Designer: Chuti Prasertsith
Managing Editor: Gina Kanouse
Project Editor: Anne Goebel
Copy Editor: Gayle Johnson
Proofreader: Williams Woods Publishing Services, LLC
Indexer: WordWise Publishing Services
Senior Compositor: Gloria Schurick
Manufacturing Buyer: Dan Uhrig

www.ftpress.com

FT Press offers excellent discounts on this book when ordered in quantity for bulk
purchases or special sales. For more information, please contact U.S. Corporate and
Government Sales at 1-800-382-3419, corpsales@pearsontechgroup.com. For sales
outside the U.S., please contact International Sales at international@pearsoned.com.

Printed in the United States of America
Fourth Printing July 2009
ISBN-10: 0-13-235469-1
ISBN-13: 978-0-13-235469-1

Pearson Education Ltd.
Pearson Education Australia PTY, Limited.
Pearson Education Singapore, Pte. Ltd.
Pearson Education North Asia, Ltd.
Pearson Education Canada, Ltd.
Pearson Educatiòn de Mexico, S.A. de C.V.
Pearson Education—Japan
Pearson Education Malaysia, Pte. Ltd.

Augen, Jeffrey.
   The volatility edge in options trading : new technical strategies for investing in
unstable markets / Jeff Augen.
      p. cm.
   Includes bibliographical references.
   ISBN 0-13-235469-1 (hardback : alk. paper) 1. Options (Finance) 2. Investment
analysis. 3. Securities—Prices. 4. Stock price forecasting. I. Title.
   HG6024.A3A923 2008
   332.63'2283—dc22
                          2007026094

To Lisa, whose kindheartedness and unending patience rescued me from oblivion.

CONTENTS

ACKNOWLEDGMENTS

I would like to thank the team who helped pull the book together. First and foremost is Jim Boyd, who provided sound advice that, among other things, resulted in a guide for readers and improved flow and readability throughout. That said, Anne Goebel, who carefully read every word and made final decisions about phraseology, and Gayle Johnson, who edited the original text, provided a critical eye that an author can never have for his own work. Likewise, Dr. Edward Olmstead was the driving force behind the expansion of several sections that improved overall clarity and made the book accessible to a larger audience. The options trading world is expanding at a remarkable rate, and investors are becoming more sophisticated with each financial event. Adding value to their efforts has been our principal goal.

ABOUT THE AUTHOR

J eff Augen, currently a private investor and writer, has spent more than a decade building a unique intellectual property portfolio of algorithms and software for technical analysis of derivatives prices. His work includes more than one million lines of computer code reflecting powerful new strategies for trading equity, index, and futures options.

Augen has a 25-year history in information technology. As a co-founding executive of IBM's Life Sciences Computing business, he defined a growth strategy that resulted in $1.2 billion of new revenue, and he managed a large portfolio of venture capital investments. From 2002 to 2005, Augen was President and CEO of TurboWorx, Inc., a technical computing software company founded by the chairman of the Department of Computer Science at Yale University. He is author of *Bioinformatics in the Post-Genomic Era: Genome, Transcriptome, Proteome, and Information-Based Medicine* (Addison-Wesley, 2004). Much of his current work on options pricing is built on algorithms for predicting molecular structures that he developed as a graduate student.

PREFACE

This book is written for experienced equity and index option traders who are interested in exploring new technical strategies and analytical techniques. Many fine texts have been written on the subject, each targeted at a different level of technical proficiency. They range from overviews of basic options positions to graduate-level reviews of option pricing theory. Some focus on a single strategy, and others are broad-based. Not surprisingly, many fall into the "get rich quick" category. Generally speaking, books that focus on trading are light on pricing theory, and books that thoroughly cover pricing theory usually are not intended as a trading guide.

This book is designed to bridge the gap by marrying pricing theory to the realities of the market. Our discussion will include many topics not covered elsewhere:

- Strategies for trading the monthly options expiration cycle
- The effects of earnings announcements on options volatility and pricing
- The complex relationship between market drawdowns, volatility, and disruptions to put-call parity
- Weekend/end-of-month effects on bid-ask spreads and volatility

A cornerstone of our discussion will be a new set of analytical tools designed to classify equities according to their historic price-change behavior. I have successfully used these tools to trade accounts as small as $80,000 and as large as $20M.

Ten years ago, having studied the markets for some time, I believed I could be a part-time investor with a full-time professional career. At the time I was a computer-industry executive—a director at IBM—with a large compensation package and a promising future. My goal was to develop a successful trading strategy that could be implemented as an income supplement. It was a naïve idea. Successful investing is a demanding pursuit. The work described in this book took more than ten years. It involved writing hundreds of thousands of lines of computer code, constructing numerous financial-history databases, creating new data visualization tools, and, most important, executing more than 3,000 trades. During that time I also read dozens of books and thousands of technical articles on economic theory, technical analysis, and derivatives trading. The most important result was not the trading system itself, but the revelation that nothing short of full-time effort could possibly succeed. The financial industry is populated with bright, hard-working, well-educated professionals who devote every waking hour to making money. Moreover, there is virtually no limit to the funds that can be made available to hire outstanding talent. An amateur investor should not expect to compete with these professionals in his or her spare time. The market is a zero-sum game—every dollar won must also be lost. Option trading represents the winner-take-all version of the game. Consistently making money requires focus and dedication. That said, experienced private investors often have a distinct advantage over large institutions in the equity options world. The advantage relates to scale. A private investor trading electronically can instantly open or close typical positions consisting of tens or even hundreds of option contracts. Conversely, institutions often manage very large positions worth hundreds of millions of dollars. Efficient execution becomes a barrier at this level. Furthermore, many equity option issues do not have enough open interest to support trades of this size. The result is that institutional traders tend to focus on index options— which are much more liquid—and some of the more heavily traded equity options. Large positions take time to negotiate and price. They have an element of permanence because they can't be unwound with the press of a button. Liquidity and scaling are central to this work, and we will return to this discussion many times in the context of trading logistics.

Generally speaking, the work is not done—not even close. But I've come a long way. Today I can comfortably generate a return that would make any investment bank or hedge fund proud. Needless to say, I no longer work in the computer industry, and I have no interest in a salary. I'm free. My time belongs to me. I trade for a living.

A GUIDE FOR READERS

This book introduces a charting technique that is designed to help option traders visualize price change behavior. Although the form is new, the underlying mathematics are that of standard option-pricing theory. Many of the charts presented in this book contain a series of bars that measure individual price changes in standard deviations against a sliding window of predetermined length. The exact method for creating these charts is described in the "Profiling Price Change Behavior" section of Chapter 3. All the charts presented were created using standard Microsoft desktop tools and readily available data sources. If you subscribe to a data service and you want to create charts of the same form, you will find that Excel's statistical analysis and charting functions support these efforts very efficiently and that no programming is necessary.

Many readers who are familiar with the Microsoft Office environment will also want to construct a database containing historical price change information and volatility calculations for thousands of securities and indexes. For the present work, price and volume information was downloaded to a Microsoft Access database from a variety of readily available public and subscription-based data services. A large number of calculations were generated across the dataset and results for individual tickers were exported to Microsoft Excel, where the charts were created. The complete infrastructure is described in Chapter 9.

Just a few years ago desktop computers lacked the capacity and performance to support the work described in this book. Recent improvements in these machines' size and performance have significantly reduced the complexity of such work. The change has been dramatic. Today's multigigahertz multicore CPU desktop computers often come equipped with 3 gigabytes or more of memory and hundreds of gigabytes of disk storage. Microsoft desktop products such as Excel, Access, and Visual Basic provide all the necessary tools to build an infrastructure for managing millions of stock records on such a machine. These changes have been a welcome advance for those of us who previously programmed exclusively in C and C++ and struggled with the complexity and expense associated with a large computing infrastructure.

If you want to replicate the database system described in Chapter 9, you will discover that Microsoft Access can support relatively large designs. Most programmers will find the performance of the VBA programming language to be quite acceptable. The actual design includes a large number of Access VBA programs, macros, and SQL queries in addition to modeling tools written in Excel VBA.

Finally, the past few years have witnessed a leveling of the playing field in the sense that a serious private investor can, at reasonable cost, obtain all the tools necessary to build a sophisticated infrastructure. Information sources such as Bloomberg provide a robust set of programming interfaces for capturing and analyzing tick-by-tick data. They can become the content source for custom databases built with Microsoft SQL Server, Oracle, or IBM DB2, whose single-user versions are relatively inexpensive. Depending on the size, such systems can run on a single desktop computer or a cluster of machines linked with publicly available free Linux software. Five years ago this level of computing infrastructure was available only to financial institutions. Today, hundreds of thousands of private investors and small hedge funds are developing customized data mining and analysis tools as part of their effort to gain a technical edge in the market. This trend has become a dominant force in the investment world.

This book begins with an introduction to pricing theory and volatility before progressing through a series of increasingly complex types of structured trades.

The chapters are designed to be read in sequence. No particular technical background is required if you start at the beginning. However, you might find value in reading them in a different order. The following table will help you. It relates the level of technical background that is most appropriate for the subject matter presented. The two categories are option trading experience (Opt) and computer software skills (Comp):

Opt 1: No prior knowledge of pricing theory or structured positions.

Opt 2: Some familiarity with option pricing and basic trades.

Opt 3: Familiarity with option pricing concepts, including the effects of time decay and delta. Experience with structuring option positions.

Comp 1: Familiarity with basic software tools such as Microsoft Excel.

Comp 2: Experience using trading tools such as stock-charting software.

Comp 3: Experience building customized spreadsheets and moving data between software packages. The ability to download and use data from a subscription service. Familiarity with basic database concepts.

	Comp 1	Comp 2	Comp 3
Opt 1	Chapters 1, 2, and 3		
Opt 2		Chapters 4 and 5	
Opt 3		Chapters 6, 7, and 8	Chapter 9

If you plan to study the chapters out of sequence, you should become familiar with the method for creating price spike charts that is outlined in Chapter 3. Because these charts are used throughout the book, it will be helpful for you to understand how they are calculated. Chapter 3 also includes a related discussion of variable-length volatility windows that will be helpful to most option traders. It builds on the discussion of pricing theory presented in Chapter 2.

Chapter 4 contains practical trading information that is often lost to oversimplification. Many authors have written about complex trades without mentioning the effects of bid-ask spreads, volatility swings, put-call parity violations, term structure, and changes in liquidity. Chapter 4 also discusses price distortions generated by earnings and options expiration—topics that are covered in greater detail in Chapters 7 and 8. We close with a discussion of the level II trading queue, which is now available to all public customers. Chapter 4 is meant to stand alone and can be read out of sequence if you're an experienced trader who understands the basics of pricing.

Chapters 5 and 6 present a broad review of structured positions. Beginners will learn to create mathematically sound trades using a variety of pricing strategies. Advanced traders who are already familiar with the material will find the approach unique. Particularly important are the discussions of dynamic position management and the use of price spikes as trade triggers. Price-spike charts of the form presented in Chapter 3 are used throughout. Chapter 6 also includes an analysis of the VIX as a hedging vehicle—a topic that has recently come sharply into focus on Wall Street.

Chapters 7 and 8 present new information not found anywhere else. The strategies revealed in these discussions leverage price distortions that are normally associated with earnings and options expiration. They are tailored to investors seeking substantial returns with limited market exposure. The focus, as always, is practical trading. Chapter 8 also includes a review of the "stock pinning" phenomenon that has become the driving force behind the expiration day behavior of many securities. Some investors exposed to these methodologies have found that they can generate a substantial return on expiration day and remain out of the market the rest of the month.

Chapter 9 was written for the large and growing population of traders who want to optimize their use of online data services. The database infrastructure described in this chapter was built using the Microsoft desktop tools and databases mentioned previously. Detailed descriptions of the tables and data flows are included, and the layout is modular so that you may replicate the portions that best fit your needs. Investors who are primarily interested in bond, currency, future, or stock trading will also find value in the design elements presented in this chapter.

1

INTRODUCTION

On October 27, 1997, the Dow Jones Industrial Average (DJIA) fell a breathtaking 554 points, or 7.2%, to close at 7161. This massive collapse represented the largest absolute point decline in the history of the index and the tenth-largest percent loss since 1915. That evening, the financial news featured a parade of experts, each prepared to explain exactly what had happened and why. Despite the confusion, they all seemed to have two things in common: their failure to predict the drawdown before it happened, and their prediction that the next day would be worse. They were dead wrong. The next day the market resumed its decline before rallying sharply to close up 337 points (4.7%) on then-record volumes of over a billion shares. The experts were back that evening to explain why. Such is always the case with market analysts—they tend to be short on accurate predictions and long on after-the-fact analysis.

October 27 was also the first time that the cross-market trading halt circuit-breaker procedures had been used since their adoption in 1988. By 2:36 p.m., the DJIA had declined 350 points, triggering a 30-minute halt to the stock, options, and index futures markets. After trading resumed at 3:06 p.m., prices fell rapidly until they reached the 550-point circuit-breaker level, causing the trading session to end 30 minutes early. The Division of Market Regulation of the Securities and Exchange Commission launched an investigation to reconstruct the events of these two days and to review the effects of the circuit breakers on the velocity of price movements. The study concluded that the sell-off was prompted by concerns over the potential impact on U.S. corporate earnings of the growing market turmoil in Asia and repercussions from the potential economic slowdown and deflationary pressures. The Asian market turmoil evidently caused a number of institutional and professional traders to attempt to reduce their equity exposure or increase their hedges in the U.S. markets, either directly through stock sales or indirectly through trades in futures. When the sell-off reduced U.S. stock prices to attractive levels on the morning of October 28, a broad-based buying trend emerged to support a strong rebound in share prices.

As significant as it might have seemed at the time, this one-day 554-point decline is nearly invisible in the relentless march that took the Dow from 828 in March 1982 to 11,750 in January 2000. However, the October 1997 drawdown was important for many reasons. Most important among these was the lesson that all bubbles eventually burst. In this case the bubble was caused by a huge influx of foreign money into Asian markets that lasted for a decade and resulted in a credit crisis. Moreover, the ripple effect clearly demonstrated the importance of balanced trade between regions and the risks implied by deficits and surpluses. It also signaled the beginning of a hyper growth era that lasted for three years and nearly doubled the value of the U.S. equity markets.

My goal was to develop an investment strategy based on the fundamental mathematical properties that describe financial markets. Properly executed, such a strategy should provide excellent returns in a variety of market conditions. It should also be persistent in the sense that it transcends short-term trends. A perfect strategy would embody risk-management mechanisms that allow an investor to precisely calculate the expected return and worst-case loss for a given set of trades. Finally, and most important, a successful strategy should not depend in any way on personal opinion. As we shall see, the strategies that ultimately emerged from this work involve trading positions without regard to underlying financial assumptions about the performance of any particular company, index, or industry.

The work was enormously complex and time-consuming, because there was much less scientific analysis to build on than I had expected.

Unfortunately, the financial world has chosen to substitute careful scientific analysis with something far less precise—the opinions of financial analysts. These analysts are the same "experts" who have failed to forecast every major equity market drawdown in history. Most often their analyses are based on untested relationships, infrequent events, or both. It is easy to point to the last time interest rates rose by a certain percentage or oil prices fell more than a certain amount, but it is impossible to compare the effects of hundreds of such events. The modern era, characterized by electronic trading of equities, futures, options, fixed-income securities, and currencies is simply not old enough.

A significant example of the problem occurred at the very moment these words were being written. The Chairman of the U.S. Federal Reserve, the largest central bank on Earth, declared publicly that he could not explain why the yield on ten-year treasury notes had fallen 80 basis points during a time frame marked by eight consecutive quarter-point increases in the Federal Funds rate (the interest rate charged on overnight loans between banks). He used the word "conundrum" to describe the phenomenon that continued, to the surprise of many, for another year as rates continued rising.

Unfortunately, the lack of well-defined mathematical models that describe the world's economy is more than an academic problem. In June 2005, for example, GLG Partners, the largest hedge fund in Europe, admitted that flaws in the mathematical model it used to price complex credit derivative products caused a 14.5% drop in its Credit Fund over the span of a single month. Unfortunately, the model did not comprehend the tremendous market swings that followed ratings downgrades of General Motors and Ford. The problem arose because risk simulations based on historic data were blind to moves of this magnitude. The fund sent letters to all investors, assuring them that the model had been fixed. Such destruction of wealth is not nearly as rare as you might imagine because even the best financial models can be confounded by news. During the past several years, many billions of dollars have been lost in self-destructing hedge funds with faulty trading models. The risk is enormous. The U.S. gross domestic product (GDP) is approximately $13 trillion, the world's GDP is $48 trillion, and the world's derivatives markets are generally estimated to be worth more than $300 trillion. It's no longer possible to recover from a true crash.[1]

Such observations shaped my thinking, and over time my focus narrowed. Today it matters very little to me whether an individual stock rises or falls, because I am much more concerned with fundamental mathematical properties such as the shape of the curve that describes the distribution of daily price changes. Furthermore, it is often more important to have an accurate view of the potential change in a stock's implied volatility than to be able to predict short-term changes in its price. Volatility is also much easier to predict than price. This simple concept was almost lost during the great bull market of the '90s, when thousands of successful investors declared themselves geniuses as they rode a tidal wave of equity appreciation. However, those who missed (or misunderstood) the sharp rise in the implied volatilities of NASDAQ technology stocks during the second and third quarters of 2000 were putting themselves at extreme risk. Many continued to hold on to these stocks throughout the ensuing NASDAQ crash because they misinterpreted small bear market rallies as technical bottoms. These investors were repeating the mistakes of an earlier generation that was decimated during the prolonged crash that began in October 1929 and ended three years later in 1932. It has been suggested that the likelihood of a significant market crash increases with time as older investors who remember the previous crash drop out of the investment community. Very few victims of the 1929 crash were still around to invest in the NASDAQ bubble of the late 1990s.

The strategies I describe in this book are entirely focused on analyzing and trading fundamental mathematical properties of stocks and indexes. Options are the trading vehicle. Our focus is the underlying pricing models that are firmly rooted in the mathematical constructs of volatility and time. Furthermore, a reliable strategy for dynamically managing option positions has turned out to be as important as a strategy for selecting and structuring trades. Adaptive trading is a central theme of this book, and a great deal of space is devoted to discussing specific processes built on precise metrics and rules for making adjustments to complex positions. Unbiased use of these rules and a thorough understanding of the mathematical basis of option pricing are core components of this approach.

Unfortunately, few if any of today's books on option trading devote any space to this complex topic. Without these tools, an option trader simply places bets and either wins or loses with each trade. In this scenario, option trading, despite its solid mathematical foundation, is reduced to gambling. The rigorous approach that I will describe is much more difficult; fortunately, hard work and persistence usually pay off.

Not surprisingly, our discussion will focus on a precisely bounded and closely related set of option trading strategies with a great deal of rigor. Developing these strategies has revealed many inconsistencies in the models used to price options. At first it seemed counterintuitive that such inconsistencies could exist, because they amount to arbitrage opportunities, and such opportunities normally are rare in modern financial markets. Not surprisingly, brokerage houses that write option contracts are taking advantage of precisely the same opportunities on a much broader scale. Moreover, it is not surprising to find inconsistencies in a market that is barely 30 years old. The Chicago Board Options Exchange (CBOE) began trading listed call options on a scant 16 stocks on April 26, 1973. The CBOE's first home was actually a smoker's lounge at the Chicago Board of Trade. Put options were not traded until 1977. The Black-Scholes model, the underlying basis for modern option pricing, was not fully applied to the discipline until the early 1980s. Other sophisticated pricing models have also come into existence, and the CBOE recently retuned its mechanism for calculating the incredibly important volatility index (VIX). Option trading is an evolving discipline, and each new set of market conditions provides opportunities for further tuning of the system.

However, before we embark on a detailed option pricing discussion, I would like to examine the most basic assumptions about the behavior of equity markets.

Price Discovery and Market Stability

The crash of 1987 and the prolonged NASDAQ drawdown of 2000 clearly contain important but somewhat obscure information about the forces that regulate the behavior of equity markets. Three relatively simple questions come to mind:

- Why do markets crash?

- What are the stabilizing forces that end a crash?

- What, if anything, differentiates a "crash" from a typical drawdown?

The answers to these questions are rooted in the most basic assumptions about why an individual stock rises or falls. Simply stated, a stock rises when buyers are more aggressive than sellers, and it falls when sellers are more aggressive than buyers. Basic and simple as this concept might seem, many investors incorrectly believe that a stock rises if there are more buyers than sellers and falls if there are more sellers than buyers. The distinction is important. By definition there are always an equal number of buyers and sellers, because every transaction has two sides. The sole determinant of the next transaction price in any market is always the highest bid and lowest ask. When these two prices align, a transaction takes place regardless of the number of other offers to buy or sell. More precisely, the transaction takes place because an aggressive buyer raises the price that he or she is willing to pay or an aggressive seller lowers the price that he or she is willing to accept. In most markets such price adjustments take place over long periods of time; in the stock market they occur instantaneously.

Uninterrupted smooth execution of a continuous stream of transactions creates market liquidity. High levels of liquidity fuel the price discovery engine that keeps the market running. Without a price discovery mechanism, both individual stocks and the entire market would be prone to uncontrolled crashes or runaway rallies. The mechanism occasionally fails with catastrophic results. The U.S. equity market crashes of 1929, 1987, and 2000 are notable examples, as is the collapse of the Nikkei index from 38,915 in December 1989 to 14,194 in August 1992. The September 1929 crash was especially significant. The Dow Jones

Industrial Average fell from 386 in September 1929 to 40.6 in July 1932. The market did not fully recover until December 1954, when the Dow Jones Industrial Average finally rose above the September 1929 level. However, even during the prolonged crash of 1929–1932, price discovery allowed the market to plateau many times, and, in some cases, short-term rallies ensued. These rallies made the crash particularly devastating, because optimistic investors reentered the market believing that the collapse had ended. Contrary to popular belief, the largest losses were not experienced in a single one-day event. They happened over long periods of time by investors who were fooled by bear market rallies disguised as a stable rising market. Stabilization events and bear market rallies are triggered by the same price discovery mechanisms that set everyday trading prices in healthy markets. Without these mechanisms, the 1929–1932 crash would have happened in a single day.

Price Discovery Is a Chaotic Process

Surprisingly, price discovery cannot operate properly unless the market is chaotic. It must be characterized by large numbers of investors pursuing divergent strategies based on different goals and views of the market. On a microscopic scale, a particular situation might appear as follows: Investor #1, on hearing a piece of bad news, decides to sell a stock. The stock falls slightly and triggers another investor's (#2) stop-sell limit order. This new sell order causes the price to fall further. However, investor #3, who has a longer-term view of the company and believes that the stock is undervalued, has been waiting for a dip in the price. He aggressively buys a large number of shares, momentarily stabilizing the price. However, a large institutional investor with a computer program that tracks this particular stock, looking for such behavior, suddenly receives notice that a sell-short trigger has been activated. The large institutional sell order causes the stock to fall rapidly. It also triggers stop-sell limit orders from other investors who are protecting their profits. The sell-off accelerates as investors aggressively run from their positions in the stock. However, a small group of speculators who previously anticipated the bad news and sold short now begin buying the stock to cover their short sales and lock in a profit. They are using automated systems with triggers that generate a buying decision as soon as a certain profit level has been reached. The stock begins to climb again as aggressive buy-to-cover orders accumulate. As the stock climbs, short sellers begin to see their profits evaporate. They become increasingly aggressive about buying back the stock. The trend begins to slow as short sellers take themselves out of the market by unwinding positions. The price does not stabilize, however, because other investors witnessing the sudden rise and looking at particular chart patterns interpret the emerging rally as a buying opportunity and flock to purchase the stock before it runs up too much. The process continues indefinitely because price discovery is a dynamic and never-ending process.

Although it is meant as a simple illustration, this example embodies many important market drivers including program trading, short selling and buying to cover, technical charting with triggers, stop-buy and stop-sell limit orders, and a variety of complex buying and selling behaviors. If in the very first moments of the scenario every investor had made the same sell decision as investor #1, the stock would simply have plummeted. A new fair-market value would not have been discovered until a very low point had been reached. In this scenario the lack of market chaos would have caused a small drawdown to become a crash. Such events occur regularly. The size of the resulting decline is closely related to the lack of chaos exhibited just prior to the sell-off. Major crashes that begin as minor drawdowns are rare but certainly not unknown. The initial days of the '29, '87, and '00 crashes all had a distinctly nonchaotic character. So did the prolonged Nikkei crash and the general collapse of the Asian markets that occurred during the late 1990s (sometimes referred to as the Asian Miracle Bubble). Furthermore, the word "chaotic" in this context should be taken in the true mathematical sense—a system that appears random but behaves according to a well-defined set of rules. If liquidity is the fuel that powers the price discovery engine, chaos is certainly the principal ingredient in that fuel.

It is not surprising that many different types of events can affect the level of chaos exhibited by individual equities and entire markets. For example, if tomorrow morning, just before the opening bell, company X reported surprisingly strong earnings with an even more surprising outlook for the next quarter, the stock would surely rise as soon as the market opened. This effect might seem obvious, but the underlying dynamics are complex. During the first few moments of trading, new buyers would aggressively bid up the stock, but not nearly as fast as panicked short sellers trying to cover their positions. Not all short sellers, however, would be forced to cover. Some might consider the run-up to be an acceptable risk—especially if they maintain a contrary view of the company's future performance. Others might view the immediate run-up to be inflated, and at the first pullback they might sell short again. Finally, other investors who own the stock might decide to sell and realize a profit. The early-morning run-up could easily be halted by a mad rush to take profit or establish new positions on the short side at discounted prices. Such behavior almost always generates a high level of frustration for investors, who interpret the news in a straightforward way and try to make a rational buy or sell decision based on financial metrics. This is also why markets often appear confusing and unpredictable. We will return to a detailed analysis of the relationship between market chaos and equity prices, with a focus on predicting crashes and rallies (both minor and major).

Practical Limitations of Technical Charting

Equity markets are event-driven. In a highly liquid environment, investors are constantly reacting to events, news, and each other. Even the most seasoned technical analyst would concede that large unanticipated events trigger large unpredictable moves in stock prices. Like many investors, I have spent thousands of hours staring at chart patterns, trying to predict the next move of a stock or index. Sometimes it works, and sometimes it doesn't. Like any discipline, technical charting has its strengths and weaknesses. In the absence of major corrective events, stocks tend to trade within predictable ranges. Well-characterized support and resistance lines certainly have some predictive value, as do many of the more rigorous mathematical techniques. However, it would be unfair not to mention the numerous studies showing that stock picks by technical analysts tend to lag behind the leading benchmark indexes by a significant margin. In 2003, for example, the S&P 500 increased by 26% and the NASDAQ by 50%, while an imaginary portfolio built on the recommendations of an average Wall Street analyst increased by only 11%. In 79 of 81 market sectors, an investor would have outperformed the experts by simply purchasing the stocks in an index and holding them. This data suggests the importance of adopting a balanced view of technical analysis.

Operationally speaking, the stock market behaves like a school of fish. The lead fish behaves like a well-informed investor by reacting quickly to changes in the environment. The other fish react to both the environment and the direction and speed of the lead fish. In the absence of a major event, the school's behavior is somewhat predictable. However, if you drop a pebble in the water, the lead fish will suddenly change direction—and the rest of the school will almost certainly follow. Betting on the fish's direction and speed is somewhat like investing in a stock. The human eye is remarkably adept at finding patterns in charts and pictures. It is easy to be fooled by randomness. Figure 1.1 is a response to those who will undoubtedly disagree. It contains two charts. The first was created using a computer program that randomly generates the numbers 0 or 1. Each tick of the chart was created by summing 100 such numbers and dividing by a number less than 100. Changing the divisor can make the charts appear more or less volatile. The starting point was chosen at random. The second chart, the real one, is a New York Stock Exchange stock. So far I have not found a single technical analyst who can tell the difference. The reaction is always the same: "This one has a support line here and a resistance line there, this one is trending above its 50-day moving average, this one is real because it contains a well-formed breakout pattern followed by a move to a new trading level..." I have had many opportunities to show such charts to professional investors. None has ever found a reliable way to spot the fakes.

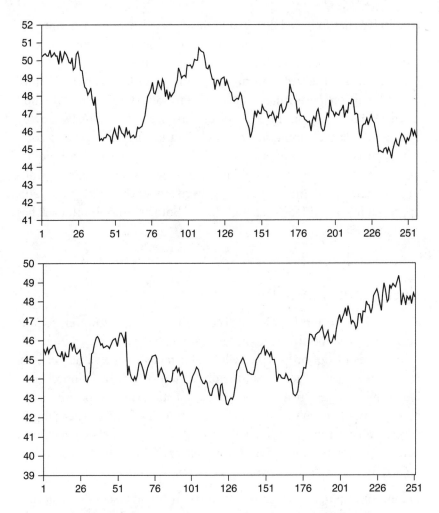

Figure 1.1   One random and one real stock chart. A random-number generator was used to generate the first chart. The second is real (250 days of Kellogg Co. stock). Nobody has ever found a reliable way to spot the fake.

I have also tried to learn from forecasters in other technical areas. Weather forecasting techniques are especially relevant. There are two basic strategies for predicting the weather. The first involves analyzing basic physical principles—cloud physics, thermals, temperature gradients, and so on. The second involves building a database containing historical information about atmospheric parameters and the weather conditions that followed. Predicting the weather involves searching the database for a set of parameters that correspond closely to those currently being observed. If the theory is correct, the weather will follow the previously observed pattern. Both techniques have some relevance to predicting the performance of stocks. Proponents of the first method often refer to financial metrics, price-earnings ratios, 50-day moving averages, relative strength, stochastics, and the like. The second approach typically involves unbounded pattern discovery techniques, neural network software, genetic algorithms, and a variety of data-mining strategies to identify repeating patterns in stock market data. This approach has a decidedly statistical flavor. Both are important. Each has been overused.

Background and Terms

This book is written for experienced option traders. However, serious beginners with an interest in understanding and exploiting the technical nuances of option pricing will realize many of the same benefits. Although somewhat technical, the discussion should be comprehensible to anyone with a firm grasp of basic statistics. We will focus on a relatively small number of trading strategies while spending a considerable amount of time discussing execution-related technical details such as bid-ask spreads, put-call parity, and price distortions related to weekends, holidays, expiration cycles, and earnings releases.

Before continuing, however, we need to define and discuss some terms:

Call options are contracts that entitle the buyer to purchase stock at a predetermined price, also known as the *strike price*. They are priced according to a model that takes into account the price and volatility of the underlying equity or index, time until the contract expires, and the risk-free interest rate that the money could otherwise earn.

Put options entitle the buyer to sell stock at a predetermined strike price. The value of a put option is related to its corresponding call through a relationship known as *put-call parity*. Put-call parity presents a striking opportunity. It is important to note that the original theory on which today's option pricing methodologies are built did not comprehend puts. We will discuss option pricing strategies and the implications of put-call parity in great detail throughout this book. For now, suffice it to say that the pricing strategy is designed to prevent a risk-free arbitrage. For example, if the put side were to be priced out of proportion to the call, a savvy investor would sell the put and buy the call while simultaneously selling the stock and buying a riskless zero-coupon bond maturing in the option's expiration time frame. The position would be unwound at the time of options expiration for a guaranteed profit. Although such trades are beyond the scope of this book, the important point is that a true disruption in put-call parity can automatically generate a profit. However, public customers who buy at the asking price and sell at the bidding price are unable to take advantage of these price distortions because they normally are accompanied by uncharacteristically wide bid-ask spreads. Parity distortions also present an opportunity to option traders who do not seek completely riskless arbitrage.

A trade consisting of puts and calls where both sides have the same strike price is commonly called a *straddle*. When the strike prices differ, the position is called a *strangle*. Positions that result from selling options are known as *short* positions. When the seller does not own a protective position, either stock or options, the position is referred to as being *uncovered* or *naked*. We will spend a considerable amount of time discussing strategies for trading and dynamically managing naked straddles and strangles. Very few options texts devote any space to such a strategy. There are two reasons. First, because the positions are uncovered, the seller has no protection against large unanticipated price movements. Such positions normally are considered very risky, because there is no limit to the amount that a stock can rise or fall. Practically speaking, though, there are limits. Effective risk management is a cornerstone of successful option trading, and we will spend extensive amounts of time discussing risk management strategies. That said, certain stocks are more prone to unanticipated price changes than others, and the magnitude of the risk varies over time. Moreover, option prices are often inflated with excess volatility to guard against unanticipated price changes. Therefore, accurate volatility assessment is central to a successful option trading strategy. Furthermore, a thorough analysis reveals that many investment strategies thought to be safe are actually riskier than most investors believe. For example, some stock portfolios lost more than 10% of their value during the September 11, 2001 terrorist attacks. Conversely, naked call sellers profited tremendously as all the options they sold expired worthless and they were able to keep the premium. Surprisingly, many put option sellers also profited, because the market remained closed for several days and the options lost much of their remaining time value. Many out-of-the-money options lost more time value than they gained from downward price movements. Short combinations were the most stable. In most cases the call side lost all its value, more than compensating for increases on the put side.

The events of September 11 joined many other market drawdowns by contradicting another important piece of conventional trading wisdom—the view that naked calls are riskier than naked puts. Nothing could be further from the truth; large negative price changes pose a greater risk to option sellers than large positive ones. The reason for the traditional view is that a stock can rise without limit but can only fall by an amount equal to its current price. For example, a $10 stock can suddenly fall to $0.00, making the $7.50 strike price put worth exactly $7.50 at expiration. The loss is limited. However, the same stock could theoretically rise to $50, taking the $12.50 strike price call $37.50 into-the-money—a catastrophic event by any measure. Practically speaking, both scenarios are highly unlikely. However, it is clear that a variety of events can cause investors to "panic" out of stocks, but very few news items have the capacity to drive an instantaneous catastrophic run-up. One in particular, the surprise announcement of a company acquisition at a price far above fair market value, can be very destructive to naked call sellers. One notable example was IBM's tender offer to purchase all outstanding shares of Lotus Development Corp. for $60 per share—nearly twice its trading price—in June 1995. Fortunately, there were clear indications that something was about to happen. The volume of $35 strike price calls more than tripled over three days from 672 to 2,028 contracts, the stock price climbed 10%, and volatility soared. Moreover, the $35 strike price call climbed from 1/8 to 1 15/16 during the three days preceding the announcement, and any investor short that call would certainly have closed the position. Finally, our trading strategy involves creating a statistical profile that compares the historical frequency of large price changes to the normal distribution. Lotus Development Corp. had a history of large price changes—often larger than 4 standard deviations from the mean. It would never have been a trading candidate for any uncovered positions. That Lotus might be a candidate for such an acquisition was one of the forces that caused its stock to behave poorly with regard to the standard model. Such stocks frequently respond to rumors with surprisingly large price movements. Conversely, we will see that it is entirely possible to identify stocks that are very unlikely to react in this way. Lotus notwithstanding, stocks rarely crash up, and indexes never do.

The second reason that few strategies have been built around uncovered combinations is psychological. Option traders focus on leverage and upside in their positions. If XYZ is trading at $98 and the $100 call option is selling for $1.50, a move to $102 will generate a call option price of $2.00 at expiration—a 30% profit. Moreover, because the call price depends heavily on volatility and time left before expiration, any rapid increase in the stock price will be accompanied by an increase in the option price. Option traders structure positions to capitalize on such moves. Conversely, the upside of a short position is limited to the value of the *premium*—the amount received for selling the option contracts. Short sellers maximize their profits when an option contract they have sold expires worthless. If XYZ trades below $100 at the time the call option contract expires, the seller keeps the $1.50 premium paid by the buyer. Likewise, he breaks even at expiration if XYZ trades at $101.50, because the calls will be worth precisely $1.50. Buyers have a quantifiable risk that is limited to the purchase price and an unlimited upside; sellers have an unlimited downside risk and their upside is limited to the selling price. However, an optimized volatility selling program based on a mechanism for selecting the best stocks and indexes to trade—those with a statistical history of behaving within the boundaries of the standard bell curve—can often provide an excellent return. Such systems must include a firm set of rules for timing trades and adjusting positions. Large institutional investors often favor such systems because they tend to deliver a steady, predictable return. As always, limiting risk necessarily involves limiting profit. For example, deep out-of-the-money options with little time left until expiration sell for very small amounts of money but present relatively little risk. Unfortunately, these trades do not always represent the most efficient use of collateral. (Option sellers are required to keep a certain amount of money on hand to cover the cost of closing in-the-money positions. It is important to understand the requirements and to optimize the use of collateral.)

We will also devote considerable time to complex multipart trades containing both short and long components. Part of our discussion will compare strategies that involve different expiration dates and strike prices. Many are direction-dependent in the sense that they rely on major economic trends. For example, the 28% dollar devaluation that occurred during 2002–2004 presented tremendous opportunities to option traders who understood the trend. The devaluation was an inescapable consequence of falling interest rates in the U.S. and a desire to lower the price of American goods to slow the growth of the trade deficit. It was part of a government stimulus package that was launched as a response to the recession that followed the NASDAQ crash and 9/11 terrorist attacks. Gold was destined to strengthen in this environment because it is priced in dollars. However, options on gold stocks and gold indexes were not necessarily a sound investment, because they were aggressively priced, with high volatility. Furthermore, occasional downward corrections proved dangerous to both call buyers and put sellers. The solution involved complex combinations of short and long positions with different expiration dates and strike prices. Managing such positions requires statistical insight into the dynamics of price change behavior and volatility—central themes of this book.

Finally, it is important to understand the effects of market movement on volatility. Falling markets, for example, normally are characterized by rising volatility, and short positions must be used with caution in such environments. We will review a set of strategies for trading in these markets that involve long positions on underpriced options where the amount of premium paid does not adequately compensate the seller for risk. As we shall see, the right statistical filters can be used to select "poorly behaved" stocks. Properly structured long option positions on these stocks tend to return very large profits.

Securing a Technical Edge

If options markets were perfectly efficient, it would be impossible to earn more than the risk-free rate of return. Fortunately, they are not.

Even the most refined option pricing models cannot anticipate earnings surprises, hostile takeovers, stock buybacks, fraud, wars, trade embargos, terrorist attacks, political upheavals, and the like. Conversely, the market sometimes overreacts to upcoming events by overinflating the volatility priced into option contracts. The strategies presented in this book are designed to quantify and exploit these price distortions.

Underlying this approach is a set of analytical tools that can be used to compare daily price changes. One straightforward approach involves recasting absolute price changes as standard deviations using a stock's volatility. For example, if a $100 stock exhibits 30% volatility, a 1 standard deviation price change over the course of a year will be $30. If the stock behaves in a way that is consistent with the normal distribution, there is a 68% chance that it will end the year between $70 and $130 (1 standard deviation in each direction). The chance of staying within the boundaries of a 2 standard deviation change is 95%, and the 3 standard deviation boundaries include more than 99% of all price changes. For reasons that we will discuss later, the conversion to a daily calculation involves dividing by the square root of the number of trading days in a year (252 trading days gives a divisor of 15.87). For the stock just mentioned, a one-day, 1 standard deviation change is $1.89.

Volatility on a given day is often calculated using a window that contains the previous month's price changes. However, many different-size windows are possible, and each provides a slightly different view of a stock's volatility. Comparisons are straightforward. For example, if we use a one-month window to obtain a volatility of 10%, we must multiply that number by the square root of 12 to obtain annual volatility (a year has 12 one-month time frames). Such a stock would have a 34.6% annual volatility. Using daily volatility values and the change in a stock's closing price, we can determine the number of standard deviations for each day's price change. Charts of these price changes expressed in standard deviations are excellent comparative tools for an option trader, because they take into account both the price and volatility of the underlying stock. From a risk-adjusted perspective, often seemingly inexpensive options on a low-volatility stock turn out to be overpriced. Expensive options on high-volatility stocks are just as likely to be underpriced.

The most subtle and important cases involve stocks that exhibit similar volatilities and prices but differ with regard to their price change distribution. Very few stocks exhibit a close fit with the normal price change distribution curve that underlies today's option pricing models. The discrepancies represent statistical arbitrages that can be traded for a profit. Figure 1.2 illustrates this concept by comparing the price change history of two very different stocks whose option prices are based on roughly the same volatility.

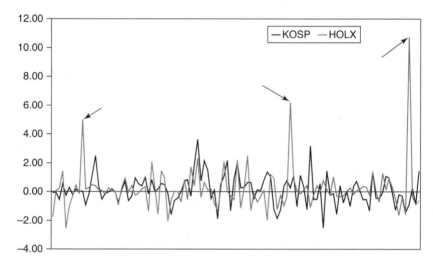

Figure 1.2   Two stocks exhibiting the same volatility but different price change behavior. The chart displays 110 daily changes measured in standard deviations. Standard option pricing models assume that each of the large spikes will occur with a frequency of less than once in 10,000 years. The largest spike should never occur.

Price changes in the chart are expressed in standard deviations calculated using a sliding 20-day volatility window. During the selected time frame, options on both stocks traded near 50% volatility. However, HOLX (Hologic, Inc.) regularly exhibited uncharacteristic spikes that are not comprehended by any option pricing model. These changes—each larger than four standard deviations—represent excellent trading opportunities. Conversely, KOSP (KOS Pharmaceuticals, Inc.) would be a reasonable candidate for short combinations consisting of out-of-the-money puts and calls.

Certain events such as earnings releases also represent excellent trading opportunities. Figures 1.3, 1.4, and 1.5 illustrate this concept using Amazon.com (AMZN). The stock predictably exhibits large price spikes with each earnings release. As a result, option prices typically soar as earnings approach and often reflect more than 3 times normal volatility. These high prices overly compensate sellers for risk. In such cases it is not uncommon for $15 out-of-the-money puts and calls to trade for more than 80 cents per contract on the day preceding an earnings release and to collapse to worthless immediately after.

Figure 1.3   AMZN: 300 days of closing prices.

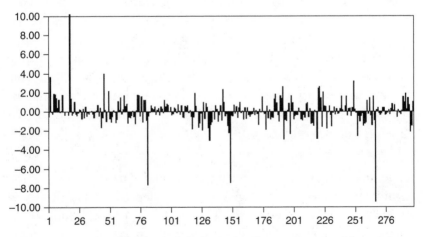

Figure 1.4   AMZN: 300 days of closing price changes expressed in
             standard deviations.

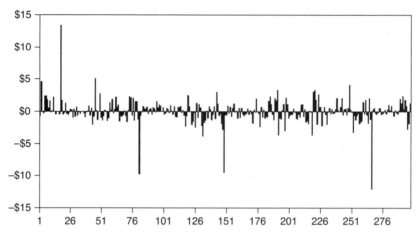

Figure 1.5   AMZN: 300 days of closing price changes translated from standard deviations into September 2006 dollars (1 StdDev = $1.31 on Sept 8, 2006).

Figure 1.3 displays daily closing prices for AMZN. Daily price changes are translated into standard deviations using a 20-day sliding volatility window. These changes are displayed in Figure 1.4. The final transformation expresses daily price changes in September 2006 dollars (a 1 standard deviation change was equal to $1.31 on September 8, 2006). The results displayed in Figure 1.5 facilitate direct comparisons between spikes. Unfortunately, many traders fall into the trap of comparing price changes in percentages rather than standard deviations. This process would have ignored the widely varying volatility that ranged from a low of 15% to a high of 95% during the time frame displayed. The data would have been skewed, causing price changes during periods of high volatility to appear much larger than those occurring during low volatility. However, when volatility is taken into account, the spikes are relatively similar in size. Armed with this information, an option trader can determine the fair price of puts and calls at each strike price.

Building on these themes, we will explore a large number of analytical techniques and trading strategies. Some will depend on specific events, and others will be more generic. In each case the goal is to link careful mathematical analysis with market reality. As always, the devil is in the details. Options don't have a price; they have a range of prices dictated by bid-ask spreads and trading queues. They don't trade at a single volatility either. The difference sometimes represents a significant put-call parity violation in which the two sides trade as if they represent different underlying stocks. Such distortions occur because the market has a view that risk is not equal on both sides. In such cases bid-ask spreads often widen, preventing public customers from taking advantage of the risk-free arbitrage that would normally accompany such an anomaly. We will discuss put-call parity and its implications at length. That discussion will form part of a more general focus on trading opportunities that arise from the underlying mathematics of the market.

Endnote

1   Lina Saigol and Gillian Tett, "Europe's Largest Hedge Fund Admits Flaws," *Financial Times*, June 13, 2005 22:12.

2

FUNDAMENTALS OF OPTION PRICING

When equity options began trading on the Chicago Board Options Exchange in April 1973, no accepted pricing methodology existed. As a result, traders relied on a variety of approaches largely based on anecdotes and rules of thumb gleaned from personal experience. The situation was not entirely new, however, because small volumes of equity options had been trading over the counter for many years.

In 1973 a landmark paper published by Fischer Black and Myron Scholes in the *Journal of Political Economy* revolutionized the world of derivatives pricing with a rigorous and extensible mathematical framework. The paper proposed a new model that quantified the influence and interaction of both time and uncertainty. This model, which was later extended in several important directions by Robert Merton, eventually became the foundation of modern option pricing across all markets—equities, indexes, and futures. Merton's extensions addressed options with dividends, nonconstant interest rate environments, and more general structures for pricing other contingent contracts. Scholes and Merton ultimately were awarded the 1997 Nobel Prize in Economic Sciences for their combined contributions to "A New Method to Determine the Value of Derivatives" (Black died in 1995).

Many of the concepts that underlie modern option pricing theory date back to the early 1900s and the work of Louis Bachelier. In his 1900 dissertation "*Theorie de la Speculation*" and subsequent publications, Bachelier described many of the concepts that later became central to the study of financial markets. Included was the assertion that prices have no memory and therefore move randomly—a concept now referred to as the random walk. He also pioneered the application of stochastic processes to pricing theory. Two important areas emerged from this work—the study of martingales,[1] and the relationship between Brownian motion[2] and financial markets.

Despite the work of pioneers such as Bachelier, the merger of economic theory and practical trading did not occur in any meaningful way before the early 1970s. At that time a variety of economic and political forces highlighted the importance of quantitative models for assessing risk and valuing financial derivatives. Relevant significant events included the following:

- The shift from fixed to floating exchange rates after the collapse of the Breton Woods agreement

- Double-digit inflation in the U.S. and massive dollar devaluation

- The creation of OPEC and an associated world oil price shock

- A 50% decline in the Dow Jones Industrial Average from 1050 in early 1973 to 580 in late 1974

Options play an important role in such unstable financial times, because they facilitate the construction of complex hedged positions with high levels of leverage. The Black-Scholes pricing model builds on these needs by offering a generalized approach that makes it applicable across a broad array of markets. Like many other financial instrument pricing and risk management strategies, it embodies the concepts of arbitrage avoidance and market equilibrium. These characteristics are familiar to students of the efficient-markets hypothesis, capital asset pricing models, and capital structure models. Generally speaking, securities with similar economic risk must exhibit similar returns. If they don't, an imbalance is created in the risk-return profile that can result in an arbitrage situation. Because arbitrages can provide automatic profit, equilibrium forces tend to erase such imbalances. This theme is central to the Black-Scholes pricing model and forms the basis of put-call parity, which we will review later in this chapter.

Like any model, Black-Scholes and its descendents have flaws. One notable assumption that has been criticized is the fixed volatility that must be priced into an option contract. Critics have pointed out that volatility can be highly variable, and different methods for estimating volatility have been proposed. The Black-Scholes model was designed around European-style options, which can be exercised only at the end of the contract time frame. The calculations can be adjusted to account for American-style options, which are always exercisable. However, because early exercise of an in-the-money option involves discarding the remaining time premium, it rarely occurs. Today's option pricing models contain many other inefficiencies as well; most are unavoidable. As we shall see, they often yield price distortions that can be traded for a profit.

Random Walks and Brownian Motion

Simply stated, the random-walk hypothesis asserts that the evolution of market prices cannot be predicted. The term was popularized by Burton Malkiel in a 1973 book titled *A Random Walk Down Wall Street*. Since then, many debates have occurred between proponents of the theory and investors/theorists who believe that they can identify chart patterns with predictive power. However, for a chart pattern to have predictive power, it must also be persistent in the sense that the market cannot learn the pattern and eliminate it. Such patterns run counter to the random walk, because they represent a market inefficiency. The random-walk concept is built on an important set of assertions known as the efficient market hypothesis (EMH). EMH predicts that such inefficiencies cannot persist. It was proposed by Eugene Fama in his Ph.D. thesis at the University of Chicago Graduate School of Business in the early 1960s.

EMH recognizes three basic forms of efficiency:

- Weak-form efficiency implies that technical analysis cannot consistently produce positive returns. However, the weak-form model recognizes the possibility of producing some return based on fundamental analysis of business performance and economic climate.

- Semi-strong efficiency implies that fundamental analysis is insufficient to yield positive returns. It assumes that share prices adjust to publicly available information almost instantaneously, making it impossible to place profitable trades using the new information.

- Strong-form efficiency is based on the assertion that share prices reflect all available information at any given moment. It is sometimes misinterpreted to imply that an individual cannot outperform the market. That is not the case. Individual traders can outperform or underperform the market as long as the entire group's performance remains normally distributed. It is also important to note that strong-form efficiency is not possible in environments where insider trading is illegal, because all information must be priced into the market. Studies have shown that the U.S. equity and bond markets are influenced by insider trading. Many people have argued that strong-form efficiency tends to be the norm rather than a theoretical possibility.

The vast amount of money spent each year on charting software and technical analysis systems provides a strong hint that most investors do not subscribe to the random-walk school of thought. Moreover, thousands of investment funds and millions of individual investors base their trading strategies on predicting the price changes of securities. It is important to recognize that moment-to-moment price changes can walk randomly without disrupting long-term trends. Gold prices, for example, rose 84% from early 2003 to late 2006 ($345 to $635) despite several large downward corrections. During the run-up, many day traders lost money while long-term investors realized large profits. The day traders were, in some sense, random-walk victims.

The random-walk model described by Malkiel in his book assumes that stock price changes are tantamount to coin tosses. The model states that future returns on a stock fit the standard normal distribution. Figure 2.1 shows the normal distribution in terms of standard deviations.[3] Looking at a few reference points along the curve, we can make the following statements:

- 34.1% of all returns fall between the mean and 1 standard deviation above the mean. Likewise, 34.1% of all returns fall between the mean and 1 standard deviation below the mean. Therefore, in a normally distributed environment, 68.2% of all returns fall within 1 standard deviation of the mean.

- 47.7% of all returns fall between the mean and 2 standard deviations above the mean, and 47.7% fall between the mean and 2 standard deviations below (95.4% total).

- 49.9% of all returns fall between the mean and 3 standard deviations above the mean, and 49.9% fall between the mean and 3 standard deviations below (99.8% total).

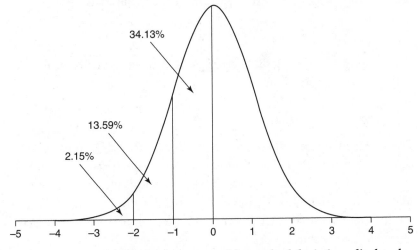

Figure 2.1 Normal distribution curve with standard deviations displayed on the x-axis.

The mathematics of geometric Brownian motion is appropriate for describing such processes. The model has its origins in the physical description of the motion of a heavy particle suspended in a medium containing many light particles. Random collisions move the heavy particle in a relatively unpredictable way with regard to both direction and magnitude. The geometric Brownian motion model asserts that the displacement of the large particle over long periods of time is normally distributed. Price change behavior is somewhat different, because prices tend to change in proportion to their absolute size. Hundred-dollar stocks can be expected to exhibit changes twice as large as fifty-dollar stocks, but the percentage change is constant. Stock returns—percentage changes in stock prices—are a better fit for the Brownian motion model than absolute price changes. Such changes are referred to as geometric (absolute changes are arithmetic).

Up to this point we have focused on stock returns and the fact that they are normally distributed. But how are a stock's future prices distributed? The answer to this question lies in the mathematics that relates stock prices and stock returns. The annualized return (R) for a stock priced today at S_{t0} and at some time in the future at S_T is

$$R = \frac{1}{T-t0} \ln (S_T/S_{t0})$$

Rearranging terms using the properties of logarithms yields the following equivalent expression:

$$R = \frac{1}{T-t0} \ln S_T - \frac{1}{T-t0} \ln S_{t0}$$

The preceding two equations are random variables representing a future return on S. Each is composed of two components: S_T (a random variable representing a stock's future price) and S_{t0} (a constant representing the current known price). We therefore can construct a new random variable that includes both the final return and the constant representing the starting price:

$$R + \frac{1}{T-t0} \ln S_{t0}$$

The new variable is also normally distributed with a mean equal to the average of the two terms. Rearranging terms allows us to restate the relationship as follows:

$$R + \frac{1}{T-t0} \ln S_{t0} = \frac{1}{T-t0} \ln S_T$$

If we multiply both sides by $1/(T-t0)$, we obtain the final form:

$$(T-t0)\, R + \ln S_{t0} = \ln S_T$$

Because the left side of the preceding equation is a normally distributed random variable, the natural logarithm of the future stock price (the right side of the equation) must also be normally distributed. Such random variables are referred to as being lognormal. Since the price change behavior of individual securities tends to adhere to the geometric Brownian motion model, it must follow that future prices are lognormally distributed. As we shall see, this assertion, commonly referred to as the lognormal hypothesis, lies at the core of option pricing theory.

The Black-Scholes Pricing Model

The Black-Scholes model was initially designed to price European-style options (those that can be exercised only at expiration). Conversely, American-style options can be exercised at any time before expiration. The distinction is less important than you might imagine, because early exercise of an option rarely, if ever, makes financial sense. Furthermore, it makes no sense to exercise an option that is out-of-the-money, because such action involves purchasing a stock above or selling a stock below its current trading price. Therefore, it is safe to assume that early exercise will occur only if an option is in-the-money. In such cases the person assigned usually gains by closing the position and keeping the excess time premium.

On very rare occasions it may be reasonable to exercise in-the-money option contracts prior to expiration, the most common reasons being lack of liquidity in the options market or excessively wide bid-ask spreads. In most cases, these conditions are driven by mixed views among investors with regard to the fairness of an underlying price. Bid-ask spreads on option contracts generally widen when sellers become concerned that risk is underpriced while buyers try to avoid overpaying. Such is often the case when a security has previously exhibited large price reversals. This situation usually corrects itself if the security moves very far beyond the strike price. However, investors should note that exercising an option and closing the final security position is more complex and expensive than simply selling the option.

Short-term equity options are usually American-style, and long-term (LEAPS) and index options are almost always European. Because early exercise rarely makes sense, the discussions in this book are based on the European-style option concept. Moreover, pricing models used by the industry are overwhelmingly based on the view that an option will be exercised only at expiration.

The Black-Scholes formulas for pricing European call and put options on non-dividend-paying stocks are as follows:

$$C = S_0 \, N(d_1) - Xe^{-rt} \, N(d_2)$$

$$P = Xe^{-rt} \, N(-d_2) - S_0 \, N(-d_1)$$

where

$$d_1 = \frac{\ln (S_0 / X) + (r + \sigma^2 / 2) \, t}{\sigma \sqrt{t}}$$

$$d_2 = \frac{\ln (S_0 / X) + (r - \sigma^2 / 2) \, t}{\sigma \sqrt{t}} = d_1 - \sigma \sqrt{t}$$

Variables:

ln = natural logarithm

C = call price

P = put price

N(x) = cumulative probability distribution function for a variable that is normally distributed

S_0 = stock price at time 0

X = strike price

r = risk-free interest rate

σ = volatility of the stock price measured as annual standard deviation

t = time remaining in the option contract, expressed as a percentage of a year

Black-Scholes calculations are relatively straightforward and can be accomplished using a spreadsheet or one of many commercially available modeling tools. In some situations it is necessary to calculate an option price using a known volatility. Conversely, if you know the option price, you can use an iterative process to discover the volatility. Volatility that is determined from an option price is commonly referred to as implied volatility. Conversely, observed volatility that is used to predict a fair option price is known as historical volatility. It is important to understand that volatility varies over time for any stock or index and that in many cases the changes can be enormous. Earnings announcements, economic and political events, expiration cycles, and dozens of other factors affect volatility. The ability to understand and predict volatility is a critical skill for successful option trading. Chapter 3, "Volatility," discusses the various nuances of implied and historical volatility in great detail.

Finally, the basic model does not comprehend dividends, which normally act to reduce call prices. This minor problem has many solutions. Fischer Black, coauthor of the model, suggested adjusting the stock price by subtracting the value of dividends likely to be paid before expiration before calculating the option price. Alternatively, investors concerned about dividend effects sometimes make small volatility adjustments to their calculations. In practice the effect tends to be very small, except in situations where dividends are very large.

If necessary, the basic Black-Scholes model can be expanded to account for dividends by substituting $S_0 e^{-qt}$ for S_0, where q is the continuous dividend yield. The expanded versions of the equations shown near the beginning of this section are shown here for completeness:

$C = S_0\, e^{-qt}\, N(d_1) - Xe^{-rt}\, N(d_2)$

$P = Xe^{-rt}\, N(-d_2) - S_0\, e^{-qt}\, N(-d_1)$

where

$$d_1 = \frac{\ln(S_0/X) + (r - q + \sigma^2/2)\,t}{\sigma\sqrt{t}}$$

$$d_2 = \frac{\ln(S_0/X) + (r - q - \sigma^2/2)\,t}{\sigma\sqrt{t}} = d_1 - \sigma\sqrt{t}$$

This relationship exists because

$$\ln(S_0\, e^{-qt}/X) = \ln(S_0/X) - qt$$

Likewise, we can write an equation that relates put and call prices. This relationship, which we will return to in Chapter 4, "General Considerations," is known as put-call parity. Put-call parity violations create arbitrage opportunities that normally disappear very quickly. For non-dividend-paying stocks:

$$C + Xe^{-rt} = P + S_0$$

C is the call price, P is the put price, X is the strike price, and S_0 is the current stock price. Not surprisingly, the dividend-containing form is a parallel construction to the first two Black-Scholes formulas just shown:

$$C + Xe^{-rt} = P + S_0\, e^{-qt}$$

For example, if the left side of the equation were relatively more expensive than the right, a savvy investor could exploit the arbitrage opportunity by essentially going long the right side and short the left side.[4] The trade would involve selling calls and purchasing both puts and stock. The small gain would then be invested in a risk-free interest-earning investment for the term of the option contract. The position would be unwound at expiration. Arbitrage opportunities are rare. When they exist, they generally are too small to be exploited by public customers who must pay trading costs.

The Greeks: Delta, Gamma, Vega, Theta, and Rho

Various characteristics of an option position can be described using parameters derived from the Black-Scholes formulas. Each parameter is an important component of the overall risk picture. As a group they relate information about the effects of price, volatility, and interest rate changes, in addition to time decay. Risk assessment of an option position commonly takes the form of descriptions that utilize the Greeks. For example, a trader might describe an option position as being "delta short 100 shares of stock." Such a position, because of its delta and size, would respond to initial price changes in the underlying as if it were 100 shares of stock. Each of the Greeks is briefly described in Table 2.1.

Table 2.1   Brief descriptions of the Greeks.

Greek	Description
Delta	The effect of a $1 increase in the underlying
Gamma	The delta's rate of change
Vega	The effect of a 1% increase in volatility
Theta	The rate of time decay (usually expressed in dollars per day)
Rho	The effect of a 1% increase in the interest rate

Although each of the Greeks is important, some figure into our discussions more prominently. Rho, for instance, tends to become significant only if interest rates are very high (such as in the early 1980s, when interest rates hovered near 20%), or if substantial interest rate changes are expected during the life of the options being traded. Conversely, delta and theta are important components of virtually every option position. Gamma, which describes the delta's rate of change, is very important for risk management and hedging. The following sections discuss each of these parameters.

Delta

Delta represents the percentage of any stock or index price change that will be reflected in the new option price. For example, suppose that an investor wants to purchase ten contracts of $100 strike price calls under the following conditions:

Current date = 01/10/2007 at 9:30 a.m.

Expiration date = 01/20/2007 at 5:00 p.m.

Days left = 10.31

Percent of year remaining = .0283

Underlying trading at $98.50

Underlying volatility = 34%

Risk-free interest = 5%

The Black-Scholes formula sets the delta of the calls at 0.42 and the price at $1.65. Because one contract represents 100 shares, the cost of the trade is $1.65 × 10 contracts × 100 shares per contract = $1,650. An instantaneous $1.00 upward move of the stock will adjust the position value by approximately 42 cents, or $420. That is, an investor who sold ten contracts of these calls would lose $420 if the stock suddenly climbed $1.00. Conversely, if the stock fell $1.00, the contracts would lose 42 cents. The situation is actually more complex, because the delta changes with the stock price. The precise Black-Scholes calculation actually reveals that the option price will move 45 cents when the stock price moves up $1.00 and 70 cents for a $1.50 move. The new deltas will be 0.49 and 0.52, respectively. The change in the delta at a fixed time corresponds linearly to the change in the price of the underlying. An investor taking a short position on ten contracts of these calls could fully hedge his or her position by purchasing 42% of the number of shares represented in the option contracts (.42 × 1,000 shares = 420 shares). However, as the stock moves, the delta changes, and maintaining a perfect hedge can become a challenge. A large upward move of the stock raises the delta to 1.00, and the size of a complete hedge to 1,000 shares. It is precisely for this reason that many investors track the gamma of a position. Many short sellers actually hedge with options so that both the hedge and the short position experience similar changes in delta. We will return to a discussion of hedging and gamma in the next section.

Delta is also affected by time. In the preceding example, if the stock stayed at $98.50 until expiration, both the delta and the value of the option would fall. At expiration the option would be worthless, because it is below the strike price. The relationship between time and delta is not linear; the decay accelerates as the contract nears expiration. Figure 2.2 depicts the relationship between time and delta for the $100 strike price option just specified.

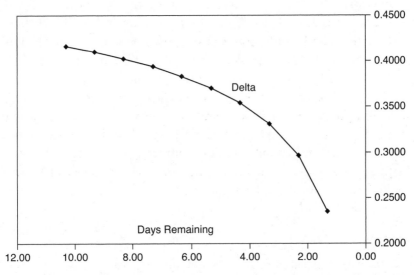

Figure 2.2   The relationship between time decay and delta. Days remaining before expiration are depicted on the x-axis and delta on the y-axis for a $100 strike price call on a stock with 34% volatility trading at $98.50 and risk-free interest = 5%.

You will notice that the figure includes precise information about the time remaining until expiration. Each data point in Figure 2.2 was calculated at 9:30 a.m. (the market open). Such precision is unnecessary when evaluating option positions that have a significant amount of time left until expiration. However, in the final few days, and especially on the last day—expiration Friday—precise calculations can be very important. Many of today's sophisticated pricing programs use the number of seconds until expiration for their calculations. Equity and index options expire at 5:00 p.m. on the Saturday following the third Friday of each month. During the final few days before expiration, a significant amount of time decay occurs each evening during the 17.5 hours that the market is closed. The effect can be very significant for options on indexes or expensive stocks where a significant amount of time value remains until the last few hours. Chapter 8, "Trading the

Expiration Cycle," contains a detailed discussion of the price distortions that emerge during the final days and hours of an option contract.

Delta can be calculated using the Black-Scholes formulas. The most straightforward method involves calculating the value of an option contract at two different stock prices separated by $1.00 and then subtracting the results. You will be able to verify that this value is equal to N(d1), the value of the cumulative normal distribution function of d1 in the Black-Scholes formula (see the third formula in the section "The Black-Scholes Pricing Model"). The following two formulas can be used to precisely calculate call and put deltas for dividend-paying stocks. In the formulas, q represents the dividend yield, and t represents the amount of time left in the option contract as a percentage of a year. Setting q to 0 for non-dividend-paying stocks reduces each equation to the cumulative normal distribution of d1.

$e^{-qt} N(d_1)$ (call)

$e^{-qt} (N(d_1)-1)$ (put)

As you would expect, put deltas move opposite call deltas—they rise when a stock falls and fall when a stock rises. Put and call deltas, however, are not symmetrical. This subtlety, which is related to the lognormal distribution, is very important to understand. Suppose, for example, that we wanted to find the delta-neutral stock price for option contracts with a strike price of $130, 192 days remaining until expiration, priced with 30% volatility and 5% risk-free interest. According to the Black-Scholes formulas, put and call deltas would each be 0.50 if the stock were trading at $123.62. Setting the stock price at $130 would generate a call delta of 0.59 and a put delta of 0.41. In both cases the option prices are different. The delta-neutral case yields a call price of $9.40 and a put price of $12.41, and the $130 stock price case yields $12.89 and $9.51, respectively. This asymmetry of price and delta is related to the lognormal distribution. In simple terms, if a $100 stock loses 50% of its value twice, the stock trades at $25. However, if the same stock experiences two 50% increases, it rises $125 to $225. This effect causes at-the-money calls in our example to be 35% more expensive than the corresponding puts. As a result, the delta-neutral point is shifted down nearly $7.00. Time also affects delta. With 20 days left until expiration, the delta-neutral point of our example shifts to $129.31.

This shift of the delta-neutral point is significant for investors who trade straddles using longer dated options. Long straddles generate a profit when a significant move of the underlying causes the delta of one side to become larger than the other. As the position becomes imbalanced, the combined value of both sides becomes larger than the value of the original trade. Eventually, if the underlying moves enough, one side of the trade is worth $0.00, and the other is worth much more than the combined value of both sides at the start. If the stock rises in concert with the delta-neutral point, the put/call prices equalize, with both sides losing value (the puts lose significantly more value than the calls). A long-dated long straddle therefore performs better in a falling price environment. Another way to think about the asymmetry is to realize that for the calls to gain more value than the puts lose, the underlying stock must rise much faster than the delta-neutral point. To some extent, the purchaser of a long-dated straddle is betting on a downward move of the underlying. The directional skew can be very significant. In our example, if a ten-contract position were purchased at the delta-neutral point of 123.62, and the underlying price rose $20 over 172 days, the value of the straddle would shrink by $7,216. Conversely, if the stock were to fall $20 during this time, the position would gain $4,214. We will return to a detailed discussion of straddle behavior in Chapter 5, "Managing Basic Option Positions."

Gamma

Gamma is a measure of the delta's rate of change with respect to the price of the underlying. It is certainly easy enough to calculate gamma. You simply determine the delta, increment the stock price by $1.00, and determine the delta again. Subtracting the first delta from the second reveals the gamma. A more precise method relies on this formula:

$$\frac{N'(d_1)e^{-qt}}{S\sigma\sqrt{t}}$$

where

$$N'(X) = \frac{1}{\sqrt{2\pi}}\,e^{-x^2/2}$$

As in the previous formulas, q represents the continuous dividend yield, t represents the percentage of time remaining, S represents the stock price, and σ is the annualized volatility priced into the option contract. As before, q is set to 0 for non-dividend-paying securities. Put and call gammas are always equal in both magnitude and sign.

Option traders who ignore the effect of gamma often underestimate risk. In the 1987 stock market drawdown, many option traders lost huge amounts of money because they were short large amounts of gamma. Traders who were short both puts and calls initially had insignificant losses if put and call deltas were similar. However, as downward price movements continued, call deltas fell quickly, and put deltas rose to 1. A short position composed of ten puts and ten calls rapidly became equivalent to a position that was short 1,000 shares of stock. A careful analysis of gamma would have caused many of these traders to tighten their stop orders in anticipation of a potentially catastrophic rise in gamma. Unfortunately, many option traders take the more simplistic view that a short option position is safe as long as the option remains out-of-the-money. However, a more careful risk assessment that takes into account the position gamma often reveals that the value of the contract can double or triple without breaching the strike price. Conversely, the most successful hedges are those that are long large amounts of gamma. Such positions benefit from rapid large stock price changes that raise the position delta. The goal is to establish a relatively inexpensive position that has the potential to grow rapidly and offset losses. An example is the purchase of a large number of inexpensive far out-of-the-money puts that can be expected to achieve a high delta in the event of a large market drawdown. A great deal of information is required to structure such a position. We will return to a more detailed discussion of market drawdowns, hedging, and the Chicago Board Options Exchange Volatility Index (VIX) in Chapter 6, "Managing Complex Positions."

Figure 2.3 compares the effect of time on delta and gamma. The risks associated with a short position rise rapidly in the final few days preceding expiration as the delta falls and the gamma rises. The implications are wide-ranging for a variety of complex positions that involve options expiring in different months. For example, a popular trade involves purchasing long-dated options and selling each month's options to pay for the time decay. The risk of such a position increases dramatically as expiration approaches, because a large move of the underlying can rapidly raise the delta of the short contracts while having very small offsetting effects on the long side of the trade. Positions that span different strike prices and months with long and short components therefore are very sensitive to the timing of moves of the underlying stock or index. We will return to this discussion in Chapter 6, which reviews a variety of complex multipart positions with an appropriate focus on risk management.

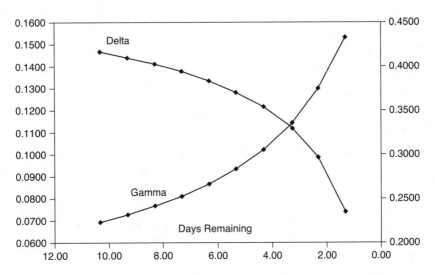

Figure 2.3   Comparison of the effect of time on delta and gamma. Days remaining before expiration is depicted on the x-axis, gamma on one y-axis, and delta on the other y-axis. The calculations are for a $100 strike price call on a stock with 34% volatility trading at $98.50 and risk-free interest = 5%.

Vega

Vega measures the effect of volatility changes on the option price. There is no letter in the Greek alphabet called "vega," so some analysts use kappa or tau instead. This book uses vega or v, but keep in mind that kappa or tau mean the same thing. Vega measures the change in option price for a 1% change in volatility. A vega of .25 indicates that the option price increases 25 cents when the volatility priced into the option rises 1%. As with the other Greeks, you can perform a simple calculation by solving the Black-Scholes formula at two different volatilities and subtracting the smaller result from the larger. Vega, like gamma, is the same for puts and calls. The formula is as follows:

$$S\sqrt{t} * N'(d_1) e^{-qt}$$

where

$$N'(X) = \frac{1}{\sqrt{2\pi}} e^{-x^2/2}$$

As before, S is the stock price, t is the percentage of time remaining, and q should be set to 0 for nondividend-paying securities.

Vega is affected by both time and price of the underlying. Far out-of-the-money and deep in-the-money options are both characterized by very small vega—neither is very sensitive to changes in volatility. Similarly, at-the-money options become much less sensitive to changes in volatility as expiration approaches. The same strike price option with several months remaining is very sensitive to volatility changes in the underlying. When you're trading positions based on anticipated changes in volatility, you must carefully track vega.

Theta

Theta describes time decay of an option contract. Many books have stated that theta is an enemy of an option holder and a friend of an option seller. This view represents a dangerous oversimplification. Although theta is certainly destructive to long positions, it also represents risk exposure to short positions. Theta will figure prominently into most of our discussions, because much of the rest of this book focuses on the dynamic management of complex positions.

Theta is written as a negative number. An option contract with a theta of −.10 loses 10 cents per day of time value. Furthermore, an option contract that has 30 days remaining before expiration and trades for

$3.00 must necessarily exhibit a theta of –.10, or 10 cents per day. With this in mind, it becomes obvious that theta is dramatically affected by the price of the underlying. As you might expect, a deep in- or out-of-the-money option has very little theta, and this effect intensifies as expiration draws near. Here is the formula for call theta:

$$-\frac{SN'(d_1)\sigma e^{-qt}}{2\sqrt{t}} - rXe^{-rt}N(d_2) + qSN(d_1)e^{-qt}$$

where

$$N'(X) = \frac{1}{\sqrt{2\pi}}\, e^{-x^2/2}$$

The calculation of theta for put contracts is similar:

$$-\frac{SN'(d_1)\sigma e^{-qt}}{2\sqrt{t}} + rXe^{-rt}N(-d_2) - qSN(-d_1)e^{-qt}$$

The parameters are identical to the previous formulas. S is the stock price, σ is volatility, t is the remaining time in percent, $N(d_1)$ and $N(d_2)$ are the cumulative normal distribution functions defined in the Black-Scholes equations, q is the dividend yield, and X is the strike price. Many analysts simply calculate the Black-Scholes formulas one day apart and subtract to find theta.

Rho

Rho relates the change of an option's value to changing interest rates. Call rho is positive and put rho is negative. As you might expect, deep out-of-the-money options are relatively insensitive to interest rate changes, and deep in-the-money options are very sensitive. Likewise, long-term options have a larger rho than short-term options. Most of our discussions will neglect the effects of interest rate changes, because they tend to be relatively small, and rate changes occur slowly—usually 25 basis points per month. However, during economic cycles characterized by persistently climbing or falling interest rates, the effect on long-term options can be pronounced.

The formulas for rho are as follows:

$Xte^{-rt} N(d_2)$ (call)

$-Xte^{-rt} N(-d_2)$ (put)

As before, X is the strike price, r is the risk-free rate of interest, t is the percentage of time remaining, and N(dx) represents the cumulative normal distribution functions defined in the Black-Scholes formulas.

Binomial Trees: An Alternative Pricing Model

In 1979 John Cox, Stephen Ross, and Mark Rubenstein published an important paper titled "Option Pricing: A Simplified Approach." The model they proposed is both versatile and straightforward. It involves constructing a binomial tree—a diagram representing different possible paths that a stock price might follow during the time frame of the option contract. The trees described in their paper are precise, discrete time analogs of the continuous-time geometric Brownian motion model. Therefore, whatever advantages or disadvantages exist in the models we have been discussing are also embodied in the binomial tree model.

The model assumes that, over any period of time, the underlying contract can move up (u) or down (d) by a given amount. The probability of an up move is given by p, and the probability of a down move is given by 1 − p. Suppose, for example, that a particular stock is trading at $50, and over the next discrete time frame, the price will move up to $52 (u = 2) or down to $48 (d = −2), and that there is a 50% chance (p = 0.5) of either outcome. If this time frame is the only one left before expiration, and we neglect interest rates, we can calculate the value of a $50 strike price call as its expected return at expiration. As always, the call will be either worth exactly the amount that the stock is in-the-money or worthless below the strike price. The expected return is: 0.5 × ($52 − $50) + 0 = $1.00. Using the same reasoning and probabilities, we can calculate the value of a $45 strike price call: 0.5 × ($52 − $45) + 0.5 × ($48 − $45) = $5.00. In this case both outcomes are above the strike price, so both have a positive value. The approach may be extended by using smaller time increments and by assuming that in each time frame the stock will move either up or down. The final result is a binomial tree with many possible price outcomes. The span of the tree (possible outcomes) relates directly to the number of discrete time frames chosen.

If we assume that the probability of an up or down move remains equal at each node, we can easily calculate the probability of each outcome at expiration. The expected return for any particular option will be equal to the sum, for each in-the-money outcome, of the difference between the price of the underlying and the strike price, multiplied by the probability of that outcome. Figure 2.4 shows a simple three-time step binomial tree with transition probabilities of p and 1 – p and up/down ratios of 4%. The value of each node is equal to the up or down ratio multiplied by the previous node's value.

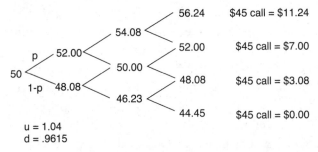

	56.24	$45 call = $11.24
54.08		
	52.00	$45 call = $7.00
52.00	50.00	
	48.08	$45 call = $3.08
48.08		
46.23		
	44.45	$45 call = $0.00

u = 1.04
d = .9615

Figure 2.4   Three-time step binomial tree ending in four different underlying prices. Each node contains a value determined by multiplying the previous node by the up (u) or down (d) ratio.

A binomial tree that approximates the lognormal distribution is built on probabilities and up and down ratios defined by the following:

$u = e^{\sigma\sqrt{\Delta t}}$

$d = 1/u$

$$p = \frac{e^{r\Delta t} - d}{u - d}$$

Variables:

 u = up ratio

 d = down ratio

 p = internode transition probability

Δt = length of the time frame in years (the total time in years / number of time steps)

σ = annual volatility

r = expected return of the stock in percent *per annum*

Our examples are overly simplistic because they contain only one or two steps. In practice, the life span of an option contract is usually divided into 30 or more steps, with each transition containing a binomial stock price movement. If we assume 30 steps, our model would contain 2^{30} (approximately 1 billion) possible pricing paths. At this level of granularity, discrete and continuous time models begin to converge. Binomial tree models, however, have some enormous advantages. Both Black-Scholes and the classical Cox-Ross-Rubenstein model are based on fixed volatility across the life of an option contract. It is possible, however, to extend the binomial model so that volatility varies with time and spot price. Binomial trees with node-specific or varying local volatility have become very popular. Sophisticated traders sometimes use such models to identify price distortions generated by fixed-volatility models. Their discussions often refer to a "volatility surface" with a unique three-dimensional shape that maps time, price, and volatility. These highly refined models can accurately represent the behavior of a stock or index as it rises or falls, or during the days preceding planned events, or in specific economic environments. The goal is to build a large library of customized binomial trees for each stock or index and to refer to the most appropriate model for any particular trading environment. You could envision having equity-specific volatility maps for the time frame that spans earnings announcements, new-product releases, options expiration, rising or falling interest rate environments, rising or falling equity markets, strong or weak dollar climates, or any other set of conditions that affects volatility in a time- or price-specific way. The possibilities are almost endless. Finally, binomial trees are effective tools for pricing exotic options (barrier options that contain threshold prices where they become active or inactive).

Summary

For the past 34 years, options have been priced using a continuous-time stochastic model based on the dynamics of Brownian motion. This model, developed by Fischer Black and Myron Scholes, assumes that future prices of an underlying stock or index are lognormally distributed. Black-Scholes pricing formulas take into account time left in an option contract, strike and spot prices, the risk-free rate of return, and volatility. Put-call parity, an important aspect of the model, is designed to prevent a riskless arbitrage. Although the model is known to have flaws, it has become the cornerstone of modern option pricing theory.

The most widely recognized deficiency relates to the assumption that volatility is constant—the so-called zero-drift assumption. Later models have addressed this issue with discrete-time approaches that allow custom volatility mapping for various time and spot price combinations.

The next chapter focuses on various approaches to analyzing and trading volatility. It also discusses the volatility smile, which has emerged as an important compensating mechanism designed to balance risk in rising and falling markets.

Further Reading

Bachelier, L., "Theorie de la Speculation," Annales de l'Ecole Normale Superiure, 1900.

Black, F. and M. Scholes, "The Pricing of Options and Corporate Liabilities," *Journal of Political Economy*, 81 (May–June 1973), pp. 637–659.

Chriss, N.A., *Black-Scholes and Beyond*, New York–Toronto: McGraw-Hill, 1997.

Courtault, Jean-Michel et al., "On the Centenary of Theorie de la Speculation," *Mathematical Finance*, vol 10, no 3 (July 2000), pp. 341–353.

Cox, J., S. Ross, and M. Rubenstein, "Option Pricing: A Simplified Approach," *Journal of Financial Economics*, 7 (October 1979), pp. 229–264.

Fama, E.F., "The Behavior of Stock Prices," *Journal of Business*, 38 (January 1965), pp. 34–105.

Malkiel, B.A., *A Random Walk Down Wall Street*, Fourth Edition, New York–London: Norton & Company, 1985.

Mandelbrot, B.B. and R.L. Hudson, *The Misbehavior of Markets*, New York: Basic Books—a member of The Perseus Books Group, 2004.

Merton, R.C., "Theory of Rational Option Pricing," *Bell Journal of Economics and Management Science*, 4 (Spring 1973), pp. 141–183.

Merton, Robert C., "Applications of Option-Pricing Theory: Twenty-Five Years Later," Nobel Lecture, December 9, 1997.

Osten, G., "Three Decades of Options," *Stocks Futures and Options*, vol 2, no 4, April 2003, pp. 26–35.

Scholes, Myron S., "Derivatives in a Dynamic Environment," Nobel Lecture, December 9, 1997.

Whaley, R., "On the Valuation of American Call Options on Stocks with Known Dividends," *Journal of Financial Economics*, 9 (1981), pp. 207–211.

Endnotes

[1] A martingale is a zero-drift stochastic process. If a financial instrument is a martingale, the best forecast for its price at some time in the future is its current price. Pricing theories based on martingales address the impossibility of profiting from a perfectly fair game.

[2] Brownian motion is a continuous-time stochastic process that describes the random movements of small particles. The associated mathematical model is referred to as the Weiner process (named after the mathematician Norbert Weiner).

[3] The standard deviation (σ) of a distribution of n occurrences where $X_i =$ each data point and m = mean is calculated as follows:

$$\sigma = \sqrt{1/(n-1) \sum_{i=1}^{n} (x_i - m)^2}$$

[4] The actual arbitrage trade is complex and involves selling calls, purchasing puts, and balancing the position with a stock-bond portfolio composed of long stock and short bonds.

3

VOLATILITY

To determine the fair price of an option contract, you must know the amount of time remaining before expiration, the current price of the underlying, the strike price, the risk-free interest rate, and the volatility. With the exception of volatility, each of these parameters has a precise known value. Unfortunately, the variable nature of volatility makes it difficult to accurately predict. Because the value of an option contract is very sensitive to the volatility component of the calculation, accurate assessment of volatility is a critical skill for an option trader. It is nearly impossible to generate a positive return without a reliable method for assessing volatility.

Long positions should be established only when you believe that the volatility priced into the option contracts is too low. The reverse is true for short positions—they make sense only when the underlying volatility is too high. Establishing a long position is tantamount to buying volatility, and short positions involve selling volatility. Because option positions are often composed of both long and short components, the terms "net long" and "net short" generally are more appropriate.

Fair volatility is an important concept. Consider the following example:

Stock price	$123.62
Strike price	$130
Days remaining	10
Volatility / price	30% / $0.54

Volatility / price	40% / $1.12
Volatility / price	50% / $1.79
Volatility / price	60% / $2.51

Doubling the volatility without any other changes causes the option price to increase more than 460%. As you shall see, volatility changes of this magnitude are not uncommon. They can happen quickly or slowly. Contrast, for example, the rapid deflation that often follows an earnings release with the slow changes that mirror the diminishing excitement after an IPO. The first happens a few minutes after the opening bell; the latter often takes several months. In this regard, it is critically important to bridge the gap between mathematical modeling and the underlying financial drivers.

Volatility takes two basic forms—historical and implied. Historical volatility is based on the past behavior of the underlying, while implied volatility is calculated from the actual trading price of an option contract. Quite often they are the same, but sometimes they can differ markedly. The discrepancy tends to be largest for stocks that exhibit a poor fit to the lognormal distribution. Such stocks are prone to occasional large price spikes. This behavior causes short sellers to bid up option prices as protection against large unanticipated price changes. Buyers, however, often are leery of overpaying for sporadic price spikes that may not occur during the life of the contract. The situation becomes especially difficult for stocks that exhibit extremely large price spikes (more than 4 standard deviations) on a very infrequent basis (perhaps two or three times each year). Options on such stocks are often very illiquid with large bid-ask spreads. We will return to this issue throughout the book in various discussions about special events, liquidity, and time points in the expiration cycle.

Volatility and Standard Deviation

Simply stated, we can define volatility as a 1 standard deviation (StdDev) price change over the course of one trading year. The value is normally expressed as a percentage of the security price. If a stock trades at $100 with a volatility of 30%, a 1 standard deviation change in a 1 year time frame will raise the price to $130 or lower the price to $70. Using the normal distribution, we can assume a 68% chance that the final price will fall within this range. Some adjustment for interest rates is also necessary. If the risk-free rate of return during this time frame is 5%, a 1 standard deviation price change at year end would be $105 × 30% = $31.50. We would expect the stock to trade between $73.50 and $136.50 68% of the time. This view, however, is somewhat simplistic. A more precise definition of volatility is the standard deviation of the return provided over one year when the return is expressed using continuous compounding.

As you saw in Chapter 2, "Fundamentals of Option Pricing," returns are normally distributed, and future prices are lognormally distributed. The distinction is important. If prices were normally distributed, a $20 stock would have the same probability of rising to $50 as falling to –$10. Clearly this cannot happen. Suppose, however, that price changes were continuously compounded. Five 10% upward price changes would raise a $20 stock by $12.21 to $32.21. The corresponding downward price changes would reduce the price by $8.19 to $11.81. The continuously compounded upward change is 61%, and the corresponding downward change is only –41%. The distribution of final prices is skewed so that no price ever falls below zero. The continuous compounding of normally distributed price changes will cause the prices at maturity to be lognormally distributed.

Assuming continuous compounding, it can be shown that volatility is proportional to the square root of time. A 1 standard deviation change for any time frame is given by the following formula, where σ is the annual volatility and Δt is the percentage of a year:

$$\sigma\sqrt{\Delta t}$$

Returning to the example of a $100 stock with 30% annual volatility, we can calculate the size of a 1 standard deviation change in one week (1/52 year):

$.30 \times \sqrt{.0192} = .0416$

$.0416 \times \$100 = \$4.16$

Much debate has occurred over the length of a trading year and the number that should be used for volatility calculations. Although a calendar year has 365 days, there are actually only 252 trading days. Throughout this book we will use a 252-day trading year when calculating volatility based on daily price changes. This approach makes sense, because there are 252 daily closing prices each year, and historical volatility is based on close-to-close price changes. However, some of our Black-Scholes calculations are more granular in the sense that they use the number of minutes remaining until options expiration. These calculations specifically take into account all the remaining time, including weekends. The difference becomes significant as expiration approaches, because the final weekend of the cycle represents two of the seven remaining days. Therefore, much of our forward modeling will be based on total time remaining, calculated in minutes, as a percentage of a year.

Calculating Historical Volatility

To calculate historical volatility, we must compute the standard deviation of the short-term returns. The following steps outline the process:

1. Select a standard time frame Δt (such as one day, one week, one month, or one quarter). Determine the number of time frames per year. The number of time frames is designated tf in the following formulas.

2. Compute the return from the beginning to the end of each time frame. If the closing price on day 1 is C_1 and the closing price on day 2 is C_2, each close-to-close return (R) is given by

   $R = \ln (C_2 / C_1)$

3. Compute the average value of the returns R0, R1, R2, ... ,Rn. If we use 21 closing prices, we will have 20 returns—thus the value of N+1 in the following formula:

$$R_{avg} = \frac{1}{N+1} \left(R_0 + R_1 + R_2 + \ldots + R_n \right)$$

4. Compute the standard deviation using N–1 statistically "unbiased" weighing. If we have 21 closing prices and 20 returns, n=19 in the following formula:

$$\sigma = \sqrt{tf} \times \sqrt{1/n \left((R_0 - R_{avg})^2 + (R_1 - R_{avg})^2 + \ldots + (R_n - R_{avg})^2 \right)}$$

In step 4 we annualize our volatility calculation by multiplying the daily standard deviation by the square root of the number of daily close-to-close price changes in one year. The number of time frames, however, is a matter of some dispute. As mentioned, there are actually only 252 trading days in a year. Some traders prefer to use this number, and others prefer to use the full 365 days. Weekends and holidays represent volatility. Some studies have shown that stocks can display as much movement between the close on Friday and the open on Monday as they would if they had traded on Saturday and Sunday. This weekend volatility would argue for a 365-day calculation. However, the effect appears to be variable. Some stocks show very little volatility over weekends and holidays when the markets are closed. Stocks that respond to world political and financial events are obviously more affected over weekends than others. For now, we will assume 252 close-to-close changes, and our annualization factor will be based on the square root of 252 (15.875).

A Sample Calculation

The sample volatility calculation shown in Table 3.1 is based on 21 trading days (20 price changes) and a 252-day trading year.

Table 3.1 Sample volatility calculation.

Close	Log Change	Mean	Deviation from Mean	Deviation Squared
86.14				
89.05	0.033224	0.004695	0.028529	0.000814
88.55	−0.005631	0.004695	−0.010325	0.000107
87.72	−0.009417	0.004695	−0.014112	0.000199
85.47	−0.025984	0.004695	−0.030679	0.000941
86.31	0.009780	0.004695	0.005085	0.000026
84.76	−0.018122	0.004695	−0.022816	0.000521
82.90	−0.022189	0.004695	−0.026883	0.000723
82.20	−0.008480	0.004695	−0.013175	0.000174
81.51	−0.008430	0.004695	−0.013124	0.000172
81.52	0.000123	0.004695	−0.004572	0.000021
80.87	−0.008005	0.004695	−0.012700	0.000161
84.84	0.047924	0.004695	0.043229	0.001869
83.80	−0.012334	0.004695	−0.017029	0.000290
85.66	0.021953	0.004695	0.017258	0.000298
85.05	−0.007147	0.004695	−0.011841	0.000140
85.47	0.004926	0.004695	0.000231	0.000000
92.57	0.079800	0.004695	0.075105	0.005641
97.00	0.046746	0.004695	0.042051	0.001768
95.80	−0.012448	0.004695	−0.017143	0.000294
94.62	−0.012394	0.004695	−0.017089	0.000292

Sum of deviations squared = 0.014450

Standard deviation = sqrt(0.014450 / 19) = 0.027578

Annualized volatility = 0.027578 × sqrt(252) = 0.43778

Using a Sliding Window to Measure Volatility

Determining the fair volatility of an option contract is a complex exercise, because historical volatility can vary tremendously for reasons that are not always obvious. Stocks generally are more unstable when prices are falling than when they are rising. Thus, in falling markets, volatility tends to rise. Volatility also tends to rise as planned events, such as quarterly earnings releases, approach. Conversely, stocks that have fallen for some time and stabilized in a new price range tend to become less volatile. Volatility also falls when stocks are steadily rising. The closely followed volatility index (VIX)—a measure of volatility priced into options on S&P 500 stocks—has become a well-accepted indicator of bullish and bearish sentiment. At the time of this writing, the VIX was hovering near an all-time low of 10% following a market rise of more than 20% in six months. Volatility also rises and falls with trading volume. A stock can trade in a relatively tight range with high volatility or move a great distance at a steady and predictable pace while exhibiting relatively low volatility. Therefore, it is very important to have a set of tools for studying historical volatility. The goal is to use these tools to evaluate option prices. A powerful set of tools can become an edge that a trader can use to spot subtle price distortions that can be traded for a profit.

The most basic tool is a sliding-window calculator that can be used to create historical volatility profiles. Table 3.2 illustrates this concept using a total of 30 days of data and a window length of 21 days (20 price changes). Volatility in the example is annualized to a 252-day trading year. The data presented is for Apple Computer (ticker AAPL). The first volatility calculation appears at the end of the first window on day 21. It corresponds to the standard deviation of the previous 20 close-to-close changes. The window then slides forward one day, and the earliest day drops out of the calculation, which now includes days 2 through 22. The process continues until we reach the end of the dataset. A 20 price change window is particularly useful, because it tends to accurately predict the volatility priced into most equity option contracts. Our example is unrealistically short. In practice, it is common to use at least one year of data, and in many cases it makes sense to use more than one year.

Table 3.2 Sliding window volatility calculation.

Day	Close	Volatility
02/23/2006	71.75	
02/24/2006	71.46	
02/27/2006	70.99	
02/28/2006	68.49	
03/01/2006	69.10	
03/02/2006	69.61	
03/03/2006	67.72	
03/06/2006	65.48	
03/07/2006	66.31	
03/08/2006	65.66	
03/09/2006	63.93	
03/10/2006	63.19	
03/13/2006	65.68	
03/14/2006	67.32	
03/15/2006	66.23	
03/16/2006	64.31	
03/17/2006	64.66	
03/20/2006	63.99	
03/21/2006	61.81	
03/22/2006	61.67	
03/23/2006	60.16	0.328
03/24/2006	59.96	0.328
03/27/2006	59.51	0.328
03/28/2006	58.71	0.313
03/29/2006	62.33	0.391
03/30/2006	62.75	0.391
03/31/2006	62.72	0.382
04/03/2006	62.65	0.366
04/04/2006	61.17	0.369
04/05/2006	67.21	0.506

Note that the volatility for the 20 price change window varied considerably from day to day. On March 29, a 3 standard deviation price change raised the 20-day volatility from 31.3% to 39.1%. An even larger price change (4.2 standard deviations) on April 5 pushed the volatility to 50.6%. Neither of these price spikes coincided with a planned event such as an earnings release. It is clear, therefore, that much more data is needed to evaluate historical volatility for AAPL. Figure 3.1 provides 300 days of AAPL volatility data using the same 20 price change window.

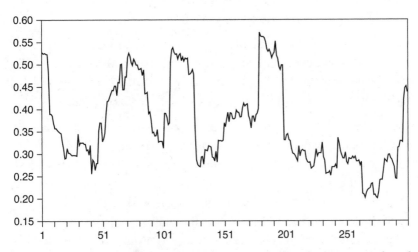

Figure 3.1   AAPL volatility 11/02/2005–01/12/2007. Calculations are based on a sliding window containing 20 close-to-close price changes.

Figure 3.1 illustrates the tremendously variable nature of volatility. On any given day an option trader must evaluate historical volatility to determine whether the volatility priced into an option contract is reasonable. The most valid approach involves finding periods of time on the volatility chart that correspond best to the current time. For example, if a major upcoming event is likely to affect oil prices, it might be reasonable to price options on oil exploration companies by viewing a period of time when similar events were playing out in the market. Apple Computer's volatility is driven by such events as microprocessor sales estimates from major chip vendors and information on consumer electronics sales revenues at major retailers. The company has transformed itself from a manufacturer and distributor of desktop computers into a consumer electronics, music, and video vendor. Although it is not always possible to identify and match specific events, a simple view of the magnitude of past volatility swings and some idea of the types of events that drove them are tremendously beneficial. Realizing that the tall peaks on the chart exceed 50%, while normal volatility averages closer to 40%, provides an important perspective. It would be impossible to successfully trade options on any stock or index without understanding the potential volatility changes that accompany major news events. It is important for an option trader to attempt to form the link between volatility and price change behavior.

The complexity of the problem becomes apparent in charts that contain both historical volatility and stock prices. Figure 3.2 illustrates this point by extending Figure 3.1 with daily closing prices. You will be quick to note that volatility alone has limited predictive power.

Nevertheless, certain trends emerge if you view a large number of volatility charts. Most notable is the relationship between high volatility and poor stock performance. In our example, Apple stock performed poorly during the time frame when volatility was high—the time frame between day 51 and day 179. After volatility peaked on day 179, however, the stock began rising. On day 271 (the final arrow), the stock closed above $90, and volatility hovered near the bottom of the chart. This behavior is mirrored in the closely followed VIX, which represents a consolidated view of volatility priced into options on the stocks that make up the S&P 500. The VIX is often used as a leading indicator of market performance, because it tends to rise as stocks fall and fall as stocks rise. However, as in our Apple example, volatility of the VIX— volatility of the market's volatility—is surprisingly high. Options on the VIX tend to be priced with more than 150% volatility. As you can see in the chart, Apple's volatility displays similar characteristics—a low of 20% and a high just below 60%. If we priced the volatility of Apple's volatility—if we sold options on Apple's volatility—those options would be priced around 300%. Underestimating the magnitude of these swings would be a critical mistake.

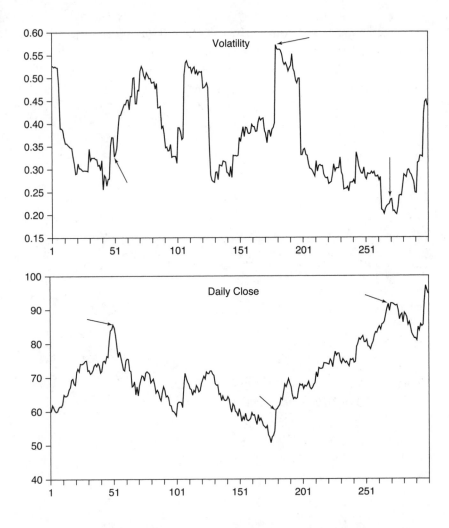

Figure 3.2   Volatility and closing price for AAPL 11/02/2005–01/12/2007.
The three arrows mark the same dates on both charts (day 51:
01/17/2006, day 179: 07/20/2006, day 271: 11/29/2006).

By varying the length of our sliding window, we can diminish the
effects of cyclical events. For example, if we extend the length of our
window to 90 days, we can expect to always have an earnings release
priced into our analysis. A chart built on a 90-day sliding window con-
veys a much more stable picture of volatility. More importantly, it tem-
pers the extremes by smoothing out the very high spikes and raising the

uncharacteristic lows. Conversely, charts built on short time frames (ten days or less) are noisy because they are influenced by small price spikes. The charts displayed in Figures 3.3, 3.4, and 3.5 are based on the same date range and closing prices as the two previous charts.

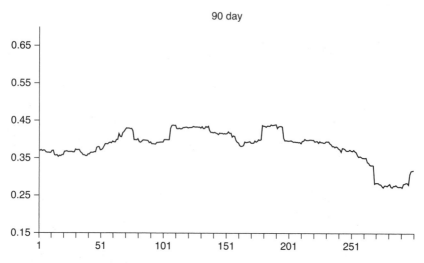

Figure 3.3   AAPL volatility: 90-day sliding window (11/02/2005–01/12/2007).

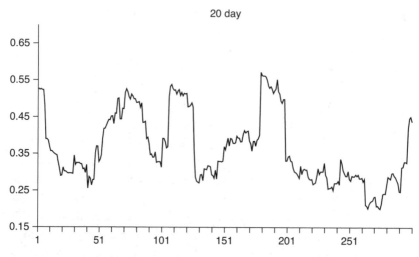

Figure 3.4   AAPL volatility: 20-day sliding window (11/02/2005–01/12/2007).

    THE VOLATILITY EDGE IN OPTIONS TRADING

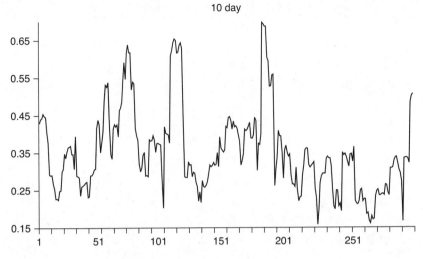

Figure 3.5   AAPL volatility: 10-day sliding window
(11/02/2005–01/12/2007).

The differences between charts created from 90-day and 20-day sliding windows is immediately apparent. The 90-day window is helpful when the goal is to gain an approximate understanding of the long-term trend. The more-active 20- and 10-day sliding-window charts are helpful when the spikes can be attributed to specific events or economic cycles. In Figure 3.5, the large upward spikes of the 10-day chart forced expansion of the scale beyond 65%. For consistency, all three charts use the same scale and represent the same dates.

Finally, the most straightforward, and often the most accurate, volatility calculation involves determining the standard deviation across a complete trading year—252 days. This calculation obviously does not need to be annualized. A balanced view of volatility should include recent long and short windows, the annual high, the annual low, and a single standard deviation that spans an entire trading year (referred to in Table 3.3 as the series volatility). The consolidated view can be surprising. Table 3.3 contains ten examples.

Table 3.3 Consolidated view of volatility for ten stocks.

Symbol	Last	Series Volatility	High Volatility	Low Volatility	20-Day Volatility	90-Day Volatility
CRL	43.45	0.29	0.62	0.11	0.12	0.27
HSP	36.97	0.33	0.76	0.08	0.17	0.40
MYOG	52.24	0.65	1.84	0.29	1.36	0.76
NAFC	25.61	0.49	1.24	0.12	0.27	0.34
BCSI	21.97	0.72	1.97	0.20	0.42	0.54
BSTE	47.27	0.40	0.86	0.15	0.28	0.35
PLT	20.44	0.53	1.28	0.16	0.48	0.55
AVID	36.17	0.41	0.69	0.14	0.38	0.45
ADRX	24.54	0.29	0.77	0.03	0.05	0.09
CECO	21.05	0.48	1.26	0.13	0.29	0.70

Estimating volatility is easiest when several of the windows agree. For example, the series, 90-day, and 20-day estimates for Plantronics (PLT) are reasonably close. However, an investor should keep in mind that PLT's volatility rose as high as 128% during the past year and fell to a low of 16%. In the short term it is reasonable for options to be priced in the range of 50%. However, investors who plan to structure longer-term trades need to recognize that volatility could rise steeply. The wisest approach involves reviewing past financial and business information to understand why volatility changed so dramatically and to use this information when making trading decisions.

Outside economic forces often affect volatility across a broad group of stocks. Such changes were apparent during the market stabilization that lowered the volatility index from 23 in June 2006 to just above 11 in mid-August. This two-month-long deflation created an excellent environment for selling naked options, because the contracts lost both time and volatility. A comparison between the VIX and a chart of historical volatility is often helpful, because it can reveal the effects of large-scale market forces on the behavior of individual stocks. It is also important to compare the volatility of related commodities and indexes to the stocks they affect—crude oil and oil company stocks, copper prices and copper mining companies, interest rate changes and mortgage companies, and so on.

Profiling Price Change Behavior

As you just saw, volatility tends to exhibit a surprising amount of variability over time frames as short as a few months. The stocks listed in Table 3.3 illustrate this behavior even though they were chosen at random. Much of the variability is caused by large price spikes whose size and frequency cause the volatility to rise. Conversely, when spike size and frequency are diminished, volatility must necessarily fall. Furthermore, volatility is often a poor indicator of price change behavior. A highly volatile stock can be relatively "well behaved" if the size and distribution of its price changes fit the normal distribution curve. Conversely, a stock that exhibits low volatility can be "poorly behaved" if its price change distribution curve has elongated tails with a surprising number of large spikes. Therefore, it is important to have both a balanced view of historical volatility and an understanding of price change behavior in terms of size and frequency of spikes.

It is critically important for an option trader to think in these terms and to resist the temptation to simply frame price changes in percent. Consider, for example, IBM stock whose options traded at 33% implied volatility in 2001 but only 16% in 2004. A 10% move of the stock in 2001 had a far smaller impact on a well-structured option position than the same size move in 2004. Option traders buy and sell standard deviations, and positional risk cannot be properly assessed by thinking in terms of percent change. The principal goal of an option trader is to arbitrage subtle differences between implied and fair volatility by structuring positions that capitalize on those discrepancies. Perfectly priced options cannot be used to generate a profit, no matter how complex the position. The underlying must rise or fall more or less than the amount priced into some portion of a trade. Therefore, both volatility and price must be taken into account during the planning phase of any trade.

Recall that we can divide a stock's annual volatility by the square root of the number of time frames in one year to determine the volatility for a single time frame. Assuming a 252-day trading year, a stock with 30% annual volatility will have a daily volatility of 30% / $\sqrt{252}$ = 1.89%. For a $90 stock with this volatility, a one-day 1 standard deviation price change would be equal to 1.89% × $90 = $1.70. We can use this simple relationship to express the price change of a stock on any given day in standard deviations. Extending this approach allows us to recast an entire stock chart so that each day's close appears as an up or down bar that corresponds to the magnitude of the change. Figure 3.6 displays one year of price changes for Cephalon (CEPH) using this format.

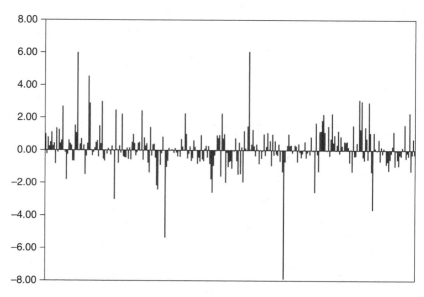

Figure 3.6   Cephalon (CEPH): one year of price changes expressed in standard deviations. Each price change is measured against the most recent 20-day volatility window—the previous 21 closes or 20 price changes.

It is important to note that each price change is measured against a window that ends just ahead of the change. That is, the change being measured does not influence the calculation. If the change being measured were part of the calculation, the value would be distorted, and the size of the distortion would be large for short windows. For example, on May 30, 2007, Apple Computer stock spiked from 114.35 to 118.77—3.03 standard deviations measured against the previous 20-day window. If we include the day of the spike as the final day of the measurement window, the magnitude is reduced to 2.6 standard deviations. The corresponding values for a five-day window would have been 2.18 and 1.60 standard deviations—nearly twice the distortion.

Looking at the chart, we can immediately determine that Cephalon experienced five very large price spikes in a single year. The spikes were −7.89, 6.06, 5.99, −5.35, and 4.55 standard deviations. Contemporary option pricing models based on the normal distribution anticipate a 5 standard deviation change only once in approximately 3 million trading days—essentially never. Furthermore, CEPH experienced 25 price spikes greater than 2 standard deviations—approximately 2 times more often than expected. This information can be enormously helpful to an option trader evaluating contract prices before a scheduled event when implied volatility is likely to be elevated in anticipation of a price spike.

Table 3.4 shows the process of calculating each point on the chart using the time frame of the first large price spike of Figure 3.6 (CEPH, December 9, 2005).

Table 3.4   Illustrated price spike calculation.

Close	Price Change	Log Change	StdDev Log Change	1 StdDev	Current Spike	Calculation
47.58						
47.78	0.20	0.0042				
48.09	0.31	0.0065				
47.52	−0.57	−0.0119				
48.47	0.95	0.0198				
48.38	−0.09	−0.0019				
49.30	0.92	0.0188				
49.61	0.31	0.0063				
50.03	0.42	0.0084				
51.65	1.62	0.0319				
51.65	0.00	0.0000				
51.57	−0.08	−0.0016				
50.60	−0.97	−0.0190				
50.45	−0.15	−0.0030				
50.83	0.38	0.0075				
51.08	0.25	0.0049				
51.26	0.18	0.0035				
50.89	−0.37	−0.0072				
50.51	−0.38	−0.0075				

Table 3.4 Continued

Close	Price Change	Log Change	StdDev Log Change	1 StdDev	Current Spike	Calculation
51.42	0.91	0.0179				
52.09	0.67	0.0129	0.0120	0.625		
55.83	3.74	0.0693	0.0188	1.050	5.98	3.74 / 0.625
55.79	–0.04	–0.0007	0.0189	1.054	–0.04	–0.04 / 1.050
56.20	0.41	0.0073	0.0183	1.028	0.39	0.41 / 1.054

As previously indicated, the calculation is based on a window containing 20 price changes. Consequently, the first calculation involves measuring the price change for record 22 against records 1 through 21. The steps required to calculate the first value (5.98) are as follows:

1. Calculate the standard deviation of the 20 price changes immediately preceding the spike (days 1 through 21). The value obtained is the one-day volatility at the end of the first 20 price change window. The result is 0.0120.

2. Multiply this number by the value of the close on day 21 ($52.09) to determine the magnitude of a 1 standard deviation price change at the end of the window. The result is $0.625.

3. Divide the day 22 price change ($3.74) by this value to recast the change in standard deviations. The result is 5.98.

After each calculation the window is moved forward one day, and the next price change is measured against the new window. Table 3.4 displays three calculations (highlighted values will ultimately be depicted on a price spike chart). For clarity, the rightmost column displays the final step in each calculation. You will note that 22 records are required to generate the first value for a 20 price change window.

It is important to recognize the significant difference between charts that measure individual price changes in standard deviations and more traditional approaches that reveal the standard deviation of the underlying price. The differences are significant in both size and meaning. As you saw in Chapter 2, option pricing theory is based on the distribution of price changes. Therefore, it makes sense for option traders to construct charts that depict the behavior of underlying securities in these terms. Charts of the form displayed in Figure 3.6 are used throughout this book because they display price changes using the same terms used to price option contracts. Stock traders, however, often use different metrics. One popular charting technique—Bollinger Bands—measures the standard deviation of the stock price using a sliding window of fixed length. A trading range is selected by symmetrically placing a pair of bands around the simple moving average of the time frame. Although the length of the sliding window and the space between the bands can both be varied, the most common approach places the upper band 2 standard deviations above the simple moving average and the lower band 2 standard deviations below. The most common window includes 20 closing prices.

Many investors mistakenly believe that Bollinger Bands measure volatility as it is priced into option contracts. However, because option pricing depends on the standard deviation of the log of the price change, the differences are quite significant. Table 3.5 reveals the differences between the two calculations for a set of stock prices. The left side of the table calculates both standard deviation and annual volatility for a set of prices using the log of each price change. The right side uses the standard deviation of the closing prices.

Table 3.5   Standard deviation of the log of the price change versus standard deviation of the closing price.

	Price Change		Bollinger Band	
Price	Log change	Diff squared	Price	Diff squared
93.87			93.87	
93.96	0.000958	0.00000849	93.96	0.74534444
93.52	−0.00469	0.00000750	93.52	0.17921111
95.85	0.024609	0.00070567	95.85	7.58084444
95.46	−0.00408	0.00000450	95.46	5.58534444
93.24	−0.02353	0.00046549	93.24	0.02054444
93.75	0.005455	0.00005491	93.75	0.42684444
92.91	−0.009	0.00004963	92.91	0.03484444
93.65	0.007933	0.00009778	93.65	0.30617778

Table 3.5 Continued

| Price | Price Change | | Bollinger Band | |
	Log change	Diff squared	Price	Diff squared
94.50	0.009035	0.00012080	94.50	1.96934444
94.27	−0.00244	0.00000023	94.27	1.37671111
94.68	0.00434	0.00003963	94.68	2.50694444
93.65	−0.01094	0.00008070	93.65	0.30617778
94.25	0.006386	0.00006958	94.25	1.33017778
92.59	−0.01777	0.00025010	92.59	0.25671111
92.19	−0.00433	0.00000564	92.19	0.82204444
90.24	−0.02138	0.00037728	90.24	8.16054444
91.43	0.013101	0.00022669	91.43	2.77777778
90.35	−0.01188	0.00009855	90.35	7.54417778
90.40	0.000553	0.00000629	90.40	7.27201111
90.27	−0.00144	0.00000027	90.27	7.9 9004444

Avg log change	−0.0019553		Avg price	93.10
Sum diff squared	0.00266972		Sum diff squared	57.19182222
StdDev	0.01185375		StdDev price	$1.73
StdDev × $90.27	$1.07			
Annual volatility			**Annual volatility**	
0.01185 × 16	**0.19**		**1.73 / 90.27 × 16**	**0.31**

The distortion becomes most apparent when a 1 standard deviation price change is annualized to a 252-day trading year as described earlier (multiply by 16). Note that the actual volatility of the series was 19% (left side) while closing price calculations indicated a value of 31% (right side). Using price changes to correctly calculate volatility, we obtain a value of $1.07 for a one-day 1 standard deviation change. The Bollinger Band calculation ($1.73) would be very misleading to an option trader trying to reconcile option prices with the underlying's historical price change behavior. Moreover, the high values obtained by substituting closing prices for price changes is the principal reason for the 4 standard deviation default spacing of the bands (2 standard deviations above and below the simple moving average). An actual 2 standard deviation price change can be expected to occur with a frequency of less than 5%, and most securities would touch one of the bands only 12 to 15 times each year. In practice the distortion causes most securities to generate many more trading signals than the width of the bands would suggest. Bollinger Bands are an excellent stock trading tool, and much work has been done to characterize the underlying stochastic behavior that generates signals. However, they should not be used as a substitute for calculations that are designed to parallel option pricing theory.

Differential Volatility

Volatility frequently has a differential component that can be visualized in price spike charts. This effect is readily visualized in Figure 3.7, which contains 310 days of price change data for Apple Computer (AAPL). In the chart, upward spikes are consistently larger than downward ones, with a surprising number of changes larger than 4 standard deviations. Conversely, the downward side of the chart fits the normal distribution fairly well, with no spikes greater than 3 standard deviations and only six spikes greater than 2 standard deviations.

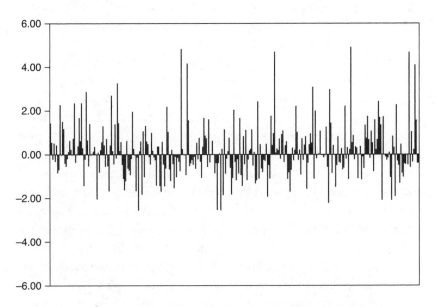

Figure 3.7   Apple Computer price spikes (10/19/2005–01/12/2007) expressed in standard deviations(10 day window).

Not surprisingly, Apple stock constantly rose during this period of time, reaching new highs on a regular basis. However, the fact that a stock is rising does not guarantee that upward price changes are consistently larger than downward ones. For example, a stock can rise when upward price changes are smaller but more frequent than downward ones. Alternatively, the frequency and size of up and down price changes could be similar, with a small number of very large exceptions on one side. Each of these scenarios is readily apparent in a price spike chart.

When this chart was created, AAPL calls were trading with implied volatility of 48%, while the puts were trading at 41%. The chart would suggest that AAPL puts are overpriced, because 7% is not enough to explain the differences in the chart. An excellent trade, therefore, might involve selling overpriced puts to pay for long calls. A skilled trader would close the position after the first large upward spike and start over. If the trend ends, and the distribution of up and down price changes begins to equalize, those changes will be evident in updated price spike charts. Large upside and downside differences in historical volatility often are not properly reflected in actual option prices. Properly priced put and call options on Apple Computer would represent an arbitrage opportunity. Professional investors would jump on the opportunity, buying calls, selling puts, and investing the difference in a stock-bond portfolio (short stock/long bonds). The arbitrage would rapidly vanish. This self-correcting effect actually prevents Apple puts from being properly priced and creates a simple trading opportunity. Statistically speaking, it makes sense to sell naked out-of-the-money puts under these circumstances, because they are overpriced and will deliver a steady profit. This analysis was validated on January 18, 2007, when Apple Computer stock opened down $2.88 after a disappointing earnings announcement the evening before. A 1 standard deviation move would have been $3.11. So, recast in these terms, Apple's downward spike was only 0.93 standard deviation. The surprisingly small downward spike on negative news validates the predictive power of Figure 3.7. A trader who sold puts before the previous evening's close at the inflated preannouncement volatility of 92% would have realized a tremendous profit, because the put price fell from $1.00 at the close to $0.40 at the open. Two trading days remained until expiration, and our investor might have attempted to realize a full $1.00 of profit by keeping the position open. That approach is a pure gamble that almost always loses money. The original idea was to trade against inflated volatility. As soon as volatility deflates, and the position is fairly priced, the trade becomes a directional bet. As it turned out, AAPL fell another $3.00 over the two remaining trading days, and the options expired in-the-money.

It is also important to understand that the overall risk of a large downward price spike is more limited than you might imagine, because naked short puts are somewhat equivalent to long stock. An investor who is unwilling to sell puts should reconsider the risks associated with long stock positions. However, options provide leverage, and it is important to remember not to oversize positions. Every ten contracts will become 1,000 shares if the stock moves deeply into-the-money. We will return to a detailed discussion of the logistics and risks associated with naked short positions in Chapter 5, "Managing Basic Option Positions."

Trading Volatility Cycles

Structured positions respond in predictable ways to rising or falling volatility. Consequently, the ability to predict rising, falling, or constant volatility can provide an important edge. Some stocks exhibit characteristic cycles composed of periods of high and low volatility. Unlike other types of cyclical behavior, repeatable volatility does not disappear as soon as it is discovered. The market lacks a mechanism for eliminating volatility swings because they do not confer a specific direction upon the underlying stock.

Periodic volatility swings can occur for many reasons. Oil company stocks, for example, become more volatile with the seasonal refinery changeover to heating oil. They also become more volatile during hurricane season when rigs in the Gulf of Mexico are in danger. Gasoline consumption for automobiles also tends to rise and fall with the seasons. Finally, volatility also tends to rise and fall on a weekly basis with the Department of Energy Oil Inventory Report. A series of regularly repeating cycles is evident in the one-year chart of Exxon Mobil volatility, shown in Figure 3.8. Generally speaking, volatility is itself a stochastic process that oscillates around a constant value—it is mean-reverting. If current volatility is low, it tends to rise, and if it is high, it

tends to fall. Mean reversion is one of the driving forces behind the
cycles displayed in the figure.

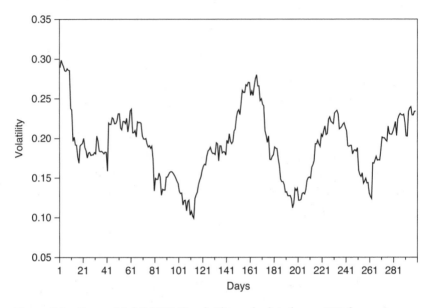

Figure 3.8 Exxon Mobil (XOM) volatility calculated over 300 days using a
20-day sliding window.

Although the cycles are imperfect, it is relatively easy to spot peaks and
troughs. For an option trader this information is invaluable, because it
facilitates relatively accurate assessment of a contract's value. The failure of implied volatility to mirror the cycles displayed in the chart creates a statistical arbitrage that can be profitably traded. Throughout
most of the year, XOM options were priced at 22% to 23%. They were
inexpensive at the peaks and overpriced at the troughs. The chart also
reveals the approximate length of each major cycle. Decisions about
structuring positions should take into account both the relative difference between implied and fair volatility and the trade's time horizon.
Underpriced contracts purchased at a peak will be affected by the
stock's increasing stability; overpriced contracts sold at a trough will
experience the effects of rising instability. Therefore, it is important to
make sure that the time horizon of a structured position does not over-
lap with the next transition between the stock's low and high volatility.

In this regard, it is often wise to close long positions when the stock's volatility falls below the options implied volatility and to buy back short positions if underlying volatility rises. However, if implied volatility begins to mirror the stock's behavior, it makes more sense to hold long positions from trough to peak and short positions from peak to trough. In this scenario long positions benefit from rising volatility—both implied and real—and short positions benefit from both volatility and time decay.

Skewed Volatility: The Volatility Smile

As we have seen, standard pricing models often fail at the extremes, where an occasional large price change can wreak havoc by suddenly placing distant strike prices in-the-money. One response to this problem has been to combine Black-Scholes-style pricing with structures known as *volatility smiles*. These hybrid models are designed to comprehend situations in which the future probability distribution of an underlying stock or index is not lognormal. The smile, which has a distinctive shape, can be visualized in a plot of implied volatility as a function of strike price for a fixed expiration. It is important to distinguish between smile and term structure, which measures the effect of time on implied volatility. Term structure can be visualized in a plot of implied volatility for at-the-money options versus expiration month. Its behavior tends to compress the shape of the smile curve as the maturity date increases. If we create a family of volatility smile curves, one curve per month, we will find that the shape of the curve becomes less pronounced as time advances. Experienced traders sometimes use this information to create a table containing the correct implied volatility for each expiration date and strike price.

The volatility smile became much more pronounced after the stock market crash of October 1987, when out-of-the-money puts climbed steeply in value. Since then, implied volatility profiles for equity and index options have taken on a distinctly negative skew—that is, volatility tends to rise as the strike price decreases. This effect causes out-of-the-money puts to be relatively more expensive than Black-Scholes theory predicts. Additionally, because put-call parity dictates that the relationship between strike price and implied volatility is the same for both types of contracts, in-the-money calls should also be more expensive. Figure 3.9 displays the February 2007 volatility smile for Apple Computer using contract prices at the market close on January 19 (AAPL traded at 88.68 at the close).

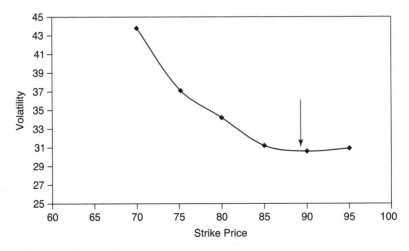

Figure 3.9 February 2007 volatility smile for Apple Computer. Data collected at the market close on January 19, 2007. AAPL's trading price is marked by a vertical arrow.

The volatility smile represents an important distortion of the Black-Scholes pricing model. As illustrated in Figure 3.9, option values decrease relative to a flat smile as the strike price increases. Near the right side of the chart they are considerably less expensive than predicted by a nonadjusted Black-Scholes model. Out-of-the-money calls, therefore, are heavily discounted. From a trading perspective this distortion can be interpreted to mean that volatility will fall if the stock (or the market) rises. Conversely, the high values placed on low strike prices indicate that volatility is expected to rise if the stock falls. This behavior is evident in most stocks, equity indexes, and the closely followed VIX. The form of the smile is different for other financial instruments. Currency options, for example, are priced with a symmetrical volatility increase centered at-the-money. Volatility increases whether an option moves into or out-of-the-money.

Skewness and Kurtosis

Skewness and kurtosis are statistical parameters that quantify the differences between an actual frequency distribution and a true normal distribution. *Skewness* quantifies the amount by which the curve is shifted about the center. A distribution is positively skewed if the curve's peak is shifted to the left and the tails on the right side are longer. Conversely, a negative skew shifts the peak to the right, leaving longer tails on the left side of the chart. In trading terms, a positively skewed curve includes an excessive number of large positive spikes that lengthen the positive tail, and a negative skew is caused by an excessive number of large negative spikes. A perfect normal distribution has a skewness of zero.

Kurtosis measures "peakedness"—that is, the extent to which the peak is tall and thin or short and flat. A distribution with a tall, narrow peak has positive kurtosis, and a low, flat peak is characteristic of negative kurtosis. In trading terms, positive kurtosis is caused by an increased number of very small and very large price changes, and a decreased number of intermediate price changes. Most markets display positive kurtosis—a large number of price spikes smaller than 1 standard deviation accompanied by a surprising number of spikes larger than 3 standard deviations. Very few stocks display negative kurtosis—very few small or large price changes and an abundance of intermediate price changes. None of today's equity indexes display negative kurtosis. The difference between high and neutral kurtosis is illustrated in Figure 3.10.

It is important to distinguish between high kurtosis and a low standard deviation distribution. Although a distribution characterized by an overabundance of small price changes would display an exaggerated peak, the tails would be smaller because of a reduced number of large spikes. Pricing less volatility into option contracts would not necessarily be appropriate, because the distribution would still be incorrect (nonlognormal). Stocks sometimes display this type of behavior after a major financial event, such as the announcement of an acquisition. Following the large price change, the stock often trades within a very tight range limited by the terms of the acquisition. It is very difficult to trade options on such stocks, because the appropriate distribution curve is unknowable, and prices are almost always skewed.

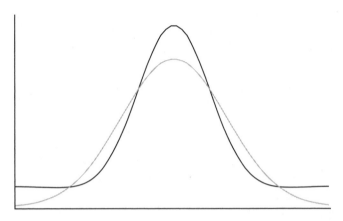

Figure 3.10 High versus neutral kurtosis. The light line traces a distribution displaying normal kurtosis; the dark line represents positive kurtosis.

Four basic parameters or moments are used to describe the shape of a distribution. The first moment defines the mean (normally 0), and the second is the variance. Skewness is described using the second and third moments, and kurtosis is defined by the third and fourth. The four moments are as follows, where X is the average price change:

$$m_1 = 1/n \sum_{i=1}^{n} (x_i - X)$$

$$m_2 = 1/n \sum_{i=1}^{n} (x_i - X)^2$$

$$m_3 = 1/n \sum_{i=1}^{n} (x_i - X)^3$$

$$m_4 = 1/n \sum_{i=1}^{n} (x_i - X)^4$$

The skewness and kurtosis of a distribution are defined using the four moments as follows:

$$skewness = \frac{m_3}{m_2 \sqrt{m_2}}$$

$$kurtosis = \frac{m_4}{(m_2)^2} - 3$$

Note that we subtract 3 from the value computed in the final equation. Neutral kurtosis has a value of 3, and the subtraction leaves what is often referred to as "excess kurtosis." For convenience, we center kurtosis at zero and measure excess kurtosis.

Summary

With the exception of volatility, each of the parameters used to price options has a precise known value. Because the value of an option contract directly depends on volatility, its accurate assessment is a critical skill for an option trader. Moreover, changes in volatility are dramatically amplified in the price of an option contract; doubling the volatility can increase the contract price several hundred percent.

Volatility is defined as a 1 standard deviation price change over one trading year. It takes two basic forms—implied and historical. Historical volatility is derived from the price change history of an optionable stock, index, or future. Implied volatility can be extrapolated directly from the price of an option contract using the Black-Scholes pricing model. The difference between implied and historical volatility often provides a statistical arbitrage opportunity that can be traded for a profit.

Volatility can be calculated using a sliding window of fixed length. Larger windows spanning longer time frames tend to smooth out major spikes. Smaller windows provide a more granular view and facilitate short-term analysis. A series of price changes measured against historical volatility can be calculated in terms of standard deviations and displayed as a series of spikes on a chart. Such charts are useful for visualizing and studying price change behavior.

Historical volatility often takes on a cyclical characteristic. If implied volatility follows the same cycles, it often makes sense to structure long option positions coincident with a trough and short positions at the peaks. Conversely, if implied volatility remains relatively constant, it is often profitable to sell overpriced option contracts when volatility of the underlying approaches a low point, and to purchase options at a peak when the underlying is more volatile than contract prices would indicate. In both cases trades should be closed when long positions are judged to be overpriced or short positions are underpriced.

The Black-Scholes pricing model is often modified using a volatility smile. The smile generally causes out-of-the-money puts and in-the-money calls to appear overpriced with regard to Black-Scholes pricing theory. It also causes high strike price contracts (above-the-money) to be underpriced. After the market crash of 1987, the smile became more pronounced due to the perceived risk associated with short put positions. From a trader's perspective, the market generally views rising prices as an indicator of stability and, therefore, discounts the future value of high strike price options. Conversely, the instability associated with falling markets places a premium on low strike price contracts.

Skewness and kurtosis are two additional measures of the shape of a distribution. A positively skewed distribution is shifted to the left, with a lengthened tail on the positive side. A negative skew has the opposite effect, shifting the peak to the right and lengthening the negative tail. Kurtosis describes the "peakedness" of a distribution. Positive kurtosis describes a tall, thin peak and large tails. Negative kurtosis is characterized by a large number of intermediate spikes and fewer large or small changes. The peak of the distribution is lower and wider, and the tails are small.

Before we move on to the dynamics of specific structured positions, the next chapter briefly discusses some of the overriding issues affecting many different types of option trades. This discussion is designed to complement our review of option pricing theory, and to serve as the foundation for the remainder of this book.

Further Reading

Gatheral, J., *The Volatility Surface: A Practitioner's Guide*: John Wiley and Sons, 2006

McMillan, L.G., *McMillan on Options*, New York–Singapore: John Wiley and Sons, 1996.

Natenberg, S., *Option Volatility and Pricing*, Revised Edition, New York: McGraw-Hill/Irwin Professional Publishing, 1994.

Rubinstein, M., "Implied Binomial Trees," *Journal of Finance* 69, no 3 (July 1994), pp. 771–818.

4

GENERAL
CONSIDERATIONS

T his book discusses various strategies for dynamically managing structured option positions. The word "structured" has important meaning in this context. All option positions, regardless of their complexity, have a structure that dictates how they behave as underlying prices change and expiration approaches. Complex positions built with long and short components can be confusing to manage. A call ratio, for example, can be net long one day and net short the next if the underlying rises quickly. Even simple trades can undergo surprising changes in character.

Understanding the behavior of an option position with regard to time decay and changes in the price of the underlying is just the beginning. You must take into account a number of other factors when establishing a new position and throughout a trade's life cycle. Following is a brief list of some of the most persistent issues:

- Bid-ask spreads: These are more variable than most traders realize and are affected by many parameters—expiration month, liquidity, behavior of the underlying, news surprises, and approaching weekends/holidays, to name just a few. For out-of-the-money options, bid-ask spreads can represent a major percentage of the potential profit. Their effect grows with a trade's complexity. Positions consisting of long and short puts and calls often have combined bid-ask spreads greater than

60 cents despite an expected return of less than $2.00. A required position adjustment has the potential to double the impact. Closing a position before expiration adds at least another 5 cents to each component.

- Volatility swings: Seemingly small changes in volatility can significantly impact option prices. Volatility often rises as earnings or other planned events approach. It also rises when the overall market becomes unstable or when the underlying price falls rapidly. Conversely, volatility can fall in the last few minutes of a trading day, as a weekend approaches, when stocks rise or the market becomes more stable, after a news event has passed, when trading volume is low, or during expiration week.

- Put-call parity violations: When the market believes that the chance of an upside move is different from the chance of a downside move, it often responds with differential pricing for puts and calls. Sometimes the differential is due to expectations that positive news will have a different effect than negative news. The market might believe, for example, that up moves are likely to be small and down moves large. Such is often the case when analysts have very high earnings expectations and a stock has been performing well. The penalty for an earnings disappointment can be excessive, and put pricing will be skewed to the upside. Moreover, as short interest falls, the chance of an extended downward spike increases (short covering often stabilizes rapid price declines). Option positions vary greatly in their sensitivity to such parity distortions. However, bid-ask spreads and commissions normally make it impossible to profit from the skew. Even very large differences can be impossible to exploit. In many cases these differences provide a hint about a stock's likely direction.

- Liquidity: Large option trades are much more difficult to execute than small ones. The level 2 option trading queue often reveals that the number of contracts bid or offered at a particular price is very small. Such illiquidity changes the real bid-ask spread when the first level in the queue will not completely fill an order. Surprisingly, this problem can impact even small positions when the underlying stock is thinly traded. It can also make it impossible to close a position in a fast-moving market. Small private investors often have an advantage in this regard because they can execute trades online. Institutional investors trading thousands of contracts must negotiate the trade and lack the flexibility to make rapid adjustments.

You will identify direct relationships between some of these items. For example, both low levels of liquidity and put-call parity violations cause bid-ask spreads to widen. It makes sense for various trading parameters to react to each other, because they are mathematically linked at every level. The purpose of this chapter is to build on these relationships to create a framework that can be used to discuss the dynamics of various structured positions.

Bid-Ask Spreads

Bid-ask spreads pose a serious challenge that scales with positional complexity. We will illustrate using a popular four-part trade known as a condor. The trade consists of a short straddle or strangle[1] with long options purchased at further out-of-the-money strike prices. It can also be visualized as a bullish vertical credit spread combined with a bearish vertical credit spread. Consider a condor position built around Sears options on the afternoon of January 25, 2007, 23 days before expiration, with Sears trading at $175.55. Data for this trade is contained in Table 4.1.

Table 4.1 Sears (SHLD) options appropriate for a condor trade, January 25, 2007.

Calls			Puts		
Strike	Bid	Ask	Strike	Bid	Ask
175	$5.00	$5.20	155	$0.25	$0.35
180	$2.70	$2.85	160	$0.50	$0.65
185	$1.30	$1.45	165	$1.05	$1.15
190	$0.60	$0.70	170	$2.05	$2.15
195	$0.25	$0.35	175	$3.90	$4.00

Several possible strike price combinations can be used to structure this trade. Assume that we go long 190 calls/160 puts and short 185 calls/165 puts. Purchasing at the ask and selling at the bid would create a position that is net short $1.00. If all went well, the short options would expire out-of-the-money, and we would collect $1.00 of profit in 23 days.

However, if we decided to immediately unwind the trade, we would need to spend $1.50. (That is, we would buy back the short side at ask prices, and sell the long side at bid prices.) The trade, therefore, represents an immediate loss, and ten days of stable time decay without any major stock moves are needed to break even. Worse still, the loss is huge—50%. In effect, 50 cents has become the cost of the trade—$500 for every 10 contracts. Furthermore, if during the waiting period Sears experiences a large price spike, we will need to make positional adjustments. These changes will cause the paper loss related to the bid-ask spread to be fully realized in addition to the much larger loss of the failed trade. This problem often causes experienced traders structuring complex positions to begin with a relatively small trade and to inflate the trade's size with each correction. The first inflation must be large enough to cover two rounds of bid-ask spreads, the initial loss from the failed trade, and trading expenses. It is also important to remember that as expiration nears, the risk/reward ratio increases. For example, if four days remain and the short side is worth only 10 cents—that is, bid $0.05, ask $0.10—it might make sense to close the trade early rather than risk a large move of the underlying. Unfortunately, closing the trade early effectively adds another 10 cents to the bid-ask spread. If we had adopted this risk-management strategy at the outset, our trade would have been worth only $0.90. The bid-ask spread would have cost 67%.

We could have selected a larger gap between long and short strike prices. If, as before, we sold 185 calls and 165 puts, but we purchased 195 calls and 155 puts, we would have been net short $1.65. The cost to unwind this trade would be $2.10—a loss of $0.45, or 27.3%. Even if we eliminate the long side and create a simple short position worth $2.35, the cost to unwind would still be $0.25, or 10.6%. However, naked short positions have higher collateral requirements, and the opportunity cost of this money must be taken into account in addition to the increased risk.[2] Many traders believe that the advantages of a simpler position with fewer moving parts far outweigh the complexity and cost of more complex hedged positions such as the condor. Others believe that it makes sense to take advantage of reduced collateral requirements by structuring more conservative hedged positions like the condor in a much larger size than would otherwise be possible. We will return to a more detailed discussion of the dynamics of complex positions in Chapter 6, "Managing Complex Positions."

Before moving on, we should address one of the most important contemporary trading issues—the practice of "legging in." Traders generally believe that they can beat the bid-ask spread by watching the stock's behavior and executing each side of the trade at just the right moment. Some wait for a piece of news, and when the stock begins to move, they execute one side, wait, and then execute the other. (If the stock is falling on negative news, they sell calls and/or buy puts; then, after some brief period of time, they buy calls and/or sell puts.) Others use a variety of technical indicators to time the execution of each side. Most traders succeed in "beating" the bid-ask spread less than 50% of the time. You should not ignore the magnitude of price change required to make up a typical bid-ask spread. For example, if the delta of an option is 0.20, a 50-cent move of the underlying would be required to make up a 10-cent differential. A trader who can reliably predict short-term 50-cent price changes should have no interest in structuring complex option positions because day trading of stocks would provide a superior return. Likewise, if a trader does not believe that he or she could generate a profit through very rapid day trading, that person should not expect to beat the bid-ask spread either. Professional traders generally caution against legging in and view bid-ask spreads as a cost of doing business.

It is also important to distinguish between different classes of investors when discussing susceptibility to the bid-ask spread problem. Small private investors trading fewer than 100 contracts often do better than hedge funds and other large investors trading hundreds or thousands of contracts. For large trades it is important to watch the queue to anticipate the bid-ask spread that is most likely to be realized at execution. Whereas small private investors normally execute their trades online at the "best" bid and ask prices, large trades often execute at lower levels in the queue, where bid prices are lower and ask prices are higher. Hedge funds typically execute through a clearing broker, and their trades are placed through an options desk. They normally experience terrible execution compared to a small private online investor. Conversely, very large institutional investors, such as investment banks, have a distinct edge, because they write option contracts and trade directly on the exchange. Unlike most private investors, they can take advantage of penny pricing on options. The edge becomes apparent on the last trading day before expiration. The final trade normally contains a few cents of time value. As a result, the last purchase of an in-the-money option normally is by a large institutional investor whose exercise cost is very small. Bid-ask spreads usually narrow to 5 cents by this point, but they can be larger.

Bid-ask spreads are also affected by very short-term volatility. When the underlying is highly unstable, bid prices tend to fall, and ask prices tend to rise. This behavior makes sense, because it is very easy for buyers to overpay or for sellers to be undercompensated for risk when the underlying displays erratic behavior. Additionally, if the instability persists, volatility will rise. Rising volatility puts pressure on buyers and forces bid prices lower.

Finally, bid-ask spreads are sometimes affected by the time remaining until expiration. Although spreads tend to widen as the expiration month is moved out, they usually fall as a percentage of the total price. This effect makes long-term options relatively less expensive. From a bid-ask perspective, short-term far out-of-the-money options are the most expensive. Most online brokerage software attempts to resolve part of this problem by calculating option contract values as the mean of the two prices when determining overall account value.

Volatility Swings

Subtle changes in volatility have enormous effects on option prices. Figure 4.1 illustrates the effect using Black-Scholes calculations based on the following parameters:

Stock price	$135
Strike price	$145
Days remaining	30
Risk-free interest	5%
Volatility	25%–33%

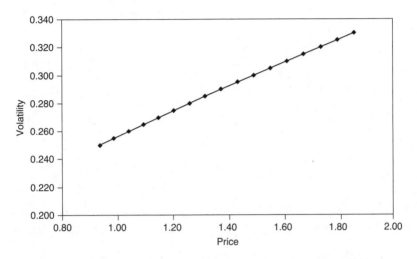

Figure 4.1   Volatility versus price for options having 30 days left before expiration.

Reducing the volatility from 30% to 27% causes the price to fall from $1.50 to $1.15—a 23% loss. The parameters used in the figure closely mirror those of the Oil Service HOLDRS Trust (OIH), an exchange traded fund composed of oil services companies. Bid-ask spreads for options on the fund normally are 10 cents. Because the calculation normally yields the midpoint, we would need to add 5 cents to the purchase price and subtract 5 cents from the real value. A sudden 3% volatility swing therefore would reduce the price from $1.55 to $1.10—a 29% loss.

OIH is one of many stocks that frequently experience such rapid changes in implied volatility. On January 23, 2007, for example, OIH rose $1.53 in the first 30 minutes of trading after opening $1.13 higher than the previous day's close. Call buyers should have realized the benefits of an overnight 2% rise in the stock. However, the calls lost 3% of their volatility while the stock was climbing. Worse still, the change in implied volatility compounded a 2% decrease that apparently occurred overnight. Out-of-the-money $145 strike price calls traded for less after the overnight and early-morning stock price increases than they did at the previous day's close. The problem was further compounded by 6 cents per day of time decay and bid-ask spreads that fluctuated between 10 and 15 cents. An investor who purchased calls at noon the previous day, when the stock traded at $133.24, would have paid $1.25. After the 2% increase in stock price, he or she would have had an unrealized loss of 25 cents per contract (calculated at the bid price). Table 4.2 contains the relevant data for this trade.

Table 4.2   OIH $145 strike calls, January 22–25, 2007.

Date	Time	Stock Price	Implied Volatility	Bid	Ask
01/22/2007	12:00:00 p.m.	$133.24	0.33	$1.15	$1.25
01/22/2007	4:00:00 p.m.	$132.49	0.33	$1.00	$1.10
01/23/2007	9:30:00 a.m.	$133.62	0.31	$0.95	$1.05
01/23/2007	10:00:00 a.m.	$135.15	0.28	$0.95	$1.05
01/24/2007	4:00:00 p.m.	$136.25	0.25	$0.80	$0.90
01/25/2007	4:00:00 p.m.	$133.25	0.30	$0.70	$0.80

The curve steepens in terms of percent change as distance to the strike price increases. If we had been trading the $150 strike price, our options would have declined from $0.65 at noon on January 22 to $0.35 at 10:00 a.m. on January 23 despite a 2% increase in the stock price. We would need the stock price to increase nearly $4.00 to offset this loss (the delta would increase from 0.09 to 0.12). Because 1 standard deviation for OIH was approximately $2.35 on January 22, a $4.00 increase is substantial.[3] We should not forget that the volatility decrease we are attempting to offset was caused by an increase only half this large. Furthermore, over the next 24 hours, OIH's trading price continued to rise, and implied volatility fell another 2% before finally stabilizing just above 25%. During this time frame, both puts and calls lost value. At the close on January 24, the stock traded at $136.25—up 2.3% from where we started—and $145 strike price calls fell to $0.85. The next day, when the stock fell from $136 to just over $133, implied volatility returned to 30%, partly buffering the decrease in call values. Two days of time decay, bid-ask spreads, and a 3% decrease in volatility eroded $0.55 from our original $1.25 call price—a loss of 44%. Conversely, while the stock was rising, put volatility remained constant around 36%. During the fall from $136 to $133, long puts benefited from both a falling stock price and rising volatility. This asymmetric behavior is very significant for investors who purchase straddles, because the trade's performance is skewed to the downside. We will return to a detailed discussion of the dynamics of straddles and strangles in Chapter 5, "Managing Basic Option Positions."

As we saw in the preceding chapter, implied volatility can also rise and fall over longer time frames ranging from days to months. The changes are usually large, and the effect on option prices can be dramatic. One of the most notable examples is the distortion that accompanies most earnings releases. Option prices generally rise in proportion to the perceived risk of a certain size spike, and implied volatility is merely a representation of the price. For example, if a $100 stock has a history of spiking 10% with each earnings release, sellers will assign a high risk to $110 calls and $90 puts. Variability with regard to the size of previous spikes tends to increase the perceived risk and drive option prices even higher. Table 4.3 contains data for five earnings releases for Sears (SHLD).

Table 4.3   Price change data for five earnings releases for Sears (SHLD).

Date	Percent Change	Change in StdDev
11/16/2006	−0.055	−3.600
08/17/2006	−0.058	−3.100
05/18/2006	0.130	9.700
03/15/2006	0.128	11.600
12/06/2005	0.054	2.900

Spikes range from 5% to 13% (2.9 to 11.6 standard deviations).[4] Because short sellers confronted with this data have no reliable way of predicting the size of the next earnings spike, they tend to err on the side of caution. Even the most cautious short seller would likely have lost a significant amount of money in the March 2006 spike. Conversely, option buyers who established long positions for the August or November earnings releases dramatically overpaid and lost virtually 100% of their investment in the volatility collapse that followed each event.

We can calculate the option volatility that would have been appropriate for the March 2006 spike. At the market close on March 14, just before earnings were announced, Sears was trading at $117.27. Expiration was four days away—Saturday, March 18, at 5:00 p.m. We know that the post-earnings $15.02 price spike would place the $120 calls $12.29 in-the-money. Using the following parameters, we can calculate a fair price for the calls:

Stock price	$117.27
Strike price	$120.00
Days left	4.042 (1.1%)
Risk-free interest	4.5%
$120 strike-call price	$12.29

Not surprisingly, the implied volatility would be extraordinarily high—274%. As the strike price increases, the magnitude of the price distortion decreases. $125 strike price calls would have been fairly valued at 211% volatility, and a short seller with a crystal ball would have defensively valued $130 strike price calls at 132% ($2.29). The $135 strike price remained out-of-the-money and was fairly valued at bid $0.00, ask $0.05.

Considering the size of the March 2006 price spike, it is not surprising that sellers would be extremely cautious as the May earnings release approached. Likewise, buyers hoping for another spike were willing to purchase very high volatility. The buyers were correct. The stock experienced another enormous price spike—9.7 standard deviations. Market prices generally remained too low to adequately compensate sellers for risk. As a result, prices were bid even higher for the August release, when the stock moved only 3 standard deviations. Sellers won in August.

Sears, like many companies, tends to report earnings only a few days before options expiration. The rapid time decay of these last few days tends to exaggerate the price distortion. As expiration day approaches, implied volatility tends to rise sharply, keeping option prices nearly constant by offsetting time decay. In effect, sellers and buyers are trading the absolute spike size, not the underlying volatility. Each trade represents an agreement on the anticipated price change. An interesting strategy involves structuring a long position that benefits from increasing volatility and closing the trade just before earnings are released. Heavily traded stocks are the best candidates, because their options tend to experience disproportionately large increases in implied volatility. Table 4.4 illustrates this effect for five different stocks approaching earnings during an expiration week.

Table 4.4   Volatility for five stocks approaching earnings during an expiration week.

Ticker	Base Volatility	Day 4 Volatility	Day 3 Volatility	Day 2 Volatility	Day 1 Volatility
GOOG	0.28	0.64	0.73	0.91	1.30
SLB	0.41	0.56	0.64	0.66	0.68
AAPL	0.37	0.59	0.66	0.88	0.96
YHOO	0.31	0.45	0.54	0.72	0.81
EBAY	0.43	0.57	0.68	0.90	0.99

The Base Volatility column displays the average implied volatility priced into at-the-money options on these stocks during the preceding month. The columns labeled Day 4 through Day 1 contain implied volatilities for the final four days (Day 1 is the final day). The value labeled *Day 1* is the implied volatility during the final few minutes of trading before the announcement. Price distortions are large because each company reported earnings during expiration week (data of July 2006).

Although the effects are additive, earnings releases have a much more pronounced impact on option prices than close proximity to an expiration date. The difference is evident in Figure 4.2. It displays implied volatility data for Google options during two different expiration cycles—one with an earnings release and one without.

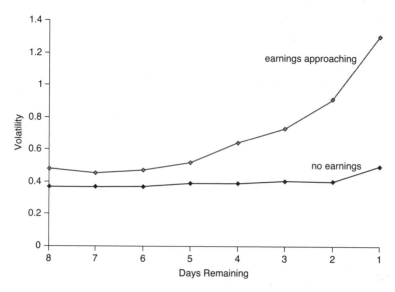

Figure 4.2 Implied volatility profile for Google options during the final days of two different expiration cycles. In both cases, the final data point represents implied volatility for at-the-money call options calculated at the close on Thursday preceding the final trading day in the expiration cycle—expiration Friday. In the first case (the upper line), earnings were announced after the market close on Thursday, July 20, 2006. The lower line displays implied volatility data for the final days of the August 2006 expiration cycle.

Reading from the right side of the chart, we see that Google call options were priced with 130% volatility just before earnings were announced. More specifically, $390 strike price calls were trading at $13.70. Because the stock closed at $387.12, we can say that the options market anticipated a $16.58 price spike—the precise amount priced into the $390 call options. Google opened the next day—after earnings were released—at $386.14. It traded near this price all day, ultimately closing at $390.11. $390 strike price calls that sold for more than $13.00 the previous day were ultimately worth only a few cents. Sellers won, and buyers lost. One final note: we could have extended each line one more day to show volatility priced at the close on Friday. However, because in both cases Friday was the final trading day for options in this cycle, implied volatility fell to nearly zero. We will further explore strategies for trading the expiration cycle and its price distortions in Chapter 8, "Trading the Expiration Cycle."

Put-Call Parity Violations

Put-call parity violations are common, but for a variety of reasons they are virtually impossible to trade for a public customer. In most cases bid-ask spreads narrow the arbitrage by increasing buying prices and decreasing selling prices. At the time of this writing, 143 strike price calls on SPDR Trust (an exchange traded fund composed of the S&P 500 index stocks) were trading with implied volatility of 11.6%. SPDR puts, however, were worth only 7.6%. Unfortunately, each side also had a 10-cent bid-ask spread. On the call side, 10 cents equaled 10% of the $1.00 price, and on the put side it was close to 7%. Add trading costs and expenses associated with a complex arbitrage trade that includes long and short positions on options and the underlying fund, in addition to bond trades, and all potential profit vanishes for a public customer.

SPDRs exhibit very small parity violations compared with common stocks and some special indexes. Call options on the VIX, for example, sometimes trade near 200% implied volatility, while puts trade below 50%. These extreme differences occur when the VIX nears its practical lower limit around 10, as it did during the second half of 2006. Knowledgeable traders understood that the index couldn't fall much lower, so they assigned very low implied volatility values to puts. However, because any market instability would have sharply raised the value from historically low levels, calls were priced much more aggressively. Moreover, it would have been perfectly reasonable for the VIX to rise into the 20s. In the event of a sudden large market correction, the index could easily rise to 80, 90, or beyond. For these reasons, call and put prices are completely decoupled. Arbitrage traders cannot profit from these huge differences because the underlying cannot be purchased or sold—it is a calculated index.

The VIX is an extreme example but a good one, because the parity violations are persistent and prohibit many types of option trades. For example, if a trader felt certain that a stock would rise, he or she might purchase calls and sell puts to pay the time decay. That trade fails for the VIX when the index is at very low levels because the puts have virtually no time value. The trader would be forced to sell in-the-money puts, which simply move up and down with the value of the index. Most parity differentials are much more subtle but still disruptive to complex trades.

Option prices for Goldman Sachs stock (GS) will serve to illustrate. In late December 2006, puts and calls traded at parity—around 24%. However, a spectacular earnings release and rapid increases in the stock price raised implied volatility for at-the-money calls to just over 29% by late January. Puts continued trading at 24% because the market had a very positive view of the stock. Traders who sold puts and purchased calls benefited from a 20% gain in call prices independent of any changes in the underlying. However, the trade becomes very risky if the parity violation unwinds. A sudden drop in GS would erase the extra 5% of implied volatility on the call side while driving a corresponding rise in put volatility. Suppose call volatility fell 5% and put volatility rose by the same amount. Such a change would lower call values by 20% and increase put values by approximately the same amount—a 40% swing in the total position value. Add the damage caused by the drop in stock price, and it becomes apparent that an unfortunate trade placed at the wrong time could lose 100% or more.

Traders should exercise caution when structuring positions on rising or falling stocks with put-call parity discrepancies. If the trade is designed to profit from a continued move in the direction anticipated by option prices, the damage caused by a reversal will be amplified by a return to parity. A reversal that results in a new parity violation in the other direction will be especially destructive. Surprisingly, it is often safer to exploit parity violations by selling potentially overpriced out-of-the-money options on the expensive side.

Liquidity

Liquidity of both the underlying and its options is a critical factor that determines whether it makes sense to structure a trade. Open interest, the number of outstanding option contracts in a particular series, is a critical component affecting liquidity. However, open interest can be misleading, because on any given day, total trading volume can exceed open interest if a powerful event is unfolding. Volumes of this magnitude frequently occur when a stock trades very close to a strike price on the last day of an expiration cycle. Some stocks regularly behave this way. That is, they tend to trade near a strike price on the last day of each expiration cycle while displaying very high levels of option contract liquidity for at-the-money options.

When trading volumes of both the underlying and its options are high, and price changes of the underlying are small, bid-ask spreads tend to narrow, and trade execution is rapid. These conditions obviously are beneficial to traders. Certain levels of liquidity are necessary to support various trade sizes. If the goal is to buy or sell a small number of contracts, low levels of liquidity are rarely a problem. However, institutional customers rarely find enough contracts for smooth execution on standard equity options. As a result, hedge funds and other large investors frequently focus on indexes and stocks with very high trading volumes. Another approach involves placing large negotiated trades that are individually capitalized through an options desk at a major clearing broker. These trades, unfortunately, cannot provide the level of flexibility that can be achieved by small private investors who trade online. Table 4.5 represents the tremendous variability that characterizes option contract liquidity. The table contains volume and open interest data for several stocks collected at the close on January 29, 2007.

Table 4.5 Liquidity parameters for several stocks (market close 01/29/2007).

Ticker	Price	Share Volume in Millions	At-the-Money Call Volume (Current Month)	Open Interest
DELL	$23.85	18	3530	66,690
OIH	$131.71	8.7	3687	26,591
IBM	$98.54	7.3	4200	21,769
DIA	$124.82	6.7	2973	12,788
SHLD	$176.54	1.5	607	5,830
ISRG	$97.52	0.59	281	2,426
BSC	$162.05	1.54	477	959
BOT	$171.03	0.202	262	407
BLK	$168.58	0.198	3	65
FFH	$179.70	0.194	0	21

You will notice that stock price does not correlate with open interest, and that open interest does not drive trading volume. Dell, a $23 stock, has far more open interest than Sears, which trades at nearly 9 times the price. Moreover, Fairfax Financial Holdings (FFH) traded just below $180 with virtually no option volume or open interest. FFH's vanishingly small option contract liquidity parallels the stock's relatively low volume (194,000 shares). Although you might expect open interest and option volume to scale in relative proportion, they frequently do not. The discrepancy is apparent in the volumes and open interest levels for Bear Sterns (BSC), Oil Service HOLDRS Trust exchange traded fund (OIH), IBM, and Dell. Each displays a distinctly different ratio of call volume to open interest for the day depicted in the table. As previously mentioned, private investors can successfully trade all but the last two entries in the table—Black Rock (BLK) and FFH. Large investors would avoid all but the top four entries, and institutional traders would find limitations everywhere. Surprisingly, even options on DIAMONDS Trust (DIA)—an exchange traded fund that mirrors the Dow Jones

Industrial Average—present limitations to very large investors. A 1,000-contract trade would represent one-third of the day's volume for the particular series listed in the table.

It is sometimes helpful to view the level II queue to understand the depth in terms of the number of contracts comprising the bid and ask for a particular series. Table 4.6 contains volume, open interest, and bid-ask data for around-the-money strike prices for Apple Computer (data recorded at the close on January 29, 2007, with AAPL trading at $85.94).

Table 4.6 Level II trading queue for AAPL around-the-money (current expiration) call options.

Strike	Open Interest	Contract Volume	Bid	Bid Size	Ask	Ask Size
80	10949	2142	$6.60	190	$6.70	144
			$6.50	354	$6.80	1041
85	32373	9308	$3.00	3360	$3.10	291
					$3.20	45
90	63672	16821	$1.05	2811	$1.10	1009
					$1.15	87

Much information can be gleaned from the level II queue. For example, the large open interest and volume associated with the $90 strike price make sense, because Apple traded below, and then significantly above, and ultimately below this price during the three weeks preceding this time point. The large volume associated with this strike price is not simply a reflection of the open interest. We know this because open interest on the put side of the $85 strike was considerably larger (54,682 contracts), but the daily volume was much smaller. Table 4.7 shows level II queue data for puts.

Table 4.7   Level II trading queue for AAPL around-the-money (current expiration) put options.

Strike	Open Interest	Contract Volume	Bid	Bid Size	Ask	Ask Size
80	67909	4147	$0.50	13	$0.55	3112
			$0.45	4884		1041
85	54682	6015	$1.90	1293	$1.95	357
			$1.85	448	$2.00	813
90	29167	3935	$4.90	2350	$5.00	263

Although there is no precise set of rules for interpreting the data, the bullish market view is readily apparent. Note, for example, that the daily volume for out-of-the-money calls is approximately 4 times larger than the volume of out-of-the-money puts ($90 calls versus $80 puts).

The important conclusion is that high levels of liquidity provide both an efficient trading environment and useful data. Many experienced traders believe that it is impossible to have a balanced view of a stock's behavior without studying both sides of the options queue for several strike prices and expiration dates. Day traders often use the queue as a technical indicator. They track trading speed, bid/ask size, depth of the queue, and general interest in each strike price. They also use the queue to determine the true bid-ask spread for a trade of a particular size. In some instances, it is necessary to step down one or two levels in the queue to find enough contracts to complete a trade. Each step down is normally met with a significant widening of the bid-ask spread.

Summary

Pricing theory fails to address a small number of key issues that impact the profitability of option trades. Bid-ask spreads, rapid volatility swings, put-call parity violations, and varying liquidity levels can each affect both pricing and profit. Sensitive dependence on initial conditions is the theme, because small changes in any of these parameters can have a significant impact on a position's value.

Bid-ask spreads plague complex trades because they are individually realized on every part of the trade. It is not unusual for the spread to cost more than 30% of the total value of a position; a single correction can sometimes take virtually all the profit. Bid-ask spreads also increase with position size because it sometimes becomes necessary to execute large trades at lower levels in the queue, where bid prices are lower and ask prices are higher. This problem is significant for institutional traders, who often are forced to capitalize their trades with new money using negotiated prices. Very large institutions benefit from reduced costs because they can trade directly on the exchange. Hedge funds, trading through a clearing broker, must bear the full cost. Hedge funds normally attempt to mitigate the risks associated with slow online execution of very large trades by submitting them to an options desk for execution. Small private investors who trade online can sometimes achieve excellent execution as their trades are swept up and executed by their broker as part of a larger block. Moreover, very large trades can affect option pricing, but small trades normally do not.

Bid prices tend to fall, and ask prices tend to rise, in unstable or illiquid environments. The effect represents insecurity and caution on the part of traders. As weekends approach, bid-ask spreads tend to widen to accommodate risks associated with volatility and time decay. Sellers are cautious about the risk that a weekend event will result in a large move of the underlying, and buyers are leery of paying for two additional days of time decay while markets are closed.

Volatility, the only imprecise variable priced into option contracts, is also highly variable. Volatility can rise or fall for a variety of reasons. Traders are sometimes surprised when call prices fall despite a rise in the underlying stock. This effect results from falling volatility that accompanies an increasingly stable rising stock. The closely followed

VIX mirrors this behavior and, as a result, has become a benchmark of market stability. Earnings releases affect volatility more than almost any other planned event. Implied volatility tends to rise at a steady rate as earnings approach and deflate immediately after. In the final few days, option values are driven by the perceived risk of a particular size spike rather than by historical volatility. Implied volatility rises simply because the option price is rising. The effect is dramatic when companies report earnings during an expiration week. One potential trading strategy that capitalizes on this scenario involves purchasing puts and calls several days before an earnings release, riding the volatility curve to the top, and closing the position just before the announcement. More traditional strategies are executed by short sellers who take the risk of selling inflated volatility on the last day before earnings, or buyers who pay inflated prices to purchase options because they expect an uncharacteristic move of the underlying. It is important to analyze data from past earnings releases to determine a reasonable implied volatility range. Recasting the data in standard deviations is key to the analysis because it levels the playing field across times when the stock price and/or volatility were different.

Put-call parity violations often occur when the market has a bullish or bearish view of a stock or industry. Trading costs and bid-ask spreads normally make it impossible to profit from the arbitrage. However, it is possible to realize a profit or loss, depending on the position, if the parity disruption unwinds and volatilities equalize or reverse.

Liquidity is important because it affects the other parameters and ultimately determines whether a trade can be executed smoothly. The best way to track liquidity is to watch the level II options queue, which contains open interest, volume, and bid-ask information in terms of both size and price for each exchange and strike price. Many traders watch the queue for hints about bullish or bearish sentiment. Day traders sometimes use the level II queue as a technical indicator. They tend to superimpose market speed on other parameters such as depth of the queue and bid-ask sizes at various prices. The picture is complex and requires experience to interpret.

Chapter 5 begins to analyze specific structured positions. Our initial discussion will focus on the basics—long and short puts and calls, straddles and strangles, and covered stock trades. Our analysis will build on your understanding of pricing, volatility, and some of the special trading considerations mentioned in this chapter. Our goal will be to develop an extensible framework for the dynamic management of both simple and complex option positions.

Further Reading

Chicago Board Options Exchange, "Hedge Funds and Listed Options: Portfolio Management Strategies," *CBOE Investor Series,* paper no 5, 2001.

Cohen, G., *The Bible of Options Strategies: The Definitive Guide for Practical Trading Strategies,* Australia–Malaysia: Pearson Education publishing as Financial Times–Prentice Hall, 2005.

Thomsett, M., *Getting Started in Options,* New York: John Wiley & Sons, 1993.

Thomsett, M., *Options Trading for the Conservative Investor,* Australia–Malaysia: Pearson Education publishing as Financial Times–Prentice Hall, 2005.

Endnotes

[1] A straddle is composed of short or long puts and calls at the same strike price. A strangle uses different strike prices.

[2] The requirement is 25% of the value of the underlying stock represented by the contracts on the more valuable side plus the value of the option contracts. When a trade involves short and long contracts, the collateral requirement is based on the difference between the strike prices. If the long position involves the same or better strike price and expiration date, there is no collateral requirement.

[3] January 2007 calculated volatility for OIH was 28.8%, and 1 standard deviation was $2.35.

[4] Measured using the most recent 20-day volatility window for each spike.

5

MANAGING BASIC OPTION
POSITIONS

his chapter focuses on basic option positions—long calls or puts, short calls or puts, long straddles, covered calls or puts, and a variety of variants employing simple combinations of stock and options. The words basic and simple are misleading. Volatility swings, bid-ask spreads, earnings announcements, expiration cycles, liquidity, and a variety of other complex issues affect so-called simple trades just as they do complex ones. Every trade, large or small, simple or complex, requires the trader to select a strike price and an expiration month. Strike price selection is impacted by many variables, time and underlying volatility being the most prominent. Sometimes seemingly simple trades can become very complex because they involve both a view of the direction of the underlying and its fair volatility.

It has become common to think about a trade in terms of the return at expiration. If a call is purchased for $3.00, the trade will be profitable if the stock is at least $3.00 above the strike price at expiration. Although this view is certainly accurate, it does not address the dynamics of an option position. Because options tend to amplify changes in the underlying, most trades experience significant swings in value during their life cycle. It is not uncommon for a call or put to double or triple in price, only to retreat from the strike price and ultimately expire worthless. In many cases, option contracts experience wild price swings without ever being in-the-money.

Simple or complex, option positions are always subject to the effects of time and volatility. During calm periods, volatility tends to fall, compounding the destructive effects of time decay on long positions. Conversely, short positions tend to benefit in such environments. The following discussions abandon the popular, but overly simplistic, view that focuses on the value of a position at expiration. Treating option positions as static entities that have a range of values at expiration has been the downfall of many books on the subject. In real life, a trader must make daily management decisions in response to unanticipated price changes, volatility swings, world financial news, market conditions, and even time decay. Our discussion will focus on position dynamics because they come into play for virtually every trade. As we shall see, opening a position and leaving it until expiration is rarely the best strategy. The exceptions are positions designed to profit from time decay (short straddles) and complex hedged positions with long and short components. We will discuss both.

Single-Sided Put and Call Positions

It is often the case that a long put or call position is most profitable at some point in the middle of its life cycle. Short sellers, on the opposite side of the trade, are sometimes surprised to find that they are losing large amounts of money and are forced to take corrective action for option positions that remain out-of-the-money. It is important to recognize that whether or not the stock has crossed the strike price is irrelevant. Only the value of the option matters.

Consider the price history shown in Figure 5.1. The options were $80 strike price calls expiring on March 18, 2006, purchased with 100 calendar days remaining, for $4.25. The calls reached their peak price ($9.20) on trading day 26.[1] A buyer could have realized a profit in excess of 100% by closing the trade at the peak, but he or she would have lost 100% by waiting until expiration, when the stock traded well below the strike price. Conversely, a seller forced to buy back his or her short position at the peak would have lost nearly $5.00—$5,000 for every ten contracts. In general, it makes much more sense to stop out early and avoid a loss. However, many option traders keep their positions relatively small, steering clear of the leverage, and allowing more flexibility with regard to tolerating losses. This strategy often helps short sellers, who, if they limit the size of their positions, often find that reversion toward the mean allows them to recover. During the time frame of Figure 5.1, the stock sold off and the calls expired worthless. It is important to point out that if the stock had remained at $85, the options would still have lost nearly half their value, declining to $5.00 at expiration. Additionally, a $5.00 drop in stock price would have delivered a 100% improvement in the position value—$9.20. It is generally a good idea to balance risk with leverage by taking some advantage of the power of options but being mindful of position size. In our example, a short seller of $80 strike price calls initially traded a delta of 0.42 (ten contracts were equivalent to 420 shares of stock). At the peak, when the options were $5.00 in-the-money with 64 days left, the delta rose to 0.71. Ten contracts were now equivalent to 710 shares of stock. If such a move had occurred only two days before expiration, the delta would have risen to 0.99, and the trade would have been short 1000 stock-equivalent shares for every ten contracts. It's important to keep a balanced view of the delta, its potential range, and the number of shares represented by the trade. At any point in time, a short seller must ask himself whether he feels comfortable being short the number of shares represented by the options. Furthermore, scenario planning is important, because a sudden change can dramatically alter the trade's complexion by increasing the delta.

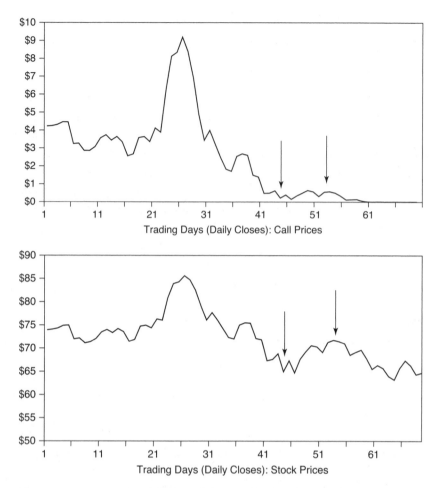

Figure 5.1   Comparison of $80 call (upper chart) and stock (lower chart)
prices for Apple computer. The stock traded between $63.19 and
$85.59 during the 100 calendar days that the position was open.
The long position was most profitable on trading day 26
(01/13/2006), when the options were worth $9.20—more than
twice their purchase price. The arrows mark ten days when the
stock rose $6.80 and the calls climbed from 20 to 55 cents
despite being nowhere near the strike price. The peak occurred
on trading day 53 (02/23/2006). For this example, fair option
values were calculated using the average volatility for the time
frame – 40%.

Note that the stock increase of $6.80 that occurred between days 44 and 53 (marked by arrows in the chart) had a comparatively small effect on the options, which had already lost nearly all of their value. It is important to realize, however, that although the effect was small compared to the original purchase price ($4.25), it would have been large if the buyer had purchased the options just before the price change (the option price rose from $0.20 to $0.55). Assuming a 5-cent bid-ask spread, the options could have been purchased for $0.25 on day 44 and sold for $0.50 on day 53 for a 100% profit, despite their never having been in-the-money.

Option sellers sometimes make the mistake of becoming complacent if the strike price is far out-of-the-money. However, as we just saw, large amounts of money can be made or lost even if the stock never approaches the strike price. In this regard it is important to recognize the leverage offered by options and to focus on trading the option and not the underlying. A short seller who ignores a significant increase in the option price because he or she believes that the strike price will not be reached before expiration is choosing to gamble. On the long side, a trader might be tempted to treat the change as the beginning of a trend and keep the position open. That decision also represents a gamble. In each case, other factors might add weight to the decision. In our example, the contracts had 23 calendar days (17 trading days) left before expiration, and the stock had just risen to $10 below the strike price. On the long side, a trader might keep the position open if the increase is related to a piece of positive news and he or she believes that the underlying will continue to rise. However, time decay for these 55-cent options was 4 cents per day. Stock traders might also have decided to take profit on the uptick, especially because the stock had fallen 17% from its recent high. Holding on to a rapidly eroding deep-out-of-the-money long call position, on a stock that has been falling, is usually a bad decision. On the short side, keeping the position open involves a calculated risk that the stock will not rise rapidly enough to place the calls in-the-money before expiration.

Both views must be considered somewhat flawed if you believe that the market is efficient. The decision to keep open either a long or short position after a significant change in the option price reflects a belief that the derivative is mispriced. It might well be. Suppose, for example, that the magnitude of the recent price change is experienced by the underlying fewer than three times each year. Also assume that in the absence of another large spike in the short time remaining, it is unlikely that the stock could rise enough to place the option in-the-money. Furthermore, suppose that the price change history reveals a quiet period or even a reversal after each large spike. This sort of information represents a refined view that might not be adequately priced into the option. In effect, the option price is distorted, and a knowledgeable trader can take advantage of this distortion—in this case by keeping a short position open.

On the long side, the decision not to take profit must represent a view that the option is underpriced and will rise, either because volatility will increase or because the underlying will rise fast enough to offset time decay in the option contract. Again, the importance of trading the option and not the stock becomes apparent, because the stock can rise significantly and still leave the option out-of-the-money and worthless. A focus on the option and its remaining time, volatility, and distance from the strike price becomes more critical as expiration approaches. If the trade is relatively small and the risk is contained, the potential loss on either side—short or long—might be considered insignificant, and it might be appropriate to take some risk. On the other hand, if the trade is very large, and the potential loss is unacceptable, stopping out on the short side or taking immediate profit on the long side is essential. This particular issue impacts option traders more than almost anything else. Unfortunately, option traders often create positions that are large enough to distort their judgment—especially on the short side, where a rising delta can be very harmful.

Figure 5.2 reveals details about the price change behavior of Apple Computer during the same time frame. The arrows mark the tops of the peaks—the large spike ending on day 26 (01/13/2006), and the small spike ending on day 53 (02/23/2006).

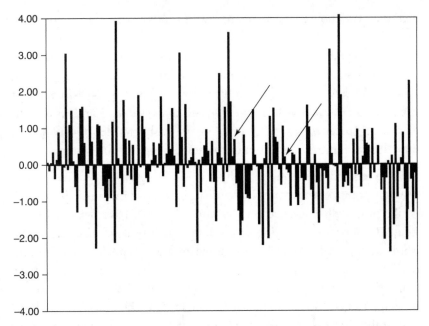

Figure 5.2   Price spike chart for AAPL. The data includes 200 trading days (08/22/2005–06/07/2006). Each spike is measured in standard deviations against the current volatility. The arrows mark the peaks of days 26 and 53.

A quick review of the chart reveals that short call positions on this stock are relatively dangerous. Up spikes are much more common than down spikes in addition to being much larger. The upper half of the chart contains eight spikes larger than 2 standard deviations. Six are larger than 3 standard deviations, and two are approximately equal to 4 standard deviations. Based on the frequency, an investor who remained short at the first peak would have been risking another 3 standard deviation spike (approximately $6.45) before options expiration. As it turned out, the investor would have been right to take that risk, because the intraspike period was slightly lengthened in this time frame. The timing of the second peak coupled with the stock price—17 trading days remaining until expiration and $9 out-of-the-money—might convey an impression of safety to a short seller. Nothing could be further from the truth. Judging from the price change profile, a large spike was overdue. We know that 3 standard deviation upward spikes are relatively common; such a spike at the time of the second peak (approximately $5.25) would have raised the $80 call option price from $0.55 to $2.05. A 4 standard deviation spike, certainly not out of the question for this stock, would have taken the price to $2.80—a 410% increase. If we look just a few days further down the chart, we see 3 and 4 standard deviation spikes separated by only 5 days. A short seller of calls would have lost a significant amount of money during this time frame.

As is often the case, long and short positions each gained and lost at various points in the expiration cycle. A long position consisting of $80 strike price calls launched on December 7 would have delivered more than 100% profit at the top of the January 13 peak. Conversely, going short at the peak would have resulted in a $9.20 profit at expiration. However, it is important to point out that most short sellers would have attempted to take advantage of the 3.6 standard deviation spike on January 10 that took the call price to $6.30. This trade would have been a mistake, because the next day's spike of 1.7 standard deviations further pushed the call price to $8.15, and two days later, at the top of the peak, the price climbed to $9.20—a 46% loss for the trade. Most short sellers would have been forced out before the peak was reached. Ignoring the spikes and recognizing the absolute top of the peak as a selling point would have been nearly impossible, because the top was characterized by a very small spike of only 0.66 standard deviations— essentially a nonevent. A similar scenario played out later in the chart with $10 out-of-the-money options that climbed from 25 cents to 50 cents before rapidly falling to zero. However, in this case selling anywhere near the top would have been profitable as rapid time decay quickly eroded the option value to zero over the next few days. The distinction is important. Selling deep out-of-the-money options near expiration is usually profitable, but the low values force larger trades that make the positions sensitive to small moves of the underlying. As always, reduced risk is met with reduced reward, and if the position is scaled to increase the reward, the risk rises appropriately. Therefore, the common view that selling deep out-of-the-money options near expiration is a safe way to generate profit is not necessarily valid.

The differences between the upper and lower portions of the price spike chart are very important. Because Apple exhibited 3 or 4 standard deviation upward spikes on a regular basis during the time frame in question, short call positions were inherently dangerous. It would be virtually impossible for AAPL calls to be priced with enough volatility to compensate sellers for the risk of randomly occurring 3 and 4 standard deviation upward price spikes. For example, using the $9.20 price peak achieved on January 13 as a starting price on December 7 would have raised implied call volatility from 40% to 72%. A more reasonable approach would involve selecting a volatility that would reduce the size of the largest upward spikes to those of the largest downward spikes—approximately 2 standard deviations. Call volatility would need to rise from 40% to more than 60% for this accommodation to have meaning. Such large differences between put and call volatility are virtually unheard of for heavily traded stocks, where arbitrage opportunities would immediately erase the discrepancy. Apple is no exception. Its puts and calls are priced exactly at parity. In other words, call sellers must take much more risk than put sellers.

As revealed in Figure 5.3, the differential between up and down price spikes for Apple Computer has persisted through significant up and down trends in the stock price. The stock price is displayed in the upper chart, and the price spike history in the lower chart. The time frame of our previous discussion is marked by the dashed lines.

Despite lengthy up and down trends in the stock price, the lower chart contains only one very large downward price spike. Short call positions tend to be riskier than short put positions because uptrends are characterized by uncharacteristically large price spikes that do not fit the normal distribution. Price declines can be considered more orderly because their behavior fits the normal distribution much more closely. From a statistical perspective, calls are consistently underpriced but puts are fairly priced. Call sellers are undercompensated for risk. Even when the stock is falling, put sellers are fairly compensated.

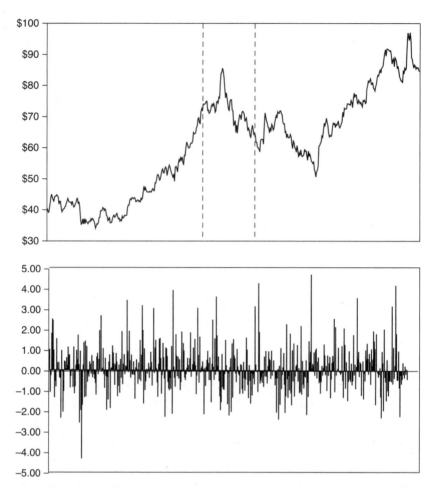

Figure 5.3   Stock price (upper chart) and price spike history in standard
              deviations (lower chart) for Apple Computer (500 trading
              days). The dashed lines in the upper chart mark the time frame
              discussed in the text and displayed in Figures 5.1 and 5.2. The
              time frame represented is 02/08/2005–02/02/2007.

Table 5.1 shows a more complete view of the time frame in the context
of call prices. Each row contains information about the behavior of an
out-of-the-money call option beginning 100 days before expiration.
The table shows every expiration date in the two-year range of Figure
5.3. In each case, for consistency, an out-of-the-money strike with a
delta near 0.30 was selected.

In 20 of 21 expirations, the peak option price exceeded the entry price; 16 of the peaks were more than double the entry price. Short sellers who did not stop out would have suffered catastrophic losses in 13 of the scenarios. Despite these extraordinary statistics, option prices ultimately fell to zero in half of all expiration cycles. Some of the reversals were quite spectacular; during the February 2006 expiration cycle, the value of a $70 strike price call rose from $1.75 to $16.05 before falling back to nearly zero.

Table 5.1   Out-of-the-money call prices spanning 100 days for each of 21 expiration cycles for Apple Computer.

Start Date	Expiration	Strike	Delta	Initial Stock Price	Expiration Stock Price	Initial Call Price	Peak Call Price	Expiration Call Price
02/09/2005	05-May	45	0.33	39.37	37.55	1.70	4.10	0.00
03/09/2005	05-Jun	45	0.34	39.35	38.31	1.75	3.35	0.00
04/06/2005	05-Jul	50	0.29	42.33	41.55	1.55	1.95	0.00
05/11/2005	05-Aug	40	0.33	35.61	45.83	1.30	7.70	5.85
06/08/2005	05-Sep	40	0.38	36.92	51.21	1.55	11.45	11.20
07/13/2005	05-Oct	45	0.23	38.35	55.66	0.80	11.15	10.65
08/10/2005	05-Nov	50	0.29	43.38	64.56	1.40	14.95	14.55
09/07/2005	05-Dec	55	0.32	48.68	71.11	1.80	20.00	16.10
10/12/2005	06-Jan	55	0.35	49.25	76.09	2.10	30.65	21.10
11/09/2005	06-Feb	70	0.27	60.11	70.29	1.75	16.05	0.30
12/07/2005	06-Mar	85	0.31	73.95	64.66	2.80	6.35	0.00
01/11/2006	06-Apr	100	0.28	83.90	67.04	3.00	3.45	0.00
02/08/2006	06-May	80	0.31	68.81	64.51	2.80	3.30	0.00
03/08/2006	06-Jun	75	0.32	65.66	57.56	2.50	3.65	0.00
04/12/2006	06-Jul	75	0.34	66.71	60.72	2.85	4.15	0.00
05/10/2006	06-Aug	80	0.34	70.60	67.91	2.95	2.95	0.00
06/07/2006	06-Sep	65	0.37	58.57	74.10	2.85	9.20	9.10
07/12/2006	06-Oct	60	0.32	52.96	79.95	1.90	19.95	19.95
08/09/2006	06-Nov	70	0.34	63.59	85.85	2.10	15.85	15.85
09/06/2006	06-Dec	75	0.38	70.03	87.72	2.40	17.00	12.70
10/11/2006	07-Jan	80	0.32	73.23	88.50	1.90	17.15	8.50

Surprisingly, the initial price was equal to the peak only once. During this particular expiration cycle (August 2006), the stock fell from $70.60 on 05/10 to $50.67 on 07/14 before rallying back to just under $70. A short $80 call position could have been safely established at any point in the expiration cycle. The stock fell continuously before finally staging a rally after the 07/19/2006 earnings release. However, the initial sharp decline caused a collapse in the price of $80 calls during the first two weeks, and accelerated time decay as expiration approached prevented them from regaining any significant value. During the first week, the call price fell approximately $2, making the short selling window very brief.

Many investors mistakenly believe that the risk profiles for short calls and long puts (long calls/short puts) are similar. Nothing could be further from the truth. While the risk of a long position is limited to the purchase price, a short position has no practical limit on the potential for loss. The reverse is also true: a short position can only return the value of the options at the time of sale. Unfortunately, the potential loss is essentially unlimited.

Furthermore, the risk is not equal for puts and calls. Negative news tends to drive down stock prices much faster than positive news drives them up. Practically speaking, markets do not crash up. Negative news frequently elicits a much larger reaction than positive news (with the exception of acquisitions). Call sellers who avoid possible acquisition candidates generally take less risk than put sellers who have very broad news exposure. These sentiments are represented in the volatility smile, which places high values on out-of-the-money puts. However, the smile cannot account for dramatic price spikes larger than 3 standard deviations. Distortions this large would make option trading impossible.

Intraday Volatility

Intraday volatility is a factor that should not be overlooked. It is very difficult to trade simple unhedged positions—that is, long or short puts or calls—on stocks that exhibit high levels of intraday volatility. Complex positions are often designed to absorb price swings within a specified range, but simple positions are not. The intraday volatility question has many dimensions. Some analysts measure high-low as a percent of the closing price and chart this number to watch for periods of instability. The most common approach involves calculating the average for some period of time (such as 20 days) and using a sliding window to roll the calculation forward. More sophisticated calculations use weighted averages to emphasize the most recent changes. However, for our purposes the method falls short, because our principal concern is that intraday volatility could be substantially higher than the close-to-close volatility that underlies option prices. More specifically, we are concerned that high levels of intraday volatility could result in large price swings that are not comprehended in the prices of the options we are trading. We need a method for accurately comparing intraday and closing price volatilities.

We can calculate intraday volatility in much the same way that we calculate daily volatility. Because the trading day is 6.5 hours long, the time frame in question is approximately one-fourth the length of a normal close-to-close cycle. That is, there are 3.7 × 252 such time frames in a trading year.[2] We can easily adjust our volatility calculations by multiplying the 20-day standard deviation by the square root of the number of 6.5 hour time frames in one trading year—932. Comparing intraday and daily volatility can yield important clues about the behavior of a stock or index. If the ratio between intraday and daily volatility is high, overnight price gaps tend to be less variable than intraday changes. When the ratio is small, the risk of a surprise overnight spike is larger than the risk of a surprise intraday spike. Close-to-close price changes, however, are already represented in standard volatility calculations.

Large intraday price variability can be very destructive to simple long or short positions. Figure 5.4 illustrates this point with daily high and low call prices for Express Scripts (ESRX) during a period when intraday volatility was considerably higher than close-to-close volatility. The chart spans 50 calendar days (36 trading days) beginning on October 26, 2006 and ending on December 15. On the first day, the stock closed at $66.15, and we selected the $70 strike price for our analysis. The stock experienced modest price changes during this time frame, falling $6 and then rising $8 to ultimately close at $68.66 on the final day of the December expiration cycle.

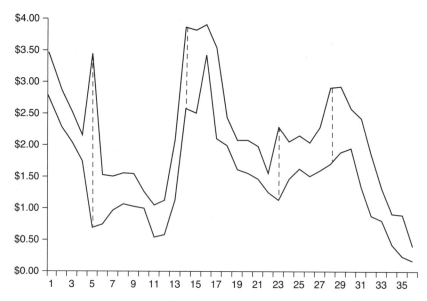

Figure 5.4   Express Scripts' daily high and low prices for $70 strike price
calls. The top line traces the option's high price, and the bottom
line traces the low. Prices are shown on the y-axis, and the x-axis
represents trading days. The dashed lines mark some of the
largest gaps between high and low call prices.

During the time frame of the trade, intraday volatility averaged 68%,
and daily close-to-close volatility averaged only 44%. Any simple long
or short position would have been impossible to manage through the
large, randomly spaced, intraday swings. Consider, for example, the
enormous price swing on day 5 that pushed the $70 call as high as $3.45
before dropping it to 70 cents. This behavior is typical of stocks that display very high levels of intraday volatility. On October 31, ESRX closed
at $63.72. The next day, the stock opened nearly $4.00 higher at $67.30,
climbed to $67.89, fell below the previous day's close to $58.79, and ultimately closed at $59.99. This dramatic high-low transition completely
spanned the previous day's prices on both sides. Although the close-to-
close price change was only 2 standard deviations, the intraday move
was more than 5. (The normal distribution predicts a 2 standard deviation change approximately once each month. A 5 standard deviation

change should never occur and cannot be comprehended by any option pricing methodology.) Furthermore, no planned events occurred during this time frame, and the next earnings announcement was two weeks away.

Although high levels of intraday volatility can be destructive to simple long or short positions, certain types of trades tend to benefit, because they are essentially underpriced. Most obvious are long straddles in which the buyer seeks large price changes regardless of direction. Such positions can be considered underpriced when intraday volatility is very high and implied volatility of the contracts mirrors the more traditional close-to-close calculation. We will return to a more detailed conversation about long and short straddles and strangles in the next section.

Using Price Spikes as Triggers

For stocks that exhibit occasional large spikes followed by calm periods or trend reversals, it often makes sense to use the spikes as selling (or buying) points. Figure 5.5 displays both price spike and stock price data for Goldman Sachs (GS) for 75 trading days beginning on 10/24/2006. Bullish investors placing short put or long call positions would have maximized their profit by trading the occasional downward price spikes. An excellent strategy would have been to use spikes greater than 2 standard deviations as triggers for opening new positions. For each trade marked in the figure, reversion to the mean coupled with continued upward movement of the stock would have generated a significant positive return.

A conservative investor who set his or her trade threshold at 3 standard deviations would have realized a significant profit by opening a position coincident with the November 27 (day 24) price spike. Details of both long call and short put trades are revealed in Figure 5.6. The upper chart traces the price of the $195 call, and the lower chart the $190 put. The arrows mark the November 27 entry point—the 3 standard deviation downward spike visible in Figure 5.5.

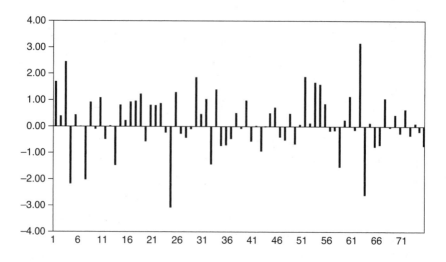

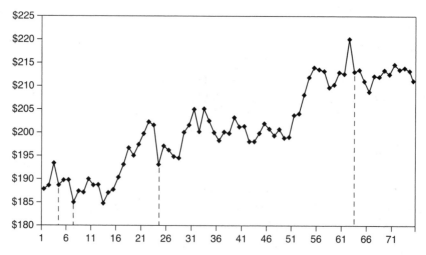

Figure 5.5   Goldman Sachs price spikes and stock price
10/24/2006–02/12/2007 (75 trading days). The upper chart displays standard deviations for each day on the y-axis, and the
lower chart displays the stock price. Vertical dashed lines mark
downward spikes greater than 2 standard deviations.

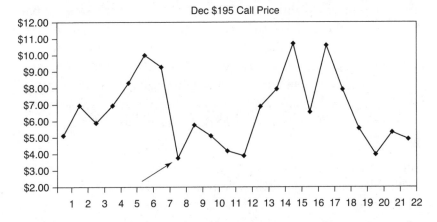

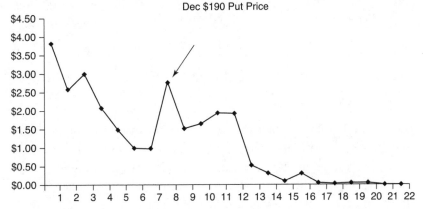

Figure 5.6 $195 call and $190 put prices for Goldman Sachs stock (11/15/2006–12/15/2006). Arrows mark the 3 standard deviation downward spike depicted in Figure 5.5. For this example, fair option values were calculated using the average volatility for the time frame – 25%.

It is important to note the dramatic differences between the two trades. Seven days after the spike, when the stock closed at $205, both trades reached their maximum value. The call, which originally traded for $3.70, had risen to $10.70. The put was worth 10 cents—a $2.70 profit for a short seller. However, if the call buyer had held the position until expiration, most of the profit would have been lost. Short trades must also be collateralized with 25% of the value of the underlying stock plus the value of the options. You can reduce the collateral requirement, which can be quite significant for expensive stocks, by purchasing a less favorable strike price. If an account is short $100 calls and long $120 calls, the collateral requirement is based on a $20 potential loss instead of the full stock price. No collateral requirement exists if the account is long options that have a more favorable expiration date and strike price.

Short puts can also be adversely affected if the stock falls rapidly and implied volatility rises. Likewise, long calls can lose value if an upward movement of the stock drives down implied volatility. The effect can be significant. During the second half of 2006, a 20% increase in the value of IBM stock was met with a 25% decrease in implied volatility.

Other Considerations Regarding Expiration Date and Strike Price

Investors often believe that they are better off opening long positions that have several months remaining before expiration and short positions that expire in the current month. Generally speaking, pricing mechanisms are efficient enough to erase any particular advantages or disadvantages of time decay acceleration. Furthermore, the tendency for reversion toward the mean tends to make long-term deep out-of-the-money options a slightly better bet for short sellers, because they are less affected by short-term price changes that have some tendency to reverse. For example, in mid-February 2007, when Google stock traded at $470, January 2008 calls at the $750 strike price were worth $2.75, and $290 strike price puts traded for $2.95. The tendency for mean reversion often causes price distortions at these extremes. Some investors specialize in analyzing these distortions and trading them. We will return to this concept in our discussion of short strangles.

Trading Deep In-the-Money Options

Another important but frequently overlooked possibility is the deep in-the-money options trade having a delta of 1.00. Such positions are similar to synthetic stock; their key advantage is price. At the time of this writing, IBM stock traded for $99.00, and $70 strike price calls were trading for $29.10 (29 days left before expiration). The price included only 10 cents of time premium. An option trader could have effectively purchased 3 times as many shares as a stock trader for the same price. Because the delta is 1.00, they move dollar for dollar with the stock and, if the stock moves toward the strike price (in the wrong direction), the delta shrinks and slows the rate of loss. As always, the maximum loss is equal to the initial position value—another advantage of long options over stock. Until recently, if the goal was to short a rapidly falling stock, the uptick rule stalled the transaction until the stock stabilized. Investors often purchased puts as a proxy for short stock. This issue frequently came into play for day traders reacting to breaking news. The uptick rule was repealed in July 2007, and it is now possible to directly short a stock without regard to the previous trading price. With today's sophisticated tools, it is relatively easy to construct a software link that triggers a trade when a piece of news causes a volume spike or rapid price change. Despite relatively large bid-ask spreads, options day trading is often very profitable—especially when stocks with large intraday volatility are the targets.

It is important to note that short deep in-the-money puts are not the inverse of long deep in-the-money calls. As the stock price rises, the put delta shrinks, while the call delta remains at 100%. The reverse is true if the stock falls. The put delta remains at 1.00, and the call delta shrinks. The short put position has limited upside potential and unlimited downside potential. Long call positions, therefore, perform better than short put positions as a replacement for stock. However, if the strike price is far enough from the stock price, the delta remains at 1.00 even if the underlying experiences a large move. Although this dynamic affects both long and short positions, the collateral requirement on the short side can be significant and should be taken into account.

Under certain circumstances, deep in-the-money short positions have a special function that cannot be replicated with long calls. Consider, for example, trading the CBOE Volatility Index (VIX), which tends to rise rapidly when the market falls. Because there is no direct way to purchase the index, many traders who want to go long purchase out-of-the-money calls. This trade makes sense if the goal is to hedge a portfolio against a market drawdown using inexpensive options. Often the options are considered a cost of doing business—an insurance policy of sorts. Unfortunately, such positions are complex to manage, because volatility of the VIX is highly variable, and time decay can become a significant problem. However, if the goal is to invest in the VIX because of an expectation that it will rise, deep in-the-money short puts are a better choice because they are priced without any volatility. Short positions composed of these options behave almost exactly like the index itself. The positions differ in one very important way: out-of-the-money options have relatively high gamma, and they tend to magnify large moves of the underlying; deep in-the-money options have essentially no gamma, and their delta remains near 1.00 across a broad range of underlying price movement. Because an efficient hedge should be relatively inexpensive and grow rapidly in value, out-of-the-money long options are a better choice (long calls). When the goal is to own the underlying and realize profit from small price changes, deep in-the-money options are superior. The VIX is a special case because there are no deep in-the-money calls under most circumstances.

Straddles and Strangles

Straddles are composed of an equal number of puts and calls having the same strike price and expiration. Strangles are also composed of equal numbers of puts and calls expiring on the same day, but with different strike prices. The term "combination" is sometimes used to describe a position containing puts and calls that is not a straddle. Strangles represent one of many possible combinations.

Long straddles generate a profit when a large move of the underlying causes an imbalance in the deltas and one side rises in price faster than the other falls. If the move is large enough, one side falls to zero, and the other has a delta approaching 1.00. Continued movement of the underlying in the same direction mirrors the return of a long or short stock position—depending on the direction of movement—that contains the number of shares represented in the option contracts. Therefore, a

50-contract long straddle will behave the same way as 5,000 shares of stock if the underlying price rises enough to generate a call delta of 1.00. Long straddles and strangles also return a profit when volatility rises sharply, increasing the value of both sides of the trade.

Short straddles and strangles return profit through time decay, falling volatility, or both. A straddle/strangle seller hopes that the underlying stock or index does not move at all before expiration. When the underlying does move enough to cause a loss, the seller must take corrective action. Some sellers stop out of the losing side and remain short the other. Others buy back one or both sides and create a new, larger position capable of generating enough profit to pay back the first loss. Because significant inflation of the position size is often necessary, many sellers of straddles or strangles keep initial positions small with the expectation that at least one correction will be necessary. As with any short position, the potential for loss is essentially unlimited. However, there are many ways to reduce the risk. Some involve timing the trade to avoid known economic events and earnings announcements; others involve hedging with another financial instrument or option.

Overnight exposure is always the greatest risk to short option positions. News that rattles the market while option trading is closed to public customers can have devastating results. The problem is that stocks trade in before- and aftermarket sessions, but options do not. An option short seller must sometimes wait on the sidelines, watching a stock rise or fall dramatically, with no chance to take corrective action. One solution is to limit the size of short positions and, if necessary, make emergency adjustments with stock in the before- or aftermarket session. Unfortunately, this strategy can be very dangerous, because these sessions are notoriously illiquid, and price changes can be unpredictable. Prices often fall or rise dramatically during extended-hours trading, reverse themselves before the open, and continue in the opposite direction. It is important to carefully judge the news and decide if a correction with stock is the right answer. With proper risk management, short positions often generate excellent returns.

Long Straddles and Strangles

A strategy for investing in long straddles must include a methodology for selecting the underlying stocks, rules for structuring positions, and a set of guidelines for managing and closing open trades. Long straddles/strangles generally perform best in environments where rising volatility helps to offset the effects of time decay. Exceptional circumstances can sometimes drive volatility to levels where both sides of a straddle or strangle profit even if the stock does not experience a significant price change.

In some sense these positions are asymmetric. When stock prices rise, volatility often falls. Conversely, when prices fall, volatility tends to increase. Long straddles/strangles, therefore, perform best when prices are falling. Some of this behavior is related to the volatility smile which we discussed in Chapter 3, "Volatility." Prices tend to fall faster than they rise when driven by news surprises. Therefore, it is advantageous to purchase straddles/strangles where implied volatility on the put side is judged to be underpriced. Very often, stocks that have experienced extended periods of price increase fit this description. Prices eventually stop rising, the chart levels off, and investors become overly sensitive to negative news. In this scenario, downward price spikes begin to grow, and upward spikes begin to shrink. When implied volatility on both sides is judged to be fair, stocks that fit this description are often excellent candidates for long straddle/strangle positions. However, if the stock continues its ascent, the position is likely to profit on the call side. Surprisingly, stocks that have experienced lengthy price declines are notoriously poor candidates for this type of trade. Practically speaking, after a substantial sell-off, the potential for a sharp price decrease or increase tends to be limited by investor interest. Residential construction stocks behaved this way in late 2006 after a 50% price decline driven by many months of negative news, falling earnings, negative forward-looking warnings from the individual companies, and a variety of business adjustments, including cancellations of land contracts. During this time frame, short interest climbed steeply across the category. By July 2006 the stocks had stabilized in the sense that they became somewhat immune to additional negative news. Some began to rise with the general market, which was experiencing a broad-based rally. However, after the lengthy decline, implied volatility remained high, and investor interest remained low. The stocks that performed well during this time frame experienced orderly increases rather than the sharp surprise spikes that generate large profits for long straddles and strangles. Figure 5.7 illustrates this concept with a chart of closing prices for Ryland Group beginning on March 1, 2006 and ending five months later, on July 31. Near the right side of the chart, after falling nearly 40%, Ryland Group became a poor long straddle/strangle candidate, because options tended to be overpriced, and the potential for further decline was limited. Over the next few months the stock barely moved, and in mid-November the price still hovered around $45. Long put-call positions would have been terrible investments during this time frame.

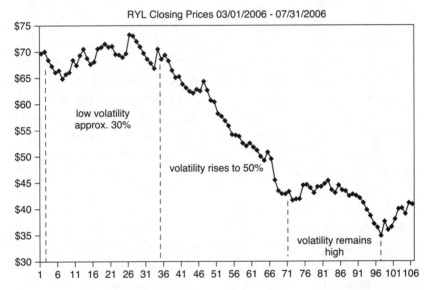

Figure 5.7   Ryland Group closing prices from 03/01/2006–07/31/2006. Near the right side of the chart, after a substantial price decline, RYL was a poor long straddle/strangle candidate.

Under the right circumstances, indexes such as the S&P 500 and Dow 30 Industrials can also be excellent candidates for long straddle/strangle positions. Just before this chapter was written, options on Spyders, an exchange traded fund that tracks the S&P 500, were priced with only

10% implied volatility. The price, although perfectly fair, did not compensate sellers for the risk of even the smallest surprise. On February 27, 2007, the S&P 500 fell more than 3%, and volatility rose to more than 19%. Such volatility spikes are not uncommon. The February 27 spike mirrored a volatility increase that occurred eight months earlier, when implied volatility of S&P 500 options increased to 23% in just a few weeks. During this time frame, long straddles and strangles on broad indexes were an excellent investment. The February 27 spike was different because it happened in a few hours. It was also much more profitable for long straddle/strangle owners with some positions experiencing increases of more than 500%.

Before structuring a long put-call position, it is important to align investment goals with the range of viable trading strategies. At one extreme we could select stocks with a history of very large price spikes that are widely spaced in time. We would likely purchase long-dated out-of-the-money options with the anticipation that, after some delay, the stock would experience a large price spike. At the other extreme are stocks that exhibit smaller spikes that are more closely spaced in time. In the most extreme cases we would open positions composed of very short-dated at-the-money options that we expect to close within a couple of days. This author occasionally opens long straddles at the close of trading when implied volatility tends to shrink somewhat and closes them the very next morning, just after the open. Targets for this particular trade include stocks with a history of large opening price gaps, high levels of intraday volatility, relatively small bid-ask spreads, and high levels of short interest. The latter is very important, because high short interest levels increase the probability of a short covering rally. This can create a spectacular upward price spike against a backdrop of positive news. Positive news before the opening bell can cause such stocks to experience a sustained rally that accelerates as short sellers bail out of losing positions. One of the best examples was the spectacular Sears rally that followed an early-morning earnings release on March 15, 2006. The stock exhibited the largest price spike in its trading history. Based on implied volatility of the time (18%), the spike was 11.6 standard deviations (12.8% above the previous close). Prior to the spike, short interest on Sears stock hovered around 14% of float—

about 9 million shares. Not surprisingly, the sharpest part of the morning rally ended as soon as 10 million shares had traded—approximately 40 minutes into the session. When this point was reached, the stock, which was trading more than $16 above the previous day's close, fell from $133 to $129.

Sears is one of many stocks that exhibit large spikes interspersed with calm periods. Its implied volatility is fair during intraspike time frames but is much too low when the stock reacts to news. Figure 5.8 displays 250 days of daily price spike data for a similarly behaved stock—USNA Health Sciences (USNA).

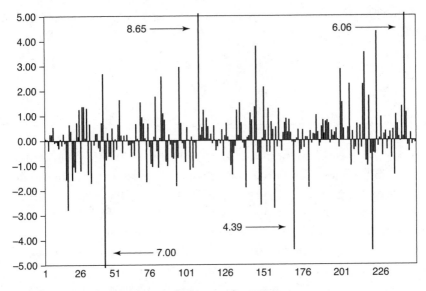

Figure 5.8   One-year price spike history for USNA
(02/21/2006–02/16/2007). Standard deviations measured against the 20-day volatility window are displayed on the y-axis, and trading days on the x-axis. Earnings releases are marked with arrows. Three of these spikes are off the scale, which is set to +/– 5 standard deviations (see Table 5.2).

USNA's trading history contains numerous large spikes. More precisely, over 250 trading days (02/21/2006–02/16/2007) the stock experienced eight spikes larger than 3 standard deviations—twice the average for stocks over $50. Recall that the normal distribution predicts 3 standard deviation spikes only 0.2% of the time. That an average stock exhibits four such spikes per year is somewhat shocking in itself when you consider that standard option pricing models do not comprehend this behavior. More surprising still, USNA exhibited three spikes larger than 5 standard deviations during the year. This number is 5 times the average for stocks in this price range. Details are provided in Table 5.2.

Table 5.2   Price spike data summary for Figure 5.8.

Standard Deviations	Occurrences
1 to 2	43
2 to 3	10
3 to 4	2
4 to 5	3
5 to 6	0
6 to 7	1
7 to 8	1
> 8	1

Although the distribution of spikes smaller than 2 standard deviations (233/250) is reasonably close to the normal distribution, the tails of the curve are exaggerated (kurtosis is positive). Despite the large number of dangerously large price spikes, implied volatility of USNA options is routinely quite low. On February 16, 2007, only a short time after successive 6, 4, and 3 standard deviation spikes (visible on the right side of Figure 5.8), implied volatility for March options was only 28%. This number was distinctly lower than the 20-day volatility window (37%), and far below the intraday value of 75%. The most important reason was the February 7 earnings release, which generated the 6 standard deviation price spike visible on the right side of the chart. As earnings approached, implied volatility rose to accommodate the risk. It fell immediately after. However, the final 35 trading days in the chart contain two spikes larger than 4 standard deviations and one larger than 3.5 standard deviations. None of these was directly related to the earnings release, but a pattern emerges. In the weeks leading up to an earnings release, price spike frequency and size both tend to increase. Option implied volatility tends to follow this pattern, rising sharply in the final days before an earnings announcement, and falling immediately after.

It is important to mention that even if we remove the four earnings release price spikes, 28% volatility does not fairly represent the risk, because the distribution of the remaining large spikes does not fit the normal distribution. However, as mentioned, the average stock in this price range exhibits four spikes per year larger than 3 standard deviations. At the detail level we can see that the most significant remaining difference is the pair of 4 standard deviation spikes that occurred in the weeks leading up to the February 7 earnings announcement.

Several viable trading strategies leverage the price change behavior evident in the chart. One approach involves waiting until earnings have passed and implied volatility deflates before purchasing a straddle or strangle. It would be wise to assume that the next large spike—more than 3 standard deviations—might be two months away. Because a standard deviation for this stock was $1.44 on February 16, we know that the next spike is likely to affect only the adjacent strike prices (3 × $1.44 = $4.32). Therefore, you must be careful not to select strikes that are too far apart. A reasonable trade might include purchasing puts and calls with three months left before expiration, one strike above and below the stock price.

Another potential trade directly involves earnings. The four announcements that occurred during the one-year time frame displayed in Figure 5.8 generated price spikes of 6.06, 4.33, 8.65, and 7.00 standard deviations. Because the market anticipates these large price changes, and implied volatility rises as the earnings release date approaches, it is wise to own a straddle or strangle during this time frame, because rising volatility will help offset time decay. If, as often happens, a price spike occurs in the pre-earnings time frame, the long position will benefit from both the underlying move and rising volatility. This author sometimes trades these events by purchasing straddles on stocks that have a history of large earnings-associated price spikes and holding them until the point of maximum implied volatility is reached (just before the announcement). For USNA it is clear that the weeks preceding an earnings announcement represent the best opportunity for long straddle and strangle positions.

USNA lies at one extreme in the sense that it exhibits defined periods of enhanced activity and a small number of enormous spikes. Some of this behavior is anticipated by the market, and some is not. Understanding the behavior at the detail level gives you an edge that you can use to structure profitable trades. Many stocks lie at the other extreme because their price change history is characterized by large numbers of randomly spaced spikes of moderate size.

Figure 5.9 shows the price change profile of a stock that fits this description—MedcoHealth Solutions (MHS). The chart uses the same parameters as those in Figure 5.8—price spikes measured in standard deviations against a 20-day moving volatility window for 250 trading days (02/21/2006–02/16/2007).

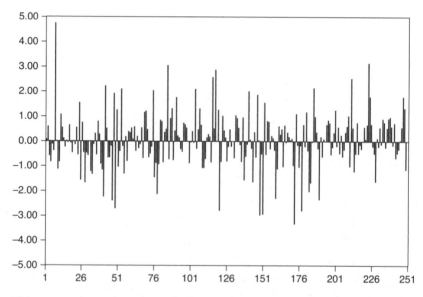

Figure 5.9 One-year price spike history for MHS (02/21/2006–02/16/2007). Standard deviations measured against the 20-day volatility window are displayed on the y-axis, and trading days on the x-axis.

Unlike USNA, MedcoHealth does not react to earnings announcements with predictably large spikes. During the time frame of the chart, earnings produced spikes of 4.74, 2.09, 2.58, and 0.52 standard deviations. The only outstanding member of the list was the large upward spike coincident with the March 1, 2006 earnings release and visible on the left side of the chart. The chart does not reveal any particular pattern or information that might be used to time entry into a long position. However, the high frequency of significant price spikes makes entry timing a minor issue.

During the trading year shown in Figure 5.9, MHS experienced 24 spikes over 2 standard deviations but only four spikes greater than 4. It is also beneficial to the analysis to rank stocks according to the size and frequency of multiday price spikes. For this purpose we can create composite days composed of a fixed number of trading days. Suppose in the case of MHS we use three-day composites. Each composite day opens at the opening price of the first day and closes at the closing price of the third day. Volatility calculations should be based on 84 three-day composites per trading year. Multiday spikes are very significant because continual movement in one direction dramatically impacts option prices. Including multiday spikes in our selection criteria helps us select stocks that are likely to experience large multiday price changes. MHS displayed eight multiday spikes (three-day composites) larger than 2 standard deviations during the measurement year.

Summarizing this data leads us to conclude that we can expect a price spike greater than 2 standard deviations twice each month, but a 3 standard deviation spike only once each quarter. We should also expect a three-day, 2 standard deviation spike eight times during the course of a year. The best strategy for such a stock is to purchase short dated straddles. Short dated options make sense for MHS because the price spike frequency is very high, and the spikes tend to be both moderate in size and evenly distributed in time. It is unlikely that we will keep the position open for an extended length of time, waiting for a spike. Straddles are a better choice than strangles because we are focused on generating profit from relatively small moves of the stock. Because MHS is a $60 stock trading with approximately 30% volatility, a standard deviation is approximately $1.15. The spike we are anticipating is likely to fall in the range of $2.30–$3.45—2 to 3 standard deviations. If the stock is trading between two strikes when the position is established, immediately adjacent strike prices are also a good choice. As always, the position should be perfectly delta-neutral at the start, because we are predicting a price spike, not a direction.

We must also consider some choices for position management. The choices fall into two broad categories. After a moderate spike we could choose to take profit and rebalance deltas by selling part of the profitable side of the trade. It is important to sell just enough to rebalance the deltas. Strictly speaking, because the two sides are no longer matched in size, the position is not considered a straddle or strangle. We could keep the position open for some time and continue selling contracts on both sides as the stock prices spike in both directions.

A simpler approach is to set a time limit and close the position whether or not a large spike has occurred. This strategy is equivalent to a stop-loss order, the loss limit being based on time. Finally, we could simply leave the position open until the first large spike. Alternatively, we might choose to leave the position open until expiration. The latter works best in a very active market characterized by rising volatility.

Table 5.3 contains data for a sample short-term trade using MHS options. As we discussed, the stock's trading history is characterized by a large number of moderate spikes. The trade outlined in the chart was launched near the close of trading on October 27, when put and call deltas were equal (the first pair in the chart). Because the trade was intended to be brief, options expiring in 22 days on November 18 were used. The stock closed very close to the delta-neutral point but began to move the next day (−1.03 standard deviations). After three trading days, the position could have been closed for a 42% profit.

Table 5.3   MHS sample short-term long straddle. For this example, fair
             option values were calculated using the characteristic volatility
             for the time frame – 30%.

Option	Date	Stock Price ($)	Option Price ($)	Delta	Value 20 Contracts ($)	Total ($)	Spike StdDev
$55 call	10/27/2006	54.67	1.55	0.50	3,100		
$55 put	10/27/2006	54.67	1.70	−0.50	3,400	6,500	
$55 call	10/27/2006	54.75	1.55	0.51	3,100		
$55 put	10/27/2006	54.75	1.65	−0.49	3,300	6,400	

Option	Date	Stock Price ($)	Option Price ($)	Delta	Value 20 Contracts ($)	Total ($)	Spike StdDev
$55 call	10/30/2006	53.68	0.95	0.39	1,900		
$55 put	10/30/2006	53.68	2.15	-0.61	4,300	6,200	-1.03
$55 call	10/31/2006	53.50	0.85	0.37	1,700		
$55 put	10/31/2006	53.50	2.25	-0.63	4,500	6,200	-0.18
$55 call	11/01/2006	50.67	0.20	0.12	400		
$55 put	11/01/2006	50.67	4.40	-0.88	8,800	9,200	-2.79

Rather than close the trade on 11/01, we could have rebalanced put and call deltas by selling all but three puts. That trade would have also generated a profit, because the stock rose $3.00 over the next three days. It would be relatively simple to assemble a lengthy table of delta-neutral trades that are likely to deliver profit within a few days. One limiting factor, however, is the requirement that the position be exactly delta-neutral when the trade is launched. It is often the case that a stock does not cross the exact neutral point for a particular straddle or around-the-money strangle during the trading day. A potential solution involves combining stock and options in the same trade—long stock/long put or short stock/long call.

This strategy guarantees that a neutral position can be structured at any time by matching the number of shares with the option's delta. This technique has advantages and disadvantages. Reduced leverage is the most important disadvantage. Because the stock already has a delta of 1.00, it can only rise or fall at a steady rate. Suppose, for example, that we purchase 200 shares of stock and ten puts with a delta of 0.2. If the stock price falls far enough, the put delta will rise to 1.00, and increases on the put side will outweigh decreases on the stock side by a factor of 5. Conversely, if the stock rises far enough, the puts will lose all their value, and the stock will continue gaining with a delta of 1.00. Unfortunately, we are giving up the leverage offered by calls which display limited loss on the downside due to falling delta, and accelerating gains on the upside due to rising delta. On the positive side, stocks normally have insignificant bid-ask spreads, are much more liquid than options, can be traded in before- and aftermarket sessions, and never suffer time decay.

Finally, long stock/long put has a slight advantage over short stock/long call. The reason relates to the tendency for implied volatility to fall when underlying prices rise and to rise when they fall. Long stock and put combinations, therefore, benefit on the downside from rising put implied volatility and do not suffer loss on the upside from falling implied call volatility. This advantage should not be overlooked, because it can have a significant impact on overall position value.

Short Straddles and Strangles

Short straddles and strangles profit from time decay. As you might expect, they perform best in falling volatility environments. While falling volatility is not a requirement, the effect cannot be overstated. It is virtually impossible to profit from short straddles/strangles in a rising volatility environment. Unfortunately, time decay is a slow process that typically generates just a few cents of profit each day.

Because a large move in either direction is destructive to short straddles and strangles, overnight exposure is a significant threat to these positions. The options market for public customers is open for 6.5 hours and closed for 17.5. This dynamic makes risk management the most important success factor for trading short put-call positions. Because it is always possible to stop out of a trade during the open session, overnight price spikes represent essentially 100% of the risk to a disciplined trader. The risk profile is dominated by two prominent characteristics:

- A significant price move by one portfolio member frequently creates a loss large enough to erase the profits earned by all the other trades.

- It is often possible to earn large profits for a long time before suffering a large loss.

The solution is to limit position size, avoid stocks with a history of opening price gaps, avoid keeping positions open during the final days of an earnings cycle, and never open short positions during times of rising market instability. These rules imply a certain level of complexity. For example, between early December 2004 and late November 2005, the overall market barely moved. During that time frame, the Dow Industrials slowly climbed as high as 10,900 and fell as low as 10,100, but in the end the index remained unchanged near 10,400. Changes during this time frame were slow, and, in virtually all cases, current month options on most stocks and indexes followed predictable paths. However, the VIX fluctuated between values as low as 10 and as high as 18, often in time frames as brief as one to two weeks. Because the VIX represents a composite of volatility priced into options on all S&P 500 stocks, we can conclude that option prices experienced substantial fluctuations during this time frame. It is important for short sellers to incorporate this information into their trading strategies, because changes in the VIX are certainly represented at the individual stock level.

That said, short straddles and strangles have the potential to deliver outstanding profits when properly traded. Almost every position needs to be adjusted at some point. It is important, therefore, to limit the initial size of each trade so that contracts can be added as changes are made. A sample trade is outlined in Table 5.4. Our scenario begins 51 days before expiration, when the stock traded at a delta-neutral point (put and call deltas were exactly matched for the chosen strike prices). Each pair of entries represents a single trading day. For each pair, the table displays information about both sides of the trade, including strike prices, the number of open contracts, option deltas, and position values. Shaded entries represent necessary position adjustments designed to keep put and call deltas balanced. Each of these adjustments involved strike price changes. The first adjustment included a 75% increase in the number of open contracts.

Table 5.4 Short combination dynamics: sample trade.

Option	Date	Stock Price	Strike	Days	Option Price ($)	Delta	Contract	Option Value ($)	Position Value ($)
Call	03/30/2006	98.90	105.00	51	1.07	0.25	20	2,140	
Put	03/30/2006	98.90	95.00	51	1.16	−0.25	20	2,320	4,460
Call	03/31/2006	96.50	105.00	50	0.56	0.16	20	1,120	
Put	03/31/2006	96.50	95.00	50	1.87	−0.37	20	3,740	4,860
Call	04/03/2006	94.50	105.00	47	0.27	0.09	20	540	
Put	04/03/2006	94.50	95.00	47	2.56	−0.48	20	5,120	5,660
Call	04/03/2006	94.50	100.00	47	1.00	0.25	35	3,500	
Put	04/03/2006	94.50	90.00	47	0.84	−0.21	35	2,940	6,440
Call	04/04/2006	95.10	100.00	46	1.13	0.28	35	3,955	
Put	04/04/2006	95.10	90.00	46	0.70	−0.18	35	2,450	6,405
Call	04/05/2006	94.60	100.00	45	0.97	0.25	35	3,395	
Put	04/05/2006	94.60	90.00	45	0.78	−0.20	35	2,730	6,125
Call	04/06/2006	93.30	100.00	44	0.66	0.19	35	2,310	
Put	04/06/2006	93.30	90.00	44	1.06	−0.26	35	3,710	6,020
Call	04/07/2006	92.50	100.00	43	0.50	0.16	35	1,750	
Put	04/07/2006	92.50	90.00	43	1.27	−0.30	35	4,445	6,195
Call	05/12/2006	92.50	100.00	8	0.00	0.01	35	0	
Put	05/12/2006	92.50	90.00	8	0.24	−0.16	35	840	840

Option	Date	Stock Price	Strike	Days	Option Price ($)	Delta	Contract	Option Value ($)	Position Value ($)
Call	05/12/2006	92.50	95.00	8	0.30	0.20	35	1,050	
Put	05/12/2006	92.50	90.00	8	0.24	−0.16	35	840	1,890
Call	05/15/2006	91.75	95.00	5	0.07	0.07	35	245	
Put	05/15/2006	91.75	90.00	5	0.24	−0.19	35	840	1,085
Call	05/16/2006	90.80	95.00	4	0.01	0.02	35	35	
Put	05/16/2006	90.80	90.00	4	0.41	−0.32	35	1,435	1,470
Call	05/17/2006	91.25	95.00	3	0.01	0.01	35	35	
Put	05/17/2006	91.25	90.00	3	0.21	−0.22	35	735	770
Call	05/18/2006	92.30	95.00	2	0.02	0.03	35	70	
Put	05/18/2006	92.30	90.00	2	0.02	−0.04	35	70	140
Call	05/19/2006	92.45	95.00	1	0.00	0.01	35	0	
Put	05/19/2006	92.45	90.00	1	0.00	−0.01	35	0	0

The first adjustment, on 04/03/2006, was necessary because the falling stock price drove the put delta to −0.48 while reducing the call delta to +.09. (Note that the put delta is represented as a negative number.) Balanced deltas are essential for buffering changes in the stock price. Leaving the position alone would have been tantamount to closing the calls and maintaining a short put position—a distinctly different trade. You will be quick to notice that we could have narrowed the position by buying back the $105 calls and selling an equivalent number of $100 calls. Although that adjustment would certainly have brought the put and call deltas closer together, it also would have increased the risk— especially since the put side was already in-the-money, the stock was falling, and 47 days were left before expiration. By adjusting strikes and inflating the position's size, we were able to closely match put and call deltas (+0.25/–0.21), keep our strike price spacing at $10, and more than cover the original loss. The original position was worth $4,460, the value climbed to $5,660 before the adjustment (a 27% loss), and after the adjustment we continued with a short position worth $6,440.

The value of our short position continued to decay with time, and the stock price continued to fall. To save space, the table skips the interval between 04/07 and 05/12. At this point, with eight days remaining, the position has decayed to $840, and we have more than 85% profit in the trade. However, call and put deltas are again imbalanced (call delta = +0.01, put delta = –0.16). We are forced to decide between closing the trade or continuing with a second adjustment. As we enter the final week before expiration, the time decay curve steepens considerably. Furthermore, 05/12 was a Friday, and the following Saturday was expiration day. Because options expire on Saturday at 5:00 p.m., the eight remaining days include three days when the market is closed—two Saturdays and a Sunday. These nontrading days represent three-eighths, or 37.5%, of the remaining time priced into the contracts. Moreover, the percentage of time that is lost between each market close and the next day's open becomes more dramatic as the final day approaches. Thursday evening before expiration marks the extreme, because at-the-money options must lose more than one-third of their remaining value while the market is closed.[3] The market often compensates for this problem with falling and rising volatility. As you would expect, the daily swings become more pronounced near the end. These distortions have many implications, and they often create an advantage for short sellers. A detailed discussion of this phenomenon appears in Chapter 8, "Trading the Expiration Cycle."

If we decide to keep the trade, the best move is to narrow the distance between strike prices by buying back the $100 calls and selling an equivalent number of $95 calls. The new position has relatively balanced call and put deltas and a strike price spacing of only $5.00. Because we are not adjusting a loss, there is no reason to inflate the trade's size with additional contracts.

Two days later, when the stock price falls to $90.80, the deltas again become imbalanced. We must weigh moving the call strike price to $90 and creating a straddle against keeping or closing the current trade. Unfortunately, creating a $90 straddle inflates the position value nearly four-fold and leaves the deltas relatively imbalanced at +0.68 (call) and –0.32 (put). Additionally, a $90 straddle would be very sensitive to any move of the underlying. In this regard it is important to recognize that 1 standard deviation is only $1.15 for a $90 stock exhibiting 20% volatility. As it turns out, we would have been forced to stop out with a slight loss the very next day on a very small move of the stock. If we continued to hold the position, it would have climbed from $5,833 at the time of the correction to $8,310 on 05/18, when the stock rose to $92.30 (less than a 1 standard deviation move). Narrowing the trade to a straddle would have made sense only if we closed most of the contracts and created a lower risk position. Conversely, keeping the delta-imbalanced position would have been equivalent to holding short puts. Closing the trade on 05/16 at a stock price of $90.80 therefore would have been the most conservative approach. Had we followed that path, we would have bought back both sides for $1470. Because, with adjustments, we sold options worth $6,290, the total profit would have been $4,820, or 76%. Had we gambled by keeping the short put position, the options ultimately would have expired out-of-the-money, delivering a 100% profit. Gambling sometimes works.

As we have seen, maintaining coupled deltas is central to the strategy for managing short put-call positions. When the difference between the deltas becomes significant, the trade can be decomposed and described as a simple long or short position. For example, if a 50-contract straddle has a call delta of 0.90 and a put delta of –0.05, that trade is effectively long 4,250 shares of stock (0.85 × 5,000). Although it is unreasonable to assume that the deltas can be kept at exact parity, a short straddle/strangle seller should set a limit based on the position size and behavior of the underlying. For example, if downward spikes tend to be much larger than upward spikes, a net short position should be considered riskier than a net long position.

VOLATILITY AND RISK
It is sometimes tempting to sell options that are priced with relatively high volatility, because the higher prices provide flexibility with regard

to strike price selection. Unfortunately, the risk of a large price spike increases disproportionately with the volatility of the underlying. The difference is dramatic. A $60 delta-neutral straddle (at-the-money options) with 30 days left until expiration and 10% implied volatility is worth approximately $1.40 (stock at $59.73 = delta neutral). At 40% implied volatility, a much wider delta neutral position ($75 call/$60 put with stock at $66.33) is worth the same amount of money. Unfortunately, high-volatility strangles where put and call strike prices are widely separated are not necessarily safer than low-volatility at-the-money straddles. Table 5.5 contains information regarding the average number of large spikes for each volatility range. The data was tabulated for all optionable stocks above $20 (1,817 stocks) over 252 trading days. The chart reveals a steep drop-off in the number of spikes greater than 3 standard deviations when volatility falls below 20%. Conversely, stocks exhibiting more than 60% volatility experience a disproportionate number of large price spikes. Between 20% and 60%, the curve is relatively flat. The comparisons are valid because the size of a spike is determined using both the stock price and volatility. A 3 standard deviation spike on a $100 stock with 40% volatility is $7.56, whereas the same size spike on a $30 stock with 20% volatility is only $1.13. As we have seen, recasting price changes in standard deviations allows direct comparison.

Table 5.5   Number of spikes greater than 3 standard deviations grouped by volatility (252 trading days).

Annual Volatility (%)	Average Number of Spikes Greater Than 3 StdDev
Fewer than 10	3.24
10 to 19.9	3.83
20 to 29.9	4.94
30 to 39.9	4.97
40 to 49.9	5.11
50 to 59.9	5.35
60 to 69.9	6.50
> 70	7.57

Statistically speaking, it is safer to sell at-the-money straddles on low-volatility stocks than very wide strangles at high implied volatility.

Covered Calls and Puts

A short position is considered "covered" if the account also contains an opposing position composed of an equivalent number of shares of the underlying security. That is, for each short contract, the account must have an opposing position composed of 100 shares of stock. The phrase "opposing position" was purposely chosen because, in this context, the terms "long" and "short" can be confusing. Short calls are balanced against long stock, and short puts are balanced against short stock. A short option position is also considered covered if the account is long a corresponding number of option contracts having more favorable terms—the same or longer expiration date, and the same or closer strike price.

Covered short positions do not have special collateral requirements, because they are not naked, and the potential loss is limited. Table 5.6 illustrates the concept using calls spaced by one strike price and one expiration month.

Table 5.6   Covered call position using only options.

Date	Closing Price ($)	Strike	Expiration Date	Days Remaining	Option Price ($)	Volatility	Delta
01/15/2007	73.00	75	03/17/2007	61	3.91 long	0.38	0.48
01/15/2007	73.00	80	02/17/2007	33	0.92 short	0.35	0.22
02/16/2007	80.00	75	03/17/2007	29	6.61 long	0.38	0.76
02/16/2007	80.00	80	02/17/2007	1	0.02 short	0.01	0.61

The first pair in the table depicts both sides of the trade when the position was first opened. The long side (top row) has 61 days left before expiration, and the short side has 33 days. The second pair of entries depicts both sides of the trade on expiration Friday, with the stock 7 points higher than when the trade was opened. Note that volatility of the short side decays to near zero at 4:00 p.m. on expiration Friday.

In this scenario the trade went well because the long side grew in value and the short side shrank. Under these circumstances, the profit of the option-option covered position is much larger than the more traditional stock-option covered trade. Initially we were long $3.91 and short $0.92—that is, net long $2.99. At expiration we were net long $6.59 for a profit of 121%. The realities of bid-ask spreads reduce the profit slightly. The opening trade would have been net long $3.05, and at expiration the position would have been worth $6.50. Overall profit would have been 113%.

The conservative approach would be to close the position and realize the full profit. However, we could also sell another batch of calls and keep the covered position. Selling the March $80 call is overly conservative—it would be worth $3.57, with a delta of 0.54. If the stock continued rising, both deltas would eventually reach 1.00. The maximum difference between both sides would be $5.00, which would yield an additional $1.96 of profit (the starting difference is $6.61 – $3.57). However, the $3.57 of downside protection is deceiving, because the starting delta is higher on the long side (0.76 versus 0.54). If the stock fell, we would be forced to stop out, and the position would be worth less than the value at the time of February expiration. The amount of the loss would be determined by the deltas, which are initially net long 0.22.

A less conservative approach would involve selling a higher strike price—probably $90. The value of these calls would be $1.67. The maximum upside of this trade is $4.94, and the delta of the short side is 0.32. We pay for the additional upside by significantly limiting downside protection.

All potential roll-forward scenarios considered, the best choice is to close the trade and realize the profit, especially since the stock has recently risen 9.5%. If the view is tremendously bullish, the best choice is to create a new position using different strikes that provide higher leverage. With the stock trading for $80 at February expiration, an excellent structure would consist of long April $80 calls and short March $85 calls, essentially a repeat of the first trade. The concept of closing a winning trade and taking profit rather than rolling forward is important. It makes sense to roll a trade forward when the new position has similar dynamics and the outlook remains the same. In our scenario that is not the case. The stock has risen sharply, placing the long side $5.00 in the money with a high delta. Any choice of short call that leaves upside room will do little to protect existing profit.

Simply stated, it does not make sense to roll forward with a new short option unless this is the structure we would launch from scratch with no existing position.

Unfortunately, most trades do not work out as well as the one we just reviewed. The trade outlined in Table 5.6 is delta long 0.26 at the time of launch. That is, it will lose 26 cents for each dollar of price decline of the underlying. As with any position, it is important to set stop limits and exit the trade without hesitation if a limit is reached. Overall, this trade was conservatively structured. Table 5.7 outlines a poorly structured, high-risk version of a covered call trade using only options.

The most significant difference between this trade and that of Table 5.6 is timing. Rather than launch the trade with a month left before expiration of the short side, we chose to wait until the final week, which forced a riskier strike price combination. This scenario was chosen purposefully, because many traders mistakenly believe that rapid time decay provides an excessive advantage that outweighs the risk of a price spike.

Table 5.7   Covered call position using only options launched in the final days before expiration.

Date	Closing Price ($)	Strike	Expiration Date	Days Remaining	Option Price ($)	Volatility	Delta
02/10/2007	73.00	75	03/17/2007	35	2.89 long	0.40	0.45
02/10/2007	73.00	75	02/17/2007	7	0.67 short	0.35	0.30
02/16/2007	85.00	75	03/17/2007	29	10.86 long	0.40	0.89
02/16/2007	85.00	75	02/17/2007	1	10.01 short	0.01	1.00

Unfortunately, in our ill-fated example, the stock rapidly rose from $73 to $85, taking the short-side delta to 1.00. We were long $2.22 before the sudden price rise, and only $0.85 after. A 50-contract position would have fallen from $11,100 to $4,250—a 62% loss. This scenario illustrates an important difference between covered positions built around options and their stock-option counterparts. Stock-option covered trades cannot lose money when the stock moves in the profitable direction, even if option volatility rises. Pure option covered positions have the potential to lose money in ether direction. Therefore, it is very important to pay close attention to the specific structure while keeping the relative frequency and size of historical price spikes in mind.

Because implied volatility can also vary enough to impact the trade, it is important to understand where current implied volatility sits on the historical scale. A rapid rise in volatility, which often accompanies a sudden price decline, can have an enormously positive effect on a pure option covered trade. Consider the two positions shown in Table 5.8. The first is a covered put position with the same time parameters and similar strike price pattern as our first example. The second position represents an instantaneous $3.00 drop in price accompanied by a 10% rise in volatility on both sides. In both cases the upper row represents the long side.

Table 5.8   Covered put position before and after a rapid downward price spike.

Date	Closing Price ($)	Strike	Expiration Date	Days Remaining	Option Price ($)	Volatility	Delta
01/15/2007	73.00	70	03/17/2007	61	3.07 long	0.40	−0.35
01/15/2007	73.00	65	02/17/2007	33	0.45 short	0.35	−0.12
01/15/2007	70.00	70	03/17/2007	61	5.39 long	0.50	−0.44
01/15/2007	70.00	65	02/17/2007	33	1.58 short	0.45	−0.26

A 50-contract position would have risen from $13,100 before the downward spike to $19,050 after. Raising the volatility alone—no price change—would have increased the net value to $16,150. In the first case we would have realized a 45% profit, and in the second 23%.

This effect is very significant because these occurrences are far more common than most investors realize. For example, during the week ending March 3, 2007, the market was particularly active. Virtually every equity option contract experienced a volatility increase greater than 10% (the VIX rose from 11 to 19 in less than one hour on February 27). An investor who is very bearish on a stock is much more likely to realize a large profit by structuring a covered put position using only options rather than the more traditional stock-option equivalent. The effect is less pronounced on the call side, because most volatility increases are also accompanied by falling prices. Moreover, caution is necessary, because rising volatility can partially obscure a loss that will be fully realized if volatility returns to normal after the decline. This scenario played out very abruptly in the case of Research in Motion stock, which fell approximately $7.00 during the February 27 decline while its call option implied volatility rose from 33% to 44%. Already-significant at-the-money call losses nearly doubled the very next day, when implied volatility returned to 33%.

Finally, the term "covered" can be somewhat misleading. The collateral requirement for a short option position that is married to a long position with a more favorable strike price but a closer expiration month is the same as that of the naked short position. Strictly speaking, these positions are not considered covered, and their trading dynamics are much different from those we have been discussing. If the trade were treated as covered, expiration of the long option would trigger a collateral requirement. For example, if the long option expires barely out-of-the-money, the longer dated short option may experience a large-enough price increase to cause a significant loss with no offset from the long side. We will revisit these structures in the next chapter as part of our review of complex trades that span multiple strike prices and expiration dates.

It is more traditional to think of covered call positions as consisting of long stock and short calls and of covered put positions as consisting of short stock and short puts. Both trades are characterized by the same dynamics as the option-option positions we have been discussing. The difference is that the stock side behaves like an option with a delta of 1.00. We could, in fact, purchase deep in-the-money calls or deep in-the-money puts as our long cover against corresponding out-of-the-money short options. One small advantage of this approach is that the loss on the long side is somewhat limited. Additionally, the shrinkage of the long delta that occurs if the stock moves far from the strike price can be helpful. Whereas long or short stock always behaves as an option with a delta of 1.00, deep in-the-money options do not. Significant moves of the underlying can reduce the delta from 1.00 and buffer the long side loss.

Covered positions built around stock have the general property of buffering losses and limiting gains for a portfolio. A covered call, for example, delivers profit if the stock falls slightly, stays at the same price, or rises to the strike price. In a flat market, covered calls and puts can deliver substantial profit on stocks that go absolutely nowhere. For example, if you were to sell out-of-the-money calls worth 50 cents, each month, against a stock trading for $50, the profit for the year would be $6.00, or 12%. If the stock also appreciated slightly in value, the profit would be accretive.

Historical price change behavior is also an important factor that should be taken into account when structuring covered positions. Stocks that exhibit occasional large spikes are inferior candidates for such positions. The short option position limits profit from a large spike in one direction but cannot effectively buffer a loss in the other. This effect is magnified by a rising delta in the profitable direction and a falling delta in the direction of a loss.

Finally, short in-the-money puts and calls can also be used in covered positions. Such positions are usually considered defensive in the sense that they can be added to a long or short stock position when the likelihood of a reversal is high but some upside potential still remains. The range of strike price choices is large, and it is important to choose short options that fit a specific investment strategy. Table 5.9 contains illustrative data for Apple Computer put options with 22 days remaining before expiration and a stock price of $88.90.[4]

Table 5.9   AAPL put data with 22 days remaining before expiration.

Strike	Put Delta	Bid ($)	Ask ($)
100	−1.00	10.90	11.10
95	−0.96	6.10	6.20
90	−0.58	2.50	2.55
85	−0.22	0.65	0.75

It is evident from the data that selling $100 or $95 strike price puts against short stock would not make sense, because falling stock prices would not generate any additional profit (both deltas are virtually –1.00). However, if we sold $90 puts against short stock, we would realize an initial net delta of –0.42. Further decline of the underlying would generate profit, initially at the rate of 42 cents per dollar of stock movement. The short delta would rise, and we can estimate from the table that a $5.00 drop in the price of AAPL would drive the put delta to nearly –1.00. This limited profit potential is offset by 58% buffering of a move in the wrong direction. If the underlying rises $1.00, we would lose only 42 cents. However, as the stock rises, the put delta shrinks until no protection is left. As with any stock position—long or short—stop orders are essential.

Synthetic Stock

It is possible to use options to structure a position that behaves essentially the same as a stock position. Pure option positions are sometimes desirable because of their reduced cost. Two strategies are possible:

- Long stock = long call/short put
- Short stock = short call/long put

Table 5.10 reveals the behavior of a synthetic long stock position established using at-the-money options with 44 days remaining before expiration. Each entry consists of a long call/short put pair at a different stock price (ten contracts on each side). Near the bottom of the chart, we see that the stock has risen to $54. The final entry contains values for the pair with the stock at $54 and only two days remaining. The initial position was net long $310. If the stock instantaneously rose to $54, we would keep approximately $300 of time premium, and the value of the position would follow the same path as it would for 1,000 shares of stock—a $4.00 increase yielding a $4,000 gain (second pair from the bottom of the table).

The final entry in the table differs by the amount of time decay that the options would experience over 42 days. Because both short and long options experience time decay, the change is modest. The position loses $940 on the call side and gains $650 on the put side. As a result, the profit shrinks slightly to $3,700, which is $300 less than the increase that would be experienced with 1,000 shares of stock.

The financial requirement to establish this trade can be calculated as follows: $300 net position cost + 0.25 × $50,000 collateral for the short put position + $1,920 collateral for the put value = $14,720. It is reasonable to compare the opportunity cost of the collateral requirement to that of the equivalent $50,000 stock purchase, because neither the collateral nor the $50,000 is lost. In either case the relevant expense is the opportunity cost. Regardless, it is clear that synthetic positions require considerably less funding.

Table 5.10   Synthetic stock example.

Stock Price ($)	Option/ Strike	Days Left	Option Price ($)	Volatility	Delta	Contract	Option Value ($)	Total ($)
50.00	Call 50	44	2.23	0.30	0.54	10	2,230	
50.00	Put 50	44	1.92	0.30	−0.46	−10	−1,920	310
51.00	Call 50	44	2.81	0.30	0.62	10	2,810	
51.00	Put 50	44	1.51	0.30	−0.38	−10	−1,510	1,300
52.00	Call 50	44	3.46	0.30	0.69	10	3460	
52.00	Put 50	44	1.16	0.30	−0.31	−10	−1,160	2,300
53.00	Call 50	44	4.18	0.30	0.75	10	4,180	
53.00	Put 50	44	0.88	0.30	−0.25	−10	−880	3,300
54.00	Call 50	44	4.95	0.30	0.80	10	4,950	
54.00	Put 50	44	0.65	0.30	−0.20	−10	−650	4,300
54.00	Call 50	2	4.01	0.30	1.00	10	4,010	
54.00	Put 50	2	0.00	0.30	0.00	−10	0	4,010

There is some asymmetry between synthetic long and short positions. Recall that the long position suffered a modest amount of time decay ($310). The reverse is true for a synthetic short position, because the short call loses more time value than the long put—the inverse of the position just outlined would gain approximately $310 over 42 days. Before July 2007, synthetic short positions also had the advantage of immunity to the "uptick" rule which prevented investors from establishing a short position while the stock price declined. The rule was designed to prevent a large investor from continually shorting a stock to drive down the price. An option trader had the advantage of being able to open a synthetic short position following a piece of negative news that caused a large drawdown. In today's fast-moving online trading environment, the difference is important. However, the uptick rule is no longer in effect, and it is now possible to short a stock while it is falling.

Investors sometimes use different strike prices to create synthetic long or short variations that are more bullish or bearish than their simple stock counterparts. For example, if you were to open a synthetic long position on a stock that was expected to rise quickly in the near term, the strike prices could be skewed so that the put is more expensive than the call. Even if the stock were to go nowhere and both sides expired worthless, the profit from the short side would be larger than the loss from the long side. As revealed in Table 5.11, such a position is not equivalent to a simple stock position.

Table 5.11 Synthetic long position with skewed strike prices.

Stock Price ($)	Option/ Strike	Days Left	Option Price ($)	Volatility	Delta	Contract	Option Value ($)	Total ($)
51.00	Call 55	44	0.83	0.30	0.27	10	830	
51.00	Put 50	44	1.51	0.30	−0.38	−10	−1,510	−680
52.00	Call 55	44	1.13	0.30	0.33	10	1,130	
52.00	Put 50	44	1.16	0.30	−0.31	−10	−1,160	−30
53.00	Call 55	44	1.5	0.30	0.40	10	1,500	
53.00	Put 50	44	0.88	0.30	−0.25	−10	−880	620

Table 5.11   Continued

Stock Price ($)	Option/ Strike	Days Left	Option Price ($)	Volatility	Delta	Contract	Option Value ($)	Total ($)
54.00	Call 55	44	1.94	0.30	0.47	10	1,940	
54.00	Put 50	44	0.65	0.30	−0.20	−10	−650	1,290
54.00	Call 55	2	0.14	0.30	0.21	10	140	
54.00	Put 50	2	0	0.30	0.00	−10	0	140

An equivalent long stock position consisting of 1,000 shares would have gained $3,000, but the skewed synthetic position outlined in Table 5.11 generated only $820. The problem is that a $3.00 increase still leaves the $55 calls $1.00 out-of-the-money. As expiration approaches, their value shrinks to nearly zero. Even the instantaneous increase (second pair from the bottom of the table) generated less value than a simple long stock position. With the underlying at $54.00, the synthetic position gained only $1,970 as opposed to $3,000 for the stock trade. However, the downside is also buffered. An instantaneous $4.00 decline in the stock price would have reduced the position value by only $2,790—a $1,210 improvement over the loss that would be experienced with long stock (put = $3.64, call = $0.17 at a stock price of $47 with 44 days remaining before expiration). As you might expect, the bullish option position held until expiration loses more in a downward move than it gains if the stock rises by the same amount.

Generally speaking, these positions are somewhat simplistic; we will explore more sophisticated bullish and bearish structures in the next chapter.

Summary

Option positions are dynamic; even the most basic positions can be complex to manage. Many books on the subject make the mistake of treating option positions as static entities that have a range of values at expiration. Nothing could be further from the truth. In real life, a trader must respond to a variety of forces that include but are not limited to price spikes, volatility swings, world financial news, market conditions, and time decay.

It is important to trade the option and not the underlying security, because out-of-the-money options can gain or lose tremendous amounts of value under the right circumstances. Furthermore, many traders lose sight of the option delta and forget that they may be moving around many more shares than they would ever trade. This problem worsens as options move toward, and ultimately into-the-money.

It is important to measure the size of each underlying price spike in terms of standard deviations and to develop a view of the frequency and size of the spikes. This information can be tremendously valuable when structuring trades. Moreover, it is often possible to use relatively large price spikes as entry point triggers for certain types of trades. When structuring long or short, bullish or bearish trades, it is helpful to view up and down price spike histories separately. Multiday composites can also aid in the analysis. Using the right annualization factor, it is possible to create multiday price spike charts that can be directly compared to single-day charts.

Earnings announcements, expiration days, and other events have characteristics that option traders can exploit, because they create subtle price distortions. It is important to interpret price change behavior in the context of these events. Some stocks exhibit predictably large price spikes with each earnings release and normally distributed price change behavior the remainder of the time. These facts can be helpful when you select expiration dates and strike prices.

Volatility swings can cause option positions to gain or lose value without any change in the price of the underlying security. Some stocks are prone to large intraday swings. We can calculate intraday volatility in much the same way that we calculate daily volatility using a different annualization factor. Stocks that exhibit large intraday swings often have underpriced options because most pricing strategies are based on close-to-close changes. Conversely, stocks that have high daily but low intraday volatility often experience large opening gaps. It is dangerous to hold short straddles on such stocks, because large changes tend to occur while the market is closed.

One of the most dangerous but common misconceptions is related to the risk profiles of long and short dated option positions. Short strangles with distant expiration dates and widely separated strike prices are not necessarily safer than their short dated counterparts. Much of the risk relates to the volatility of the underlying. It is statistically safer to sell at-the-money straddles on low-volatility stocks than very wide strangles at high implied volatility, because high-volatility stocks have a disproportionate number of large price spikes.

Finally, it is possible to create synthetic long or short stock positions using only options. These positions behave much the same as their pure stock counterparts. By selecting different strike prices and offsetting the center point of the trade, you can bias a position to be more bearish or bullish than the equivalent stock position.

The next chapter builds on these concepts to explore more complex multipart trades. The trades we have been analyzing will form the basis of more elaborate positions. Many of these can be decomposed into the basic positions that we have just reviewed.

Further Reading

Farley, A., *The Master Swing Trader*, New York–Toronto: McGraw-Hill, 2001.

Kaufman, P., *Trading Systems and Methods*, Third Edition, New York–Toronto: John Wiley and Sons, 1998.

Luft, C.F. and R.K. Sheiner, *Listed Stock Options: The Hands-on Study Guide for Investors and Traders*, New York: McGraw-Hill, 1993.

Natenberg, S., *Option Volatility and Pricing*, Revised Edition, New York: McGraw-Hill/Irwin Professional Publishing, 1994.

Olmstead, E., *Options for the Beginner and Beyond,* Financial Times Press (Prentice Hall), March 2006.

The Options Institute, *Options: Essential Concepts and Trading Strategies*, Third Edition, New York: McGraw-Hill, 1999. By staff and consultants of the Chicago Board Options Exchange.

Endnotes

1 There are three calendar days between the close on Friday and the close on Monday. As a result, 100 calendar days typically include 70 to 75 trading days or closes, depending on the number of additional holidays.

2 It is important to consistently use either a 252- or 365-day trading year if intraday and daily volatility are to be compared. The corresponding annualization factors for the 6.5-hour time frame are 30.50 or 36.71.

3 On Thursday at the close, 2.042 days remain before expiration. At the open on Friday, 1.313 days remain.

4 Data at market close on February 23, 2007.

6

MANAGING COMPLEX POSITIONS

T he preceding chapter began with single-sided trades composed of either puts or calls. As we progressed up the complexity scale, we encountered more complicated positions that contained both. We ended that chapter with a focus on trades built of long and short components—covered calls/puts and synthetic stock. This chapter continues the trend, opening with calendar spreads—which include long and short components with different expiration dates. The chapter then progresses to ratios, calendar spread ratios, and finally trades with three or more components.

This approach was chosen because it fits well with our theme of dynamic management. The simplest trades to manage consist of long or short puts or calls. Managing trades that contain both puts and calls is a more complex endeavor. Mixing long and short components raises the bar still higher, because it balances limited gain/unlimited loss against unlimited gain/limited loss. This chapter adds the dimensions of time (calendar spreads) and asymmetry (ratios). We end with a look at trades that can include various combinations of long and short puts and calls, potentially across different expiration months. Managing these trades is enormously complex, because they include many moving parts that behave differently. They are also sensitively dependent on initial conditions in the sense that subtle changes in the initial structure can have dramatic effects on the outcome.

Many investors believe that complex option trades can be structured to deliver a solid return with limited risk and virtually no need for interim management. Our theme is the opposite: we discuss the most complex multipart positions last because they are the most difficult to launch and maintain. As you have seen, market realities differ from basic theory because they include bid-ask spreads, variations in volatility, liquidity issues, intraday spikes, and a variety of market surprises. Complexity rises exponentially with each variable introduced into the system. Therefore, it is reckless to advise beginners to start with complex multipart trades under the misconception that they are straightforward to understand and well hedged against risk. Conversely, an investor who spends time modeling the effects of varying volatility, time decay, and large price changes in the underlying will likely generate a profit. Such investors always have a detailed plan and a set of rules for stopping out and making positional adjustments. Complex trades require sophisticated management schemes that can only result from careful planning. Our goal in this chapter is to lay the foundation for building these management strategies.

Calendar and Diagonal Spreads

Calendar spreads involve purchasing and selling the same strike price with different expiration dates. If the short position is also the longer dated option, the position is called a *reverse calendar spread*. When different strike prices and expiration dates are both used, the position is considered *diagonalized*. Not surprisingly, a diagonal spread that is short the more distant expiration date is sometimes called a *reverse diagonal spread*.

The preceding chapter introduced diagonal spreads in the form of covered put and call positions that were structured exclusively with options. In this context we structured positions that were long the more favorable month and strike price. An example might be a position that is short April $50 calls and long May $45 calls with a later strike price. As we previously discussed, such positions are considered covered.

The number of strike price/expiration date combinations is as large as the number of strategies. At one extreme, an investor might purchase far-dated deep out-of-the-money options and sell current-month out-of-the-money options to defray the cost. The short position is renewed each month at a new strike price that depends on the stock's performance. At the other extreme, an investor might purchase current-month out-of-the-money options and sell far-dated far out-of-the-money options to defray the time decay cost. Many previous texts on the subject have classified such trades on a scale from very bullish to very bearish. These classifications can be helpful. In our analysis we will often relate technical parameters such as delta and gamma to price change behavior to determine where a position fits on the bullish-to-bearish spectrum.

Certain structures can be deceiving with regard to risk. For example, a diagonal spread that is long the more favorable strike price but in a closer expiration date than that of the short side can lose significant amounts of money, even when the stock moves toward the strikes. The risk rises as expiration nears and the long side remains out-of-the-money. Suppose, for example, that the account is long $100 strike price calls expiring in the current month and short $120 calls with three months left, on a stock trading for $90. If the underlying rises to $98 in the final days before expiration, the long options might rise only a small amount before expiring worthless. The short options, owing to their long expiration time frame, would rise a significant amount. The position would behave very much like a naked call position with three months remaining before expiration. Worse still, if a new hedge were established for the following month (long $110 strike price calls with two months remaining), and the scenario repeated itself, the loss could easily double. A representative scenario is shown in Table 6.1.

Table 6.1 Diagonal call spread pricing scenario #1: delayed underlying price increase with $10 strike spacing.

Date	Closing Price ($)	Strike	Expiration Date	Days Remaining	Option Price ($)	Volatility	Delta
01/15/2007	71.00	90	05/19/2007	124.04	1.70 short	0.40	0.20
01/15/2007	71.00	80	02/17/2007	33.04	0.55 long	0.35	0.15
02/13/2007	75.00	90	05/19/2007	95.04	1.89 short	0.40	0.23
02/13/2007	75.00	80	02/17/2007	4.04	0.05 long	0.35	0.04
02/14/2007	77.00	90	05/19/2007	94.04	2.37 short	0.40	0.27
02/14/2007	77.00	80	02/17/2007	3.04	0.15 long	0.35	0.12
02/15/2007	79.00	90	05/19/2007	93.04	2.93 short	0.40	0.32
02/15/2007	79.00	80	02/17/2007	2.04	0.43 long	0.35	0.32

Each pair consists of a short call with a distant expiration (upper row) and a long call expiring in the near term (lower row). Time remaining at the close each day is displayed in the Days Remaining column.[1] Although diagonal spreads are traditionally long the far dated month, this position is also referred to as a diagonal spread because it involves long and short components with different expiration dates and strike prices.

The first pair in the series represents the opening trade. With 30 days left before expiration, the long call was worth $0.55, and the short call was worth $1.70. In the final days before expiration, the stock rallied to $79. The effect on the long options was limited; the price climbed only to $0.43. The short side, however, experienced a large increase in value. If we project the position forward one more day at the same stock price, the long side will decay to zero, and the short side will be worth $2.90—a gain of $1.20 for the short side and a loss of $0.55 for the long side. The trade would suffer a net loss of $1.75, or $175 per contract. This problem is very common when expiring long options are used to hedge a longer dated short position. It is also important to note that the short position is uncovered because it expires after the long side of the trade. Therefore, we must add the opportunity cost of the collateral to the cost of the trade. This amount is not insignificant. A 50-contract position on a $70 stock would consume $87,500 of collateral plus the cost of the position—in this case, $8,500. Therefore, we must add the value of risk-free interest on $96,000 for the life of the trade.

The conservative approach would have been to stop out when the stock price rose to $75 on 02/13, or the next day, when the stock price climbed to $77. As always, such decisions have much to do with predefined loss limits that are heavily dependent on the size of the trade. Many investors keep positions relatively small and rely on mean reversion to reverse the trend.

Had we taken the other side of the trade—a traditional diagonal spread—the profit would have been $1.75 (assuming expiration of the near-dated short option below the strike price). Many investors adopt this strategy for stocks that they expect will rise over a long period of time. It is not uncommon to purchase calls with six or more months left before expiration and to sell current-month calls at the beginning of each expiration cycle to offset time decay cost.

The same trade also would have yielded significantly different results if the stock price had moved to $75 at an earlier date. This scenario is shown in Table 6.2.

Table 6.2   Diagonal call spread pricing scenario #2: rapid underlying price increase with $10 strike spacing.

Date	Closing Price ($)	Strike	Expiration Date	Days Remaining	Option Price ($)	Volatility	Delta
01/15/2007	71.00	90	05/19/2007	124	1.70 short	0.40	0.20
01/15/2007	71.00	80	02/17/2007	33	0.55 long	0.35	0.15
01/17/2007	75.00	90	05/19/2007	122	2.61 short	0.40	0.27
01/17/2007	75.00	80	02/17/2007	31	1.35 long	0.35	0.29

Table 6.2   Continued

Date	Closing Price ($)	Strike	Expiration Date	Days Remaining	Option Price ($)	Volatility	Delta
01/18/2007	77.00	90	05/19/2007	121	3.17 short	0.40	0.31
01/18/2007	77.00	80	02/17/2007	30	1.98 long	0.35	0.39
01/19/2007	79.00	90	05/19/2007	120	3.80 short	0.40	0.35
01/19/2007	79.00	80	02/17/2007	29	2.79 long	0.35	0.48

At the beginning of the trade, we are net short $1.15; after the stock price increase, the number narrows slightly to just over $1.00. Because our near-dated long options have not lost much time and are relatively close to the strike price, we experience a gain that is roughly equivalent to that of the short side. However, if the stock remains at this price, our near-dated options will ultimately lose all their value—the scenario of Table 6.1. In scenario #2, we might consider closing our long position for a $2.24 profit and establishing a new hedge, at a higher strike price, for the short side. There is no loss because the overall position value has not materially changed (the short side increased $2.10 and the long side increased $2.24). The $2.10 increase on the short side would be rolled into the new position. We might also decide to keep both sides of the trade open while the stock is rising and, if the stock rises enough, close both sides for a profit. The contrast between scenario #1 and scenario #2 illustrates the destructive nature of time on option positions.

It is important to establish goals for the trade up front and to adjust the position to achieve those goals. If the goal is to sell out-of-the-money options to profit from time decay or a large opposing move in the stock price, less-expensive long options are the best choice. However, if the goal is to profit from appreciation in the value of the long side and to use the short side to offset some of the time decay cost, more-expensive near-the-money long options are usually better. As always, the collateral requirement for the short side is unchanged if the long option has a closer expiration date.

Table 6.3 addresses the strategy that is designed to deliver profit on the long side while using the short side to offset some of the time decay cost. The stock price increase occurs at the same time as in scenario #2, but because we purchase a much closer strike price ($75), the profit is significant. The trade, which is initially even on both sides (net short 13 cents), is net long $1.85 after the stock rises to $79—a profit of $1.98. In this scenario it makes sense to realize the profit by closing both sides of the trade and to establish a completely new position.

Finally, if the stock price had initially fallen, the position would have behaved as a simple long call with a delta of 0.14 (0.34 long side, 0.20 short side). The correct management strategy would have been to stop out if the loss exceeded a predefined limit.

Table 6.3 Diagonal call spread pricing scenario #3: rapid underlying price increase with $15 strike spacing.

Date	Closing Price ($)	Strike	Expiration Date	Days Remaining	Option Price ($)	Volatility	Delta
01/15/2007	71.00	90	05/19/2007	124	1.70 short	0.40	0.20
01/15/2007	71.00	75	02/17/2007	33	1.57 long	0.35	0.34
01/17/2007	75.00	90	05/19/2007	122	2.61 short	0.40	0.27
01/17/2007	75.00	75	02/17/2007	31	3.21 long	0.35	0.54
01/18/2007	77.00	90	05/19/2007	121	3.17 short	0.40	0.31
01/18/2007	77.00	75	02/17/2007	30	4.33 long	0.35	0.64
01/19/2007	79.00	90	05/19/2007	120	3.80 short	0.40	0.35
01/19/2007	79.00	75	02/17/2007	29	5.65 long	0.35	0.73

A similar result could have been obtained using a combination of long stock and short calls with the same initial difference in deltas. The mix would be different, however, because stock has a delta of 1.00. The long stock/short call combination would also qualify as covered, and no collateral would be required. The same dynamics apply to trades built around short stock and puts. We could, in fact, purchase deep in-the-money calls or deep in-the-money puts on the long side against corresponding out-of-the-money short options. One small advantage of this approach is that the loss on the long side is somewhat limited. Additionally, the shrinkage of the long delta that occurs if the stock moves far from the strike price can be helpful. Whereas long or short stock always behaves as an option with a delta of 1.00, deep in-the-money options do not. Significant moves of the underlying can reduce the delta from 1.00 and buffer the long-side loss.

Historical price change behavior is also an important factor that should be taken into account when structuring diagonal spreads. Stocks that exhibit occasional large spikes are inferior candidates for such positions. The short option position limits profit from a large spike in one direction but cannot effectively buffer a loss in the other. The effect is magnified by a rising delta in the profitable direction and a falling delta in the direction of a loss.

A calendar spread has all the same dynamics, but, because the strike prices are equal, it can be difficult to roll the trade forward at each expiration cycle. The problem occurs when the underlying moves far enough to breach the strike price at the end of a cycle, making it difficult to add another out-of-the-money short position. Continuing the trade would involve protecting existing profit in a long in-the-money option that also has a high delta. Table 6.4 displays a repeat of the first scenario (Table 6.1) recast as a calendar spread.

Table 6.4   Calendar call spread derived from Table 6.1.

Date	Closing Price ($)	Strike	Expiration Date	Days Remaining	Option Price ($)	Volatility	Delta
01/15/2007	71.00	80	05/19/2007	124	3.77 long	0.40	0.37
01/15/2007	71.00	80	02/17/2007	33	0.55 short	0.35	0.15
02/13/2007	75.00	80	05/19/2007	95	4.47 long	0.40	0.23
02/13/2007	75.00	80	02/17/2007	4	0.05 short	0.35	0.04
02/14/2007	77.00	80	05/19/2007	94	5.37 long	0.40	0.49
02/14/2007	77.00	80	02/17/2007	3	0.15 short	0.35	0.12

Date	Closing Price ($)	Strike	Expiration Date	Days Remaining	Option Price ($)	Volatility	Delta
02/15/2007	79.00	80	05/19/2007	93	6.36 long	0.40	0.54
02/15/2007	79.00	80	02/17/2007	2	0.43 short	0.35	0.32

In this case we are both long and short the $80 strike price. However, because this is a calendar spread, not a reverse calendar spread, we are long the far month and short the near dated option. The rapid 10% rise in stock price raised the long option from $3.77 to $6.36, while the short side decayed to 43 cents. If the underlying remains below the strike price for one more day, the short side will expire worthless.

It would be wise to close the trade and realize the full profit, which, at February expiration, would be $3.14 ($6.36 − $3.77 + $0.55). However, if we want to continue with a similar structure, the next move would be the sale of March $85 calls for $1.15. The new position is a diagonal spread because the strikes are different. The new calls, priced at the time of February expiration, would have a delta of 0.26 with 29 days remaining. Note that when we began the first trade, we were net long a delta of 0.22. Our risk, in the event of a reversal after the new position is established, would be higher, because the overall delta would be net long 0.28. The problem is caused by the in-the-money long call with a delta of 0.54. Management of the new position therefore is more difficult, and we would need a more sensitive stop limit.

As we have seen, the potential effectiveness of a long hedge in the current month against a short position in a distant month can be large. The effect is heavily dependent on strike price and time. For example, the contrast between Table 6.3 and Table 6.5 is striking. In Table 6.3 the long position had a $15 advantage with regard to strike price, whereas Table 6.5 is built around a single strike. Both scenarios involve an almost immediate 10% increase in the underlying price. Because the near option has 33 days left before expiration, its potential to increase in value is significant. Note that the position is called a *reverse* calendar call spread because the long option has the nearer expiration.

Table 6.5 Reverse calendar call spread with an immediate underlying price increase.

Date	Closing Price ($)	Strike	Expiration Date	Days Remaining	Option Price ($)	Volatility	Delta
01/15/2007	71.00	80	05/19/2007	124	3.77 short	0.40	0.37
01/15/2007	71.00	80	02/17/2007	33	0.55 long	0.35	0.15
01/17/2007	75.00	80	05/19/2007	122	5.39 short	0.40	0.46
01/17/2007	75.00	80	02/17/2007	31	1.35 long	0.35	0.29
01/18/2007	77.00	80	05/19/2007	121	6.33 short	0.40	0.51
01/18/2007	77.00	80	02/17/2007	30	1.98 long	0.35	0.39
01/19/2007	79.00	80	05/19/2007	120	7.35 short	0.40	0.55
01/19/2007	79.00	80	02/17/2007	29	2.79 long	0.35	0.48

We begin the trade short $3.22. After the sudden price increase, we find that we are short $4.56—a loss of $1.34. An unhedged short position would have lost nearly 3 times as much—$3.58 ($7.35 − $3.77). Comparing near-month call prices in Tables 6.4 and 6.5 reveals a significant decay in the effectiveness of a near-term out-of-the-money hedge as expiration approaches. In Table 6.4, if we had been long the current month, the value of our option would have changed little while the distant month increased substantially. As you might expect, the performance of the near-term long position is even more powerful in Table 6.3, where the diagonal spread included a lower near-term strike price ($75) than that of Table 6.5 ($80).

The reverse calendar spread illustrated in Table 6.5 is bearish because of its initial net short delta of −0.22. That is, a rapid rise in the stock price would be destructive to the position. Gamma, in this case, is the opposing force. The long-side gamma rose with the stock from 0.031 to 0.051, while the short-side gamma remained constant at 0.022. So despite being short delta, the trade was long gamma, and gamma was increasing. As a result, with the stock at $79 on 01/19, the trade became less bearish, and the net delta climbed to –0.07. This dynamic makes the near-term hedge effective. However, we would have stopped out before the underlying reached $79. In Table 6.4, the large price increase occurred near expiration. The gamma of the long side was essentially zero, and the net delta remained +0.22. If the underlying remained below the strike price for one additional day, the delta of the short side would have fallen to zero, yielding a net delta of +0.54. That is, the trade becomes very bullish at February expiration.

The underlying concept of structuring a bearish trade using only calls is important. You might be tempted to think of a bearish trade as being structured around puts, but that is not always the case. Table 6.6 illustrates the effect of reversing the near-expiration 10% increase of Table 6.4 with a 10% decline.

Table 6.6   Reverse calendar call spread with an underlying price decline.

Date	Closing Price ($)	Strike	Expiration Date	Days Remaining	Option Price ($)	Volatility	Delta
01/15/2007	71.00	80	05/19/2007	124	3.77 short	0.40	0.37
01/15/2007	71.00	80	02/17/2007	33	0.55 long	0.35	0.15
02/13/2007	67.00	80	05/19/2007	95	1.76 short	0.40	0.24
02/13/2007	67.00	80	02/17/2007	4	0.00 long	0.35	0.00
02/14/2007	65.00	80	05/19/2007	94	1.30 short	0.40	0.20
02/14/2007	65.00	80	02/17/2007	3	0.00 long	0.35	0.00
02/15/2007	63.00	80	05/19/2007	93	0.94 short	0.40	0.15
02/15/2007	63.00	80	02/17/2007	2	0.00 long	0.35	0.00

The trade is very profitable as it declines from being short $3.22 to being short $0.94. The bearish nature of the –0.22 net delta is evident in this behavior. However, the structure is inherently flawed. The problem is that the near-dated option will expire worthless even if the underlying rises 10%. The trade would then yield the same result as a far-dated naked short call with an added loss of 55 cents. The long option, therefore, has little capacity to buffer losses on the short side. If, as in our example, the stock declines, the cost of the long option simply detracts from the profit. At May expiration, the total cost of four months of hedges would be approximately $2.20, and the total profit would be $1.57. The opportunity cost of the collateral requirement should also be considered, because it equals approximately 20% of the profit (assuming a risk-free interest rate of 5%). Such trades, which are designed to profit from time decay and/or falling volatility, are generally structured in four parts on the put and call sides simultaneously. They are adjusted over time as needed. We will return to complex four-part trades later in this chapter.

Ratios

Broadly stated, ratio trades are long a certain number of options at one strike and short some multiple of this number of options at another. This section focuses on trades in which both sides have the same expiration date. Ratios are extremely conservative trades because they profit over a wide range of underlying prices while being buffered against losses.

Ratio trades can be constructed using stock and options or options only. Most pure option ratios are buffered against loss on one side and are completely protected on the other. Ratio call spreads are a perfect example. Such a trade might consist of ten long $70 calls and twenty short $75 calls with the same expiration. Assuming that both sides are worth approximately the same amount, the trade would be profitable at expiration, with the stock anywhere between $70 and $80 with a profit peak at $75. One very attractive characteristic is that the trade is a wash—that is, no gain or loss—if the stock is below both strikes at expiration. Table 6.7 illustrates with a stock that is often a perfect ratio call spread candidate—Sears. The table is abbreviated to preserve key days.

Table 6.7   Ratio call spread: Sears January 2007 expiration. For this example, option values were calculated using average volatility for the time frame (18%).

Date	Stock Price ($)	Strike	Days Remaining	Option Price ($)	Delta	Contract	Position Value ($)
12/21/2006	167.93	175	30	1.20	0.24	10	
12/21/2006	167.93	180	30	0.45	0.11	−20	300
01/03/2007	167.28	175	17	0.45	0.14	10	
01/03/2007	167.28	180	17	0.10	0.04	−20	250
01/09/2007	166.23	175	11	0.15	0.06	10	
01/09/2007	166.23	180	11	0.01	0.01	−20	130
01/10/2007	172.09	175	10	1.00	0.31	10	
01/10/2007	172.09	180	10	0.15	0.07	−20	700
01/11/2007	174.48	175	9	1.85	0.48	10	
01/11/2007	174.48	180	9	0.40	0.15	−20	1050
01/16/2007	179.07	175	4	4.35	0.89	10	
01/16/2007	179.07	180	4	1.00	0.41	−20	2350
01/17/2007	177.41	175	3	2.80	0.81	10	
01/17/2007	177.41	180	3	0.30	0.20	−20	2200
01/18/2007	178.03	175	2	3.20	0.90	10	
01/18/2007	178.03	180	2	0.30	0.21	−20	2600
01/19/2007	179.52	175	1	4.50	1.00	10	
01/19/2007	179.52	180	1	0.05	0.40	−20	4400

Sears was chosen for this example because the stock's price change behavior often fits the normal distribution, and option prices tend to represent risk fairly. The time frame was chosen to avoid earnings releases, which tend to be very volatile. Note that the trade was delta-neutral at launch—0.24 on the long side and 0.22 on the short side. Long-side calls cost $1.20, and the short side sold for $0.90 ($0.45 × 2). The total downside risk was only 30 cents ($300 for ten contracts). If the stock had fallen, we likely would have closed the trade near expiration, selling the long side for a small amount and allowing the short side to expire worthless. At expiration the trade was nearly $5.00 in-the-money on the long side and at-the-money on the short side.

Few trades embody this level of luck. Suppose, for example, that between 01/16 and expiration the stock had suddenly risen sharply in response to a piece of positive news. All profit to that point would have been erased, and, if the spike were large enough, the short side would have overwhelmed the long side. This behavior is time-dependent in the sense that the trade is more susceptible to such a spike early on. Table 6.8 depicts such a scenario. The stock chosen for this illustration is Apple Computer because it has a history of large upward spikes that confound all option pricing models.

Table 6.8   Ratio call spread: Apple Computer January 2007 expiration. For this example, option values were calculated using average volatility for the time frame (36%).

Date	Stock Price ($)	Strike	Days Remaining	Option Price ($)	Delta	Contract	Position Value ($)
12/20/2006	84.76	85	31	3.60	0.53	10	
12/20/2006	84.76	90	31	1.70	0.32	−20	200
01/08/2007	85.47	85	12	2.55	0.56	10	
01/08/2007	85.47	90	12	0.75	0.23	−20	1,050
01/09/2007	92.57	85	11	7.90	0.92	10	
01/09/2007	92.57	90	11	3.90	0.69	−20	100

Date	Stock Price ($)	Strike	Days Remaining	Option Price ($)	Delta	Contract	Position Value ($)
01/10/2007	97.00	85	10	12.15	0.99	10	
01/10/2007	97.00	90	10	7.40	0.90	−20	−2,650
01/11/2007	95.80	85	9	10.95	0.98	10	
01/11/2007	95.80	90	9	6.25	0.88	−20	−1,550
01/12/2007	94.62	85	8	9.75	0.98	10	
01/12/2007	94.62	90	8	5.15	0.84	−20	−550
01/16/2007	97.10	85	4	12.15	1.00	10	
01/16/2007	97.10	90	4	7.20	0.98	−20	−2,250
01/17/2007	94.95	85	3	10.00	1.00	10	
01/17/2007	94.95	90	3	5.05	0.95	−20	−100
01/18/2007	89.07	85	2	4.15	0.96	10	
01/18/2007	89.07	90	2	0.60	0.36	−20	2,950
01/19/2007	88.50	85	1	3.50	0.98	10	
01/19/2007	88.50	90	1	0.05	0.20	−20	3,400

Both examples have the same expiration month—January 2007. The market generally was rising during this time frame, and most stocks performed well. Apple, however, experienced some very large upward spikes that were disruptive to our trade. At launch the trade was slightly bearish (delta = −0.11). The short side sold for $3.40 and the long side for $3.60. Initial stock stability caused significant decay of the short side, and the trade went from being essentially flat to being long $1.05. This result makes perfect sense for a trade that is slightly bearish and experiences no significant underlying price increase. Decay of the short side yielded a slightly bullish position on January 8 (delta = +0.10).

On January 9 everything changed, because the stock suddenly experienced a 4 standard deviation upward spike that took the underlying price from $85 to $92. The profit in the trade was erased by this move. However, the buffering capacity of the long side of a ratio spread was evident, because, despite a 420% increase in the price of the short side, the trade was still absolutely flat, and, overall, no money was lost. It is often a good idea to close such a trade, especially when a stock that had previously experienced very little price change suddenly becomes active. In the case of Apple, the cause was a product announcement—the company had decided to enter the cell phone business with an exotic new product. The announcement also represented a turning point for the company that included a new focus on computing infrastructure for home entertainment. Analysts began writing reports, and Apple was continually in the news for the next several weeks. This was not a good time to own a structured position on Apple unless that position was designed to profit from large, unpredictable price spikes in either direction (a long straddle).

The next day, January 10, the stock jumped another $4.43, completely destroying the trade and creating a $2,850 loss. As it turns out, mean reversion (and mixed reviews from analysts) caused the stock to decline nearly $9.00 before expiration. In the end the trade was profitable by $3,200. Had the stock remained at $97, the trade would have been a loss. The short side would have been worth $14 and the long side only $12. On January 10, at the time of the second spike, keeping this position would have been roughly equivalent to shorting the stock, because the position had a net delta of –0.81. Unless an investor had that intention, and expected to recover the first loss by shorting the stock, the position would have been a pure gamble.

The same characteristics that cause Apple stock to be a poor candidate for ratio call spreads make it an excellent candidate for long straddles. As we have seen, however, long straddles and strangles have a time decay cost that can become excessive if the stock does not experience a price spike during the time frame of the trade. One solution is to structure a trade that has long and short components, does not suffer from time decay, and generates profit in the event of a large price spike. Ratio backspreads are a viable answer. They are structured much like the forward spreads we have been discussing. The difference is that the further out-of-the-money strike is the long side.

If we had taken the other side of the trade depicted in Table 6.8—that is, twenty long $90 calls and ten short $85 calls—we would have structured a ratio call backspread. This trade would have generated profit in the event of a very large upward spike. In the event of a downward spike, both sides would have expired worthless. At the peak on January 10, a call backspread would have been profitable. We would have closed the trade.

Forward spreads rely on slow, steady price change over time, because the goal is to allow the further out-of-the-money option to decay. Rapid moves in the direction of the strikes tend to favor the short side, causing the trade to lose money. Backspreads are exactly the opposite— large, unanticipated price changes in the direction of the strikes favor the long side. A large price spike that substantially alters the position value should trigger an exit in either case. If the position is a forward spread, the exit is a stop that prevents further loss. In the case of a backspread, the exit is a profit-taking event. Profit taking among stock investors and the general forces that underlie mean reversion typically work against backspreads after a large spike occurs. This behavior is evident in Figure 6.1, which depicts the price change behavior of Apple stock during the time frame of the trade, 12/20/2006–01/19/2007.

The first upward spike, which occurred on 12/29, is not listed in the table. It had a negligible effect on the position because, after the spike, both sides of the trade remained out-of-the-money. The close strike climbed to $3.05, and the far strike to $1.25. The two large in-the-money spikes marked with arrows had pronounced effects. The close strike climbed to $12.15, and the far strike to $7.40.

Because proximity to the strike price and time both affect the trade, backspreads should be structured differently than forward spreads. Backspreads have a better chance of generating profit if they are structured with the far strike nearly in-the-money. This behavior is evident in Table 6.9, which outlines a ratio call backspread for Apple Computer stock that corresponds to the forward spread of Table 6.8.

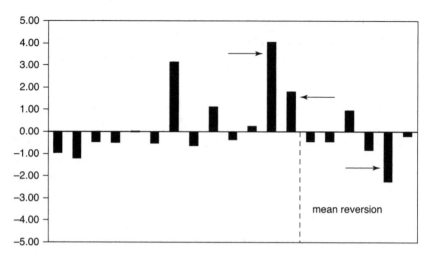

Figure 6.1   Apple price spikes in standard deviations 12/20/2006–01/19/2007.
The large upward spikes of 01/09 and 01/10, as well as the downward spike of 01/18, are marked with arrows. The early 12/29
upward spike visible on the chart is not listed in the table.

Table 6.9   Ratio call backspread: Apple Computer January 2007 expiration.
For this example, option values were calculated using average
volatility for the time frame (36%).

Date	Stock Price ($)	Strike	Days Remaining	Option Price ($)	Delta	Contract	Position Value ($)
12/20/2006	84.76	80	31	6.55	0.74	−10	
12/20/2006	84.76	85	31	3.60	0.53	20	650
01/08/2007	85.47	80	12	6.00	0.86	−10	
01/08/2007	85.47	85	12	2.55	0.56	20	−900
01/09/2007	92.57	80	11	12.70	0.99	−10	
01/09/2007	92.57	85	11	7.90	0.92	20	3,100
01/10/2007	97.00	80	10	17.10	1.00	−10	
01/10/2007	97.00	85	10	12.15	0.99	20	7,200

Date	Stock Price ($)	Strike	Days Remaining	Option Price ($)	Delta	Contract	Position Value ($)
01/11/2007	95.80	80	9	15.90	1.00	−10	
01/11/2007	95.80	85	9	10.95	0.98	20	6,000
01/12/2007	94.62	80	8	14.70	1.00	−10	
01/12/2007	94.62	85	8	9.75	0.98	20	4,800
01/16/2007	97.10	80	4	17.15	1.00	−10	
01/16/2007	97.10	85	4	12.15	1.00	20	7,150
01/17/2007	94.95	80	3	15.00	1.00	−10	
01/17/2007	94.95	85	3	10.00	1.00	20	5,000
01/18/2007	89.07	80	2	9.10	1.00	−10	
01/18/2007	89.07	85	2	4.15	0.96	20	−800
01/19/2007	88.50	80	1	8.50	1.00	−10	
01/19/2007	88.50	85	1	3.50	0.98	20	−1,500

Note that we have structured the trade with the first strike in-the-money and the second just out-of-the-money. This trade was not initially delta-neutral. On the starting day we were net long a delta of +0.32. That is, the trade was bullish in the amount of 320 shares of stock. A neutral trade would have been long only 14 contracts. Conversely, a price-neutral trade would have been long between 18 and 19 contracts. Because the price spike history of Apple stock during the time frame preceding this trade was strongly skewed to the upside, a bullish trade would have been a reasonable choice. The volatile nature of Apple stock is more evident than in the previous example because at-the-money deltas are larger and have a more pronounced effect.

The structures described in Tables 6.8 and 6.9 have different risk profiles as backspreads (recall that Table 6.8 was a forward spread). If Table 6.8 were structured as a backspread, the trade would have lost $3,200. Because the strike price arrangement in Table 6.9 was optimized for a backspread, the loss at expiration would have been smaller—$2,150. The profit on 01/10 was also much larger—$6,550. If we had structured a far out-of-the-money trade using $90 and $95 strike prices, none of the days would have been profitable.

Our second example was built around higher deltas and in-the-money strike prices. We could take one more step and structure a trade using stock and options. Both stock-option structures, forward spread and backspread, are reasonable. A ratio call spread would consist of long stock and short out-of-the-money options. A backspread would be short stock and long calls. Unfortunately, the stock's fixed delta presents some limitations.

Consider Table 6.10, which displays two different scenarios based on the previous example. Each assumes that we are long stock and short calls at the time of the first upward price spike on 01/09. Both are based on a delta-neutral position at the market close on 01/08. The first is built around the $85 strike price, and the second uses the $90 strike.

Table 6.10   Ratio call spread using stock and options: two scenarios with rising stock price.

Date	Stock Price ($)	Strike	Days Remaining	Option Price ($)	Delta	Contract/ Shares	Position Value ($)	Gain/ Loss ($)
01/08/2007	85.47				1.00	1120	95,726	
01/08/2007	85.47	85	12	2.55	0.56	−20	−5,100	0
01/09/2007	92.57				1.00	1120	103,678	
01/09/2007	92.57	85	11	7.90	0.92	−20	−15,800	−2,748
01/10/2007	97.00				1.00	1120	108,640	
01/10/2007	97.00	85	10	12.15	0.99	−20	−24,300	−6,286

Date	Stock Price ($)	Strike	Days Remaining	Option Price ($)	Delta	Contract/ Shares	Position Value ($)	Gain/ Loss ($)
01/08/2007	85.47				1.00	460	39,316	
01/08/2007	85.47	90	12	0.75	0.23	-20	-1,500	0
01/09/2007	92.57				1.00	460	42,582	
01/09/2007	92.57	90	11	3.90	0.69	-20	-7,800	-3,034
01/10/2007	97.00				1.00	460	44,620	
01/10/2007	97.00	90	10	7.40	0.90	-20	-14,800	-7,996

The first scenario loses 7%, and the second loses more than 21%. Scenario #2 suffers a larger loss because its short-side delta increases 290% versus a 76% increase in scenario #1. This problem is somewhat counterintuitive, because the second scenario short side was built around a safer strike price that is $5.00 further out-of-the-money. However, creating a delta-neutral trade decreased the size of the long side, creating additional exposure. After the large price spike, the short side gamma also increases much more severely for the $90 strike price than for the $85. On January 8, before the spike, the gammas are 0.07 and 0.05, respectively. On January 10, after the upward spike, the gammas adjust to 0.005 for the $85 strike price and to 0.029 (6 times higher) for the $90 strike. At this point the forward risk is much higher for short $90 calls than for the high-delta, in-the-money $85 calls. It is always dangerous to be short large amounts of gamma.

Our discussion would not be complete without examining the falling stock case for the stock-option ratio call spread of Table 6.10. Table 6.11 illustrates this case using the same parameters with the price changes reversed. On January 9 the stock price falls $7.10, and on January 10 the price drops another $4.43.

Table 6.11   Ratio call spread using stock and options: two scenarios with falling stock price.

Date	Stock Price ($)	Strike	Days Remaining	Option Price ($)	Delta	Contract/ Shares	Position Value ($)	Gain/ Loss ($)
01/08/2007	85.47				1.00	1120	95,726	
01/08/2007	85.47	85	12	2.55	0.56	−20	−5,100	0
01/09/2007	78.37				1.00	1120	87,774	
01/09/2007	78.37	85	11	0.25	0.11	−20	−500	−3,352
01/10/2007	73.94				1.00	1120	82,813	
01/10/2007	73.94	85	10	0.05	0.01	−20	−100	−7,913
01/08/2007	85.47				1.00	460	39,316	
01/08/2007	85.47	90	12	0.75	0.23	−20	−1,500	0
01/09/2007	78.37				1.00	460	36,050	
01/09/2007	78.37	90	11	0.05	0.02	−20	−100	−1,866
01/10/2007	73.94				1.00	460	34,012	
01/10/2007	73.94	90	10	0.00	0.00	−20	0	−3,804

As before, the first scenario is built around the $85 strike price, and the second around the $90 strike. Both positions are delta-neutral at launch; therefore, the number of shares of stock is the same as in Table 6.10. This trade also loses money. The problem is related to the falling delta of the short calls, which fail to properly hedge the constant delta of the long stock. The $90 strike price case does slightly better, because the original delta-neutral position contains fewer shares of stock.

Simply stated, ratio trades that mix stock and options are difficult to manage if the stock shows any significant movement. The traditional view that evaluates the position at expiration is flawed, because you can lose large amounts of money hoping that a rising stock does not continue rising or that a falling stock will stabilize. Traders often believe that, despite a sharp move in the underlying, their short option position will remain out-of-the-money. That gamble assumes that the options are mispriced. Additionally, as you have seen, farther out-of-the-money short options represent a larger risk, because they are balanced against fewer shares when the position is new.

Of course, adjustments are always possible. In the case of a rising stock, the short options can be repurchased and the position reset at a higher strike price. The position can also be rebalanced so that it is delta-neutral through the purchase of additional shares. A very bullish investor might choose to absorb the loss on the short side and continue holding only the long stock position in the hope that additional price increases will ultimately offset the loss from the short options. In the case of a falling stock, you could reset the short position at a lower strike price. If you choose this path, it would be wise to repurchase the first batch of short options, even if the price is only 5 cents. Leaving the original short position open is equivalent to being naked short deep out-of-the-money options. A sudden price reversal would be very damaging. However, if the investor is willing to treat the two trades as distinct, keeping the nearly worthless short options open might be acceptable. It is important to be cognizant of the collateral requirement and decide if collecting another 5 cents is worth the opportunity cost of the money. This author never leaves deep out-of-the-money short positions open, even in the final days before expiration. Active traders often feel that "cleaning up" these positions is helpful for account management purposes. Other possibilities include selling some or all of the shares of stock and leaving the short calls untouched.

In summary, the stock-option ratios we have been discussing profit most when the stock follows a smooth, steady path toward the strike price, mirroring the time decay of the short side of the trade. No movement will return the same profit as the short option side of the trade alone. Generally speaking, because most stocks experience occasional large price spikes, it is easier to find stocks that don't behave this way. We could capitalize on this characteristic of the market by taking the other side of the trade—long call/short stock or long stock/long put positions that are initially delta-neutral. Either strategy will profit from a large price spike of the underlying in either direction. We previously reviewed this strategy in our discussion of long straddles.

Our discussion of ratios would not be complete if we did not review the effects of rising and falling volatility. Rising volatility tends to favor the far strike price and falling volatility the close strike. Table 6.12 illustrates the effect.

Table 6.12 Rising volatility and ratio call spreads.

Stock Price ($)	Strike	Days Remaining	Option Price ($)	Volatility	Delta	Contract	Position Value ($)
82.20	85	29	2.30	0.36	0.41	10	
82.20	90	29	0.95	0.36	0.21	−20	400
82.20	85	29	2.85	0.42	0.42	10	
82.20	90	29	1.40	0.42	0.25	−20	50
82.20	85	29	3.40	0.48	0.44	10	
82.20	90	29	1.85	0.48	0.28	−20	−300
82.20	85	29	3.95	0.54	0.45	10	
82.20	90	29	2.30	0.54	0.31	−20	−650

Each pair of entries in the table represents a ratio call spread with 29 days left before expiration, but a different volatility. Changes in the total position value are substantial as the delta rises from neutral to net negative (−0.17).

This effect represents a trading opportunity if we can predict when volatility will rise and fall. We know, for example, that volatility rises in the days approaching an earnings release. During this time frame, ratio backspreads have a statistical advantage. That is, we would take the other side of the trade in the table by shorting the close strike price and going long the far strike price. Conversely, we could wait until the last trading moment before earnings are announced, when volatility is highest, and set up a position that is long the close strike and short the far strike. We would close this trade after earnings are announced and the volatility shrinks. This trade has some additional risk because the earnings-associated price spike could be larger than the risk priced into the options, and, even after volatility deflation, the trade could lose money. The first scenario is much safer, because it takes advantage of a price distortion that precedes an event during a period of time that tends to be quiet for many stocks. The decision can become more complex when earnings and options expiration occur within a few days of each other, because this period of time normally is accompanied by rapid volatility increases that partially offset very fast time decay. We will return to this discussion in Chapter 7, "Trading the Earnings Cycle."

The next section combines strategies by exploring ratio trades that cross expiration dates.

Ratios That Span Multiple Expiration Dates

As we have seen, ratios can be complex to manage. Ratios that span multiple expiration dates are more complex, but they often provide additional profit opportunities. The goal is to discover a pricing inefficiency that is generated by a specific combination of strike prices and expiration dates. If there is no inefficiency, there is no profit potential. Fortunately, a pricing inefficiency can almost always be found, even if it is not readily apparent. This simple fact can be verified by using 20/20 hindsight to structure profitable positions for past time frames for any stock or index. It is rare not to find a winning expiration/strike price combination for any particular set of circumstances.

Pricing inefficiencies tend to occur in the final few days before expiration, immediately before earnings announcements, or in a fast-moving market driven by news. Of course, many other circumstances can create price disparities. Regardless of the cause, subtle differences in the true value of a position can cause one side to be overpriced—that is, the risk associated with both sides is not equal. Such distortions are not adequately represented in today's pricing methodologies.

This concept is illustrated in Table 6.13. The short side of the trade suffers excessive time decay in the final few days before expiration. The long side, which has another month before expiration, continues to decay at a much slower rate. The effect becomes dramatic over the January 12 long weekend.

Table 6.13   Ratio call calendar spread.

Date	Stock Price ($)	Strike	Days Remaining	Option Price ($)	Delta	Theta	Contract	Position Value ($)
12/21/2006	167.93	175	30	1.22	0.24	−0.05	−20	
12/21/2006	167.93	175	58	2.56	0.33	−0.05	10	120
12/22/2006	167.74	175	29	1.13	0.23	−0.05	−20	
12/22/2006	167.74	175	57	2.46	0.33	−0.04	10	200
12/26/2006	166.63	175	25	0.71	0.17	−0.04	−20	
12/26/2006	166.63	175	53	1.94	0.28	−0.04	10	520
12/27/2006	168.41	175	24	1.02	0.23	−0.05	−20	
12/27/2006	168.41	175	52	2.45	0.34	−0.05	10	410
12/28/2006	168.00	175	23	0.88	0.21	−0.05	−20	
12/28/2006	168.00	175	51	2.27	0.32	−0.05	10	510
01/10/2007	172.09	175	10	1.00	0.31	−0.10	−20	
01/10/2007	172.09	175	38	3.09	0.43	−0.06	10	1,090
01/11/2007	174.48	175	9	1.83	0.48	−0.12	−20	
01/11/2007	174.48	175	37	4.17	0.53	−0.07	10	510
01/12/2007	175.22	175	8	2.08	0.54	−0.13	−20	
01/12/2007	175.22	175	36	4.51	0.55	−0.07	10	350

Date	Stock Price ($)	Strike	Days Remaining	Option Price ($)	Delta	Theta	Contract	Position Value ($)
01/16/2007	176.03	175	4	1.90	0.64	−0.16	−20	
01/16/2007	176.03	175	32	4.69	0.59	−0.07	10	890
01/17/2007	175.45	175	3	1.30	0.58	−0.18	−20	
01/17/2007	175.45	175	31	4.29	0.56	−0.07	10	1,690
01/18/2007	175.20	175	2	0.91	0.55	−0.20	−20	
01/18/2007	175.20	175	30	4.08	0.55	−0.07	10	2,260
01/19/2007	173.92	175	1	0.00	0.00	0.00	−20	
01/19/2007	173.92	175	29	3.34	0.49	−0.07	10	3,340

During this time frame, half the number of days remaining on the short side disappear. Despite an 81 cent increase in the stock price on 01/16, the short side of the trade loses money. The long side, however, gains a small amount. The result is a nearly three-fold increase in the position's value. During the final four days, the stock falls to $173.92, causing the short side to expire worthless. Despite a 29% drop in the long option price from its high, the trade value increases from $890 to $3,340. This increase is driven by the collapse of the short side from $1.90 to zero. Note that theta accelerates dramatically in the final few days before expiration, offsetting the effects of underlying price increases on the short side of the trade.

The trade can be continued by selling 20 calls at the $180 strike price for February expiration. We would then have a ratio call spread with both sides expiring in the same month. Assuming that all parameters stay constant, the correct price for the February $180 strike call would be $1.50 (delta = 0.28) on January 19 when the first batch of short calls expired.[2] Selling these options would minimize risk by locking in the existing profit and allowing us to keep the trade open. Keeping the trade open makes sense, because the basic parameters that defined the first trade have not changed substantially. The net delta of the first trade was initially –0.15, and the new net delta will be –0.07. The first trade had 30 days left on the short side, and the new trade has 29 days left on both sides. The first trade was initially long just 12 cents, and the second is long only 34 cents—it is price-neutral. Table 6.14 summarizes these parameters.

Table 6.14 Comparison of initial and secondary trades (based on Table 6.13).

	First Trade	Second Trade
Net Delta	–0.15	–0.07
Days Remaining Short	30	29
Days Remaining Long	58	29
Short Option Price × 20	$1.22	$1.50
Long Option Price × 10	$2.56	$3.34
Net Cost	$0.12	$0.34

Unfortunately, not all trades behave this well. Suppose, for example, that as January expiration approached, the stock experienced a 3 standard deviation upward spike (approximately $6.00 for a security trading at $175 with a volatility of 18%). The surprising results are displayed in Table 6.15.

Table 6.15 Ratio call calendar spread: impact of a 3 standard deviation price spike near expiration.

Date	Stock Price ($)	Strike	Days Remaining	Option Price ($)	Delta	Theta	Contract	Position Value ($)
12/21/2006	167.93	175	30	1.22	0.24	–0.05	–20	
12/21/2006	167.93	175	58	2.56	0.33	–0.05	10	120
01/16/2007	176.03	175	4	1.90	0.64	–0.16	–20	
01/16/2007	176.03	175	32	4.69	0.59	–0.07	10	890
01/17/2007	182.00	175	3	7.08	1.00	–0.03	–20	
01/17/2007	182.00	175	31	8.81	0.80	–0.06	10	–5,350

Date	Stock Price ($)	Strike	Days Remaining	Option Price ($)	Delta	Theta	Contract	Position Value ($)
01/18/2007	184.00	175	2	9.05	1.00	−0.02	−20	
01/18/2007	184.00	175	30	10.42	0.86	−0.06	10	−7,680
01/19/2007	186.00	175	1	11.02	1.00	−0.02	−20	
01/19/2007	186.00	175	29	12.13	0.90	−0.05	10	−9,910

The new scenario includes an initial 3 standard deviation spike followed by two additional small (1 standard deviation) spikes. Such a scenario is quite reasonable. The initial spike, which occurs three days before expiration of the short side, generates a 700% loss (+$890 to −$5,350). At this point the trade has a net delta of −1.20, making it equivalent to a short stock position of 1,200 shares. Maintaining such a strongly bearish position on a stock that has just risen 3 standard deviations is almost always a mistake. This assertion comes sharply into focus when the two additional price spikes that follow nearly double the loss to 1,200%. The risk was dramatically enhanced by the time spread because we were forced into trading the same strikes to achieve a price-neutral start. As January expiration approached, and the stock breached the strike price, the near-month delta exceeded that of the far month. This inversion of deltas cannot happen when both sides have the same expiration date. The difference is evident in Table 6.16, which displays the same price spike for a single month call ratio.

Table 6.16 Ratio call spread with a large price spike near expiration.

Date	Stock Price ($)	Strike	Days Remaining	Option Price ($)	Delta	Contract	Position Value ($)
12/21/2006	167.93	180	30	0.44	0.11	−20	
12/21/2006	167.93	175	30	1.22	0.24	10	340
01/16/2007	176.03	180	4	0.17	0.11	−20	
01/16/2007	176.03	175	4	1.96	0.64	10	1,620

Table 6.16   Continued

Date	Stock Price ($)	Strike	Days Remaining	Option Price ($)	Delta	Contract	Position Value ($)
01/17/2007	182.00	180	3	2.40	0.79	−20	
01/17/2007	182.00	175	3	7.08	0.99	10	2,280
01/18/2007	184.00	180	2	4.07	0.98	−20	
01/18/2007	184.00	175	2	9.05	1.00	10	910
01/19/2007	186.00	180	1	6.03	1.00	−20	
01/19/2007	186.00	175	1	11.02	1.00	10	−1,040

Not only did the position perform better than the time-separated version, but the January 17 price spike yielded a profit. Only at the very end of the time frame, after the final rise to $186, did the position finally lose money.

The dynamics are complex. Our calendar spread was initially close to price-neutral but not delta-neutral. Had it been delta-neutral, the damage from the price spike would have been smaller. Table 6.17 displays the same trade and conditions with a delta-neutral start.

Table 6.17   Ratio call calendar spread of Table 6.15 with a delta-neutral start.

Date	Stock Price ($)	Strike	Days Remaining	Option Price ($)	Delta	Contract	Position Value ($)
12/21/2006	167.93	175	30	1.22	0.24	−14	
12/21/2006	167.93	175	58	2.56	0.33	10	852
01/16/2007	176.03	175	4	1.90	0.64	−14	
01/16/2007	176.03	175	32	4.69	0.59	10	2,030
01/17/2007	182.00	175	3	7.08	1.00	−14	
01/17/2007	182.00	175	31	8.81	0.80	10	−1,102

Date	Stock Price ($)	Strike	Days Remaining	Option Price ($)	Delta	Contract	Position Value ($)
01/18/2007	184.00	175	2	9.05	1.00	−14	
01/18/2007	184.00	175	30	10.42	0.86	10	−2,250
01/19/2007	186.00	175	1	11.02	1.00	−14	
01/19/2007	186.00	175	29	12.13	0.90	10	−3,298

Note that the position was initially long $852. We must be careful not to confuse long with bullish. Unlike the calendar spread of Table 6.15, which had a negative delta and therefore was slightly bearish, the present scenario uses an unusual ratio (1.4:1) to achieve a delta-neutral start. However, despite the delta-neutral start, the position still performed poorly when the price spiked 3 standard deviations. The same-month call ratio of Table 6.16 was more stable.

Obviously, many different constructs are possible, and the number of possible positions is virtually limitless. A few basic principles apply to both ratio calendar spreads and same-month ratios:

- Forward ratios should be structured using only securities that are "well behaved" in the sense that their price change behavior tends to follow the lognormal distribution. This principle is very important for ratio calendar spreads, where the element of time requires smooth behavior across multiple expiration dates.

- Stocks that regularly exhibit large price spikes are candidates for ratio backspreads. Because backspreads are generally closed at the time of a price spike, calendar backspreads rarely provide any additional advantage.

- Ratios are asymmetric. A large move in one direction will lose money, and a large move in the other is neutral (both sides of the trade ultimately decline to zero if both strikes remain out-of-the-money).

- Risk increases for forward ratios when the deltas are high. That is, if the long delta is 1.00 and the short delta is 0.50, the long delta cannot increase as the stock continues moving toward the short strike price.

- Risk increases for ratio backspreads when deltas are low and moderate movement in the direction of the strikes does not favor the more distant option (the long side of the trade).

- Ratio calendar spreads are complex to manage because the two sides react differently to underlying price changes as the rate of time decay accelerates for one side of the trade. Risk increases sharply if the short side is simultaneously near expiration and near the strike price.

This discussion was intended to provide an introduction to some of the salient points surrounding ratios and calendar spreads. We will continue to revisit and expand on these principles throughout the remainder of the book. The next section explores more-complex constructs that are built on ratios, calendar spreads, put-call combinations, and more than two strike prices.

Complex Multipart Trades

It would be reasonable to write an entire book on the subject of this section. The book would carefully explore all the nuances of forward and reverse structures that span different time frames and combinations of strike prices. Because some of that discussion is beyond the scope of this book, our approach will be to illustrate key concepts that span multiple classes of trades.

The vast majority of complex multipart positions are designed to hedge simpler trades against a destructive move of the underlying. The one exception is a hedge against time decay for positions that are designed to profit from a large move of the underlying. Long straddles are the most notable example because they are designed to profit when the underlying makes a large move in either direction. Their principal risk is time decay, and more-complex positions can be designed to repay part of that cost with options that are expected to expire out-of-the-money.

Butterfly Spread

We will begin with a discussion of the butterfly spread, a position that is characterized by both limited risk and limited profit potential. Up to this point we have restricted ourselves to spreads with just two sides. Although these positions often have excellent profit potential, they are not fully hedged against risk. Worse still, many short positions are exposed to unlimited loss. Many option traders focus on risky trades that have the potential to deliver spectacular returns, but institutional investors often consider this approach imprudent. For investors who desire predictably smooth returns, complex trades like the butterfly spread are often a good fit.

A butterfly is composed of options at three equally spaced strike prices. All are the same type—puts or calls—and all have the same expiration date. A long butterfly trade might be constructed as follows: ten long May $100 calls, twenty short May $105 calls, ten long May $110 calls. By convention this position is considered long because the outside strikes are purchased and the inside strike is sold. The outside strikes are often called wings and the inside strike the body. The position is also considered long because it must be purchased. Long butterflies can never be worth less than zero at expiration and therefore must be purchased. Conversely, if the outside strikes are short and the inside strike is long, the position is considered short. Such positions normally are established for a credit and therefore can be worth less than zero at expiration. These relationships make sense; it would be unreasonable to establish a position for a credit if there were no chance of losing money. As always, such a situation would represent a riskless arbitrage that would disappear almost instantly.

A long butterfly can be thought of as a hedged version of a ratio spread. Consider, for example, a delta-neutral ratio call spread consisting of ten long $170 calls and twenty short $175 calls. If the underlying remains below both strike prices, all options expire worthless, and nothing is gained or lost. The profit zone lies between the strike prices with a peak at $175. Profit declines between $175 and $180, and above $180 the trade loses money. The loss grows continuously beyond this point. However, if the initial position also includes ten long $180 calls, it would be impossible, at expiration, to lose more than the original investment. This structure defines the long butterfly. Figure 6.2 depicts the trade structured with call options as follows:

Stock price 30 days before expiration	$168
Volatility	18%
$170 long calls	$2.85 × 1
$175 short calls	$1.20 × 2
$180 long calls	$0.45 × 1
Net long at launch	$0.90

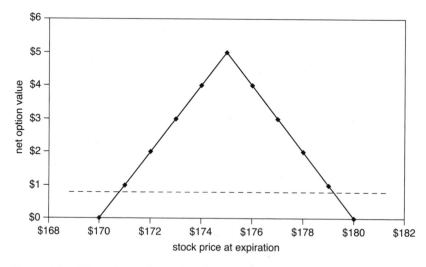

Figure 6.2   A long butterfly trade. The horizontal dashed line marks the profit cutoff for a position established on a stock trading at $168 with 30 days remaining before expiration and an implied volatility of 18%. The maximum loss ($0.90) occurs if the stock trades below $170 or above $180 at expiration.

The corresponding short butterfly has the reverse structure—ten short $170 calls, twenty long $175 calls, and ten short $180 calls. The trades are dramatically different. The long butterfly profits from time decay and moderate movement of the underlying security. At expiration the profit peak is exactly at the middle strike price, and it is never possible to lose more than the original cost. Conversely, short butterflies generate profit when the underlying trades above the highest strike or below the lowest at expiration—in our example, above $180 or below $170. The maximum profit is equal to the net value of the original position when all options expire worthless. The maximum loss occurs at expiration if the underlying trades exactly at the middle strike price. At this point the nearest strike would be in-the-money, and options at the other two strikes would expire worthless. If the strike prices were spaced by $5.00, the loss would be $5.00 minus the initial credit. A chart depicting this trade is the exact inverse of Figure 6.2, with the center being −$5.00 instead of +$5.00. It is important to point out that the profit potential of a long butterfly is equal to the risk of the corresponding short position—the difference between the strike prices. Conversely, the risk of a long butterfly is equal to the profit potential of the corresponding short position—the value of the initial trade.

Whereas most complex trades benefit from dynamic management strategies that compensate for large moves of the underlying, butterflies are best left alone until expiration. The one exception occurs when a large underlying spike takes the stock price far above or below the range of a short butterfly. If you suspect that a reversal could occur, and the stock could move back between the strikes, it might make sense to close the position for a small profit. However, more often than not, such a spike signals the beginning of a trend, and there would be no reason to suspect a reversal. Table 6.18 compares early and late moves to the maximum profit point for both types of butterfly trades. The short trade (above the gray bar) has very limited profit potential, and only two-thirds can be realized in the early downward spike depicted. In the case of the long butterfly (below the gray bar), the early spike generates very little profit, and it makes sense to continue holding the trade if the stock is somewhat stable. Both trades are heavily dependent on time decay.

Table 6.18 Comparison of early and late moves to the maximum profit point for short and long butterfly trades (short trade above the gray bar).

Stock Price ($)	Strike	Days Remaining	Option Price	Contract	Position Value ($)
167.93	170	30	2.83	−10	
167.93	175	30	1.22	20	
167.93	180	30	0.44	−10	−830
160.00	170	26	0.46	−10	
160.00	175	26	0.12	20	
160.00	180	26	0.02	−10	−240
160.00	170	1	0.00	−10	
160.00	175	1	0.00	20	
160.00	180	1	0.00	−10	0
167.93	170	30	2.83	10	
167.93	175	30	1.22	−20	
167.93	180	30	0.44	10	830
175.00	170	26	6.83	10	
175.00	175	26	3.67	−20	
175.00	180	26	1.65	10	1,140
175.00	170	1	5.02	10	
175.00	175	1	0.05	−20	
175.00	180	1	0.00	10	4,920

Short butterfly trades structured with puts have a distinct advantage in falling markets because they benefit from both rising volatility and large price spikes. Long butterfly trades structured with calls are the clear choice in low-volatility rising markets. Short and long butterflies can also be combined, and it is even possible to simultaneously generate profit from both positions if the stock trades outside the range of the short butterfly and near the center strike of the long butterfly at expiration. The reverse is also true. Investors should not forget that a long-short combination butterfly trade that expires at the midpoint of the short side will lose an amount of money equal to the strike spacing of the short side plus the initial credit of the long side, in addition to bid-ask spreads and commissions. That said, many different complex structures can be designed using various combinations of puts and calls spanning six different strike prices in long and short configurations.

The next section extends this theme by examining some of the most popular four-sided trades. As with most complex structures, these positions are designed to buffer losses at the expense of capped gains. They tend to be very popular among institutional investors who seek smooth, predictable returns that outperform the market with limited risk. Private investors often use these trades to accomplish the same goals because, properly structured, they can increase leverage by reducing collateral costs.

The Condor and Other Four-Sided Positions

A condor combines vertical bull and bear credit spreads into a single trade. The trade involves four strikes—two on the put side and two on the call side. An investor might, for example, sell a strangle composed of $90 puts and $100 calls while simultaneously purchasing the outside "wings"—$85 puts and $105 calls. Strictly speaking, condors are structured with four different strike prices. However, similar dynamics apply to trades that are built around three strikes. Our example might be reduced to a short $95 straddle and a long $90/$100 strangle. Both scenarios are designed to profit from time decay. The long outside wings serve to cap potential losses and reduce the collateral requirement.

Reduced collateral requirements can have an enormous impact on the size of trade that can be executed. For example, a 10 contract $100 naked straddle requires collateral equal to $25,000 plus the value of the options. If we were to hedge such a position with $95 puts and $105 calls, the collateral requirement would be calculated using $5 rather than $100 as the risk factor. The requirement would shrink to $5,000 plus the value of the options. This advantage exists as long as we hedge with options that have the same or further expiration. The condor is a perfect fit for investors who prefer to cap their losses and gains while creating much larger positions. Furthermore, strike price spacing can be used to balance risk against profit potential. Options on indexes are popular choices for the trade because they are viewed as being less risky than stocks. That view is flawed, because index options trade at notoriously low implied volatilities that often do not reflect their true risks. This deficiency came sharply into focus during the days preceding the writing of these words when the overall market plunged more than 5% and implied volatilities on broad indexes rose from approximately 8% to more than 22%. Traders who sold condors priced with 8% volatility lost huge amounts of money. Equity options that traded with very high volatility prior to the market drawdown were sometimes a better choice because their prices reflected a more balanced view of risk. Options on exchange traded funds often represent the best compromise. An excellent example is the Oil Services HOLDRs Trust (OIH)—a basket of stocks composed of oil field services companies. Implied volatility of the options is high enough to allow structured positions that span multiple strike prices, risk is fairly represented, and the basket of stocks behaves somewhat like an index. Additionally, because liquidity levels are high, options trade with reasonable bid-ask spreads.

Figure 6.3 displays one year (252 trading days) of price change history for the Dow Jones Industrials and OIH. As before, each spike is measured in standard deviations against the most recent 20-day volatility window.

The overall market, as represented by the Dow, exhibits a larger number of uncharacteristic spikes than OIH. The data of Figure 6.3 is summarized in Table 6.19.

Table 6.19   One year of price change data for Dow and OIH.

	Dow	OIH
StdDev		
Greater than 2	19	12
Greater than 3	5	3
Greater than 4	1	0

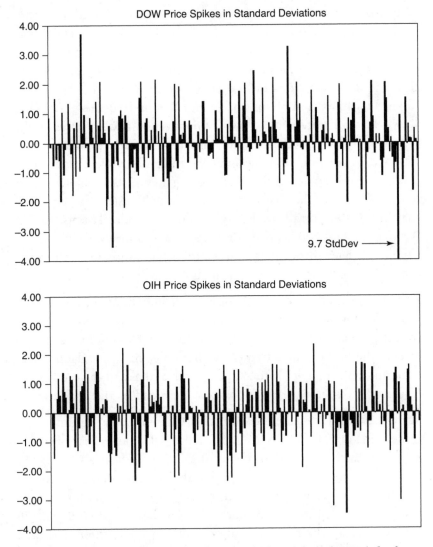

Figure 6.3   A comparison of the Dow Jones Industrials and OIH (a basket
of 20 oil field services companies) with regard to one year of
price spikes. Each price change is measured in standard deviations against the most recent 20-day volatility window. The
arrow in the upper chart points to a 9.7 standard deviation
downward spike of the Dow that is too large to represent in the
chart.

Note that the number of spikes larger than 2 standard deviations is 58% larger for the overall market than for OIH (19 versus 12). The difference is significant because one price spike per month is manageable, but one every 13 trading days is not. Additionally, throughout most of this time frame, options on the Dow were priced with 8% to 10% implied volatility, and options on OIH tended to trade near 30%. The Dow's low volatility drives down option values and compresses the maximum distance between strikes on the short side. The short side of a Dow condor would likely be an at-the-money straddle, because anything wider would have little value. Moving the strikes far enough apart to compensate for the risk of a price spike would result in a very small maximum return for the trade. It generally does not make sense to wait 30 days to realize 50 cents of time decay. Alternatively, we could use expiration dates three months or more in the future and absorb the risks associated with time and potentially rising volatility.

Just a few years before this book was written, options on the broad market traded for more than 30% volatility. Multipart trades that spanned four strikes had manageable option prices, and it was not necessary to extend the trade's time frame. Furthermore, market volatility was declining at the rate of 1% to 2% per month as the market steadily rose. The conditions were perfect for condors on broad market indexes.

Table 6.20 illustrates these concepts with a representative four-sided trade using options on DIAMONDS Trust (DIA), an exchange traded fund that mirrors the performance of the Dow Industrials. March 17 was selected as the expiration date, and the position was launched one month earlier. We were able to construct a delta-neutral position by using the 128 strike for both short sides. The hedges, 130 call and 126 put, were also delta-neutral. Had we widened the position and used four different strikes (131, 129, 127, 125), we would have barely taken in 60 cents per short side, and the hedges would have cost 20 cents each— a net value of only 40 cents per side. Either position would have ended with DIA significantly below the lowest of the two put strikes, and the final position would have been worth −$2,000 at expiration. In this sense we would have fared better by starting with a more expensive position (128 straddle) and reducing the net loss.

Table 6.20 Four-sided hedged trade for DIA.

Option	Date	Stock Price ($)	Strike	Days Remaining	Option Price($)	Volatility	Delta	Contract	Position Value
Call	02/14/2007	127.48	130	31	0.40	0.07	0.24	10	
Call	02/14/2007	127.48	128	31	1.10	0.07	0.51	−10	
Put	02/14/2007	127.48	128	31	1.10	0.07	−0.49	−10	
Put	02/14/2007	127.48	126	31	0.35	0.07	−0.23	10	−1,450
	02/15/2007	127.77		30		0.07			−1,450
	02/26/2007	126.34		19		0.06			−1,350
	02/27/2007	121.60		18		0.15			−1,850
Call	03/16/2007	121.05	130	1	0.00	0.17	0.00	10	
Call	03/16/2007	121.05	128	1	0.00	0.17	0.00	−10	
Put	03/16/2007	121.05	128	1	6.95	0.17	−1.00	−10	
Put	03/16/2007	121.05	126	1	4.95	0.17	−1.00	10	−2,000

Index-based trades have a significant advantage over their equity-based counterparts: they rarely gap up or down at the open. This characteristic would have saved our trade if we set sensitive stop orders and closed the position at the open on 02/27 (DIA opened at 125.34, down only 1 point). Kept open, the position lost 100% of its profit by the time the market closed on 02/27. Indexes have a second advantage: their futures trade around the world in various markets and are highly liquid at all times. We could have followed the markets overnight, recognized that the put side of the trade was at risk, and shorted Dow index futures to protect our position. In this particular case, Asian and European markets experienced tremendous drawdowns, and the yen had strengthened enough to cause unwinding of the infamous carry trade that funded the growth of many of these markets. It was clear that the trade needed to be closed. These facts paint an encouraging picture, because the time frame we selected was unusually destructive. The broad market experienced one of its worst downward spikes (ten standard deviations), implied volatilities more than doubled, and prices continued falling until expiration.

Some investors might think that the hedges provided a reasonable level of protection. This author would disagree, because the position ultimately lost 38%. Had we attempted a more conservative position by moving the long strikes closer, the maximum possible profit would have fallen from $1.45 to less than $0.90 (strikes 129, 128, 128, 127). In this scenario, even if the stock ended the time frame exactly at the 128 strike, we would have been forced to repurchase the short options for approximately $0.90, and bid-ask spreads would have reduced the long side value to zero eliminating all profit. We therefore had the safest possible structure. The hedges reduced our collateral requirement, but stopping out or hedging with another trade would have been the correct way to protect our investment. An excellent choice would have been the purchase of out-of-the-money, relatively inexpensive VIX calls that tend to rise sharply in value during a pronounced market decline.

Four-Part Trades That Span Different Expiration Dates

It is often possible to take advantage of various corrective forces, such as mean reversion, by selling long-dated, far out-of-the-money options on expensive stocks. Google is an excellent example because, despite occasional large price spikes, the stock tends to behave in a way that cannot be fully described by its implied or historical volatility. At the time of this writing, Google near-term at-the-money options were fairly valued at 27% as measured by the volatility of daily closing prices. However, over extended periods of time the changes tended to cancel, leaving the stock price virtually unchanged. For example, between late October 2006 and late January 2007, Google stock rose and fell more than 8%, ending up at the same price, while the overall market ended the three-month time frame more than 4% higher. During these three months, options on the S&P 500 were generally priced with 12% volatility while Google options traded between 26% and 34%. Near-dated short strangles built around closely spaced strikes were much more dangerous than far-dated positions with widely spaced strikes. Furthermore, Google volatility is strongly affected by large price spikes that are associated with earnings releases. Short positions that are established after earnings are released and closed before the next announcement generally are overpriced.

We can take advantage of this small anomaly by structuring widely spaced short strangles with three-month expiration time frames and by hedging them with very inexpensive current-month options.[3] The position becomes a condor in the final month, with the hedge dramatically reducing the collateral requirement. Table 6.21 illustrates these concepts using Google options during the three months just mentioned (10/23/2006–01/19/2007). The starting date followed immediately after an earnings release (10/19) and options expiration (10/21); the closing date was the last trading day of the January 2007 expiration cycle—12 days before the next earnings release.

Table 6.21 Hedged short strangle spanning three months using options on Google.

Opt	Date	Stock Price ($)	Strike	Days Remaining	Option Price($)	Volatility	Delta	Contract	Position Value
Call	10/23/2006	480.78	580	26	0.10	0.28	0.008	10	
Call	10/23/2006	480.78	580	89	2.65	0.26	0.096	−10	
Put	10/23/2006	480.78	400	89	2.80	0.30	−0.081	−10	
Put	10/23/2006	480.78	400	26	0.35	0.35	−0.020	10	−5,000
Call	11/17/2006	498.79	580	29	0.40	0.27	0.029	10	
Call	11/17/2006	498.79	580	64	2.65	0.26	0.106	−10	
Put	11/17/2006	498.79	400	64	1.05	0.32	−0.038	−10	
Put	11/17/2006	498.79	400	29	0.15	0.34	−0.008	10	−3,150
Call	12/15/2006	480.30	570	36	0.40	0.27	0.028	30	
Call	12/15/2006	480.30	540	36	1.60	0.26	0.091	−30	
Put	12/15/2006	480.30	420	36	1.15	0.29	−0.058	−30	
Put	12/15/2006	480.30	390	36	0.40	0.34	−0.020	30	−5,850

Table 6.21   Continued

Opt	Date	Stock Price ($)	Strike	Days Remaining	Option Price($)	Volatility	Delta	Position Contract Value	
Call	01/19/2007	489.75	570	1	0.00	0.04	0.000	30	
Call	01/19/2007	489.75	540	1	0.00	0.04	0.000	−30	
Put	01/19/2007	489.75	420	1	0.00	0.04	0.000	−30	
Put	01/19/2007	489.75	390	1	0.00	0.04	0.000	30	0

When the trade was launched, the short side had 89 days (three expiration cycles) left before expiration. The long hedge used the same strike prices and had only 26 days left. The short strangle was price- and delta-neutral. The long hedge was slightly distorted on the put side by the volatility smile. The short side of the trade was worth $5.45, and the hedge cost $0.45. The collateral requirement would have been approximately $125,000.[4]

On 11/17 the first hedge expired, and the short position had declined to a value of $3.70. A new hedge was established using current-month options and the same strikes. The new hedge was worth $0.55—15% of the value remaining on the short side. No other adjustments were necessary.

At December expiration the position was narrowed because the short calls and puts had declined to 20 and 30 cents, respectively. The new position was designed around a similar risk profile as measured by the delta, and a new delta-neutral hedge was added three strike prices from each short side. The new hedge reduced the collateral requirement for a 10 contract short strangle to $30,000 plus the value of the options. We took advantage of the reduced requirement by increasing the position size to 30 contracts on each side. Tripling the size also tripled the base collateral requirement to $90,000. The new trade was initially short $5,850 and declined to zero at January expiration.

The complete sequence generated a sizeable profit. Our initial net short value was $5,000, and we repurchased the short side at December expiration for $500. Subtracting the second hedge ($550) left a net profit of $3,950. The new December position was net short $5,850 and declined to zero. Adding together the components of the sequence gives a total profit of $9,800. This return was generated at the expense of only two months of interest on $125,000 and one month of interest on $90,000, in addition to $3,400 of hedges (the December hedge cost $2,400).

Finally, had we widened the December long strangle to $580 call/$380 put, the cost of the long side would have been reduced by $1,200, and the collateral requirement would have increased by $30,000. The risk would have been roughly equivalent to that of a naked short straddle on a $40 stock with 27% volatility. Using these parameters, we would have realized a gain of $11,000 on an investment of approximately $2,200 (hedging cost) plus interest on the collateral.

An important characteristic of the very wide, far-dated short strangle is the low relative cost of each current-month hedge. This distortion increases as the strike price moves farther from the stock price and as the expiration date moves out. At the time of this writing, Google stock traded at $447, and $600 strike price calls expiring in six months were worth $3.00 with a theta of 4 cents per day. A current-month $550 call was worth only 10 cents even though the strike was $50 closer to the stock price. Similar dynamics apply to the put side. In our example, we limited the trade to three months so that we could close the position before the January earnings release. It was also important to close the trade several days in advance because volatility tends to rise in the final days before the announcement. The final hedge lowered the collateral requirement but provided limited protection against a large price spike. It is important to calibrate this trade-off so that it corresponds to the risk tolerance of the portfolio. It is also important to remember that the protection level of any out-of-the-money hedge fades as expiration approaches. In the final few days the position should be treated as if it were naked short. This effect is exaggerated for positions with very wide strike price spacing.

Hedging with the VIX

The Chicago Board Options Exchange Volatility Index (VIX) has become an important metric of overall market volatility. Since its introduction in 1993, the index has undergone significant changes. The most recent version measures expected volatility against the prices of S&P

500 index options across a broad range of strikes.[5] The VIX is not calculated using the Black-Scholes pricing model; instead, it uses a formula that averages the weighted prices of out-of-the-money puts and calls. The contribution of a single option to the index value is proportional to its price and inversely proportional to the strike. Calculations generally span the two nearest-term expiration months. However, in the final eight days before expiration, the window is rolled forward to the second and third contract months to minimize pricing anomalies that occur just before expiration.

Building on historical information contained in its databases, the CBOE has made available calculated values of the index dating back to 1986. This data has become an important research tool for those attempting to understand the behavior of equity markets. It is also valuable to investors seeking a hedge against large market drawdowns. Trading activities are supported by investment products offered by the CBOE. On March 26, 2004, VIX futures began trading on the CBOE futures exchange, and VIX options were launched in February 2006.

Because unstable markets are characterized by high volatility, the VIX tends to rise when markets are falling. Conversely, an orderly rising market normally is characterized by a falling VIX. Much research has focused on using the VIX as a leading indicator of market direction. Some correlations have been found, and it is generally believed that a high VIX tends to precede a rally and that a low VIX tends to precede a drawdown.[6] These views are consistent with studies that reveal a link between coherent (nonchaotic) market behavior and an increased risk of a crash. Unfortunately, even the best correlations are tenuous, and investors sometimes overuse the VIX as an indicator.

Although it seems confusing to measure the volatility of volatility, that is exactly what VIX options pricing entails. The numbers are surprisingly large and highly variable. It is not unusual for implied volatility on VIX options to exceed 150%, and it can rise rapidly when sudden market changes push up the index's value. It can also fall as low as 40% in very stable markets where volatility remains constant over an extended period of time. Figure 6.4 displays the volatility of the new VIX between January 1990 and April 2007.

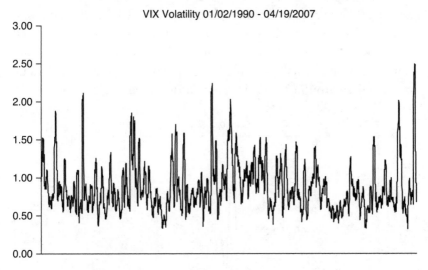

Figure 6.4 Volatility of the VIX from 01/02/1990–04/19/2007 measured using a 20-day sliding window.

The index's highly variable nature is apparent in the chart. This behavior exists at all scales and across all time frames. Even calm markets with steadily rising prices are characterized by a volatile VIX. These characteristics make trading VIX options more complex than most other securities and indexes. In general terms, if the market suddenly falls, the VIX rises, as does implied volatility of VIX options. The effect is compounded for out-of-the-money call options because they benefit from both the rising value of the index and rising implied volatility. You will note that this behavior is the inverse of that exhibited by equity options, whose implied volatility tends to fall as the underlying rises. In the event of a market crash, the magnitude of the change in value of the VIX is dramatic. Figure 6.5 displays the behavior of the VIX during the October 1987 market crash (values are for the original VIX, which is now called VXO).

During the 1987 crash, deep out-of-the-money calls that would have sold for 5 cents would have risen to more than $100. Unfortunately for investors of the time, there were no VIX options or futures to use as a hedge. It is also important to note that the value of the VIX fell by half only two days later, when the S&P 100 rebounded from 108 to nearly 127. By year end, the market stabilized around 119, and the VIX declined to 39. Volatility of the index, calculated with a 20-day siding window, rose from 46% before the event to 600% at the peak. The peak values dwarf those of subsequent market drawdowns and consequently cannot be proportionally included in Figure 6.4. By year end the value had stabilized around 125%. This data is displayed in Figure 6.6.

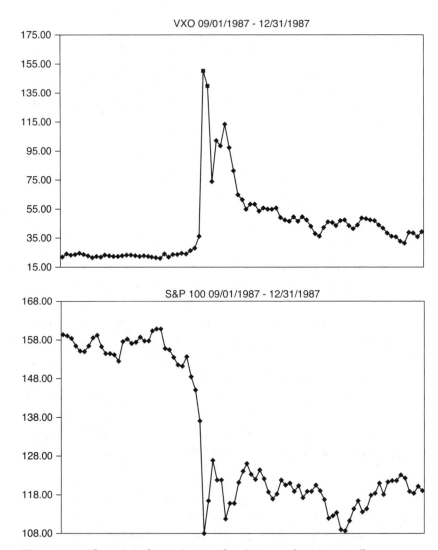

Figure 6.5   The original VIX (upper chart) versus the S&P 100 (lower chart) during the 1987 market crash. Volatility on the VIX climbed as high as 600% during the spike, which drove the index from 35 to more than 150.

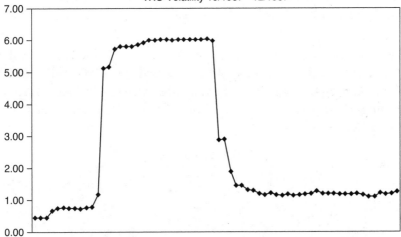

Figure 6.6   Volatility of the VIX 10/01/1987–12/31/1987 measured using a
20-day sliding window.

The 1987 decline, although long ago, was chosen for the example because it illustrates the market's behavior in a true crash. If VIX futures or options are to be used as a hedge, it is important to understand the index's behavior under these circumstances. Figure 6.7 illustrates the VIX's behavior during the smaller, but still significant, February 2007 drawdown.

Between the closes on February 26 and February 27, the market experienced a 3.5% decline, and the VIX climbed from 11.15 to 18.31. During this time frame, implied volatilities on VIX options also climbed steeply, from approximately 65% before the crash to more than 250% just after. It is important to note that these values vary tremendously between strikes. Moreover, because the market determines the price of any tradeable asset, pricing can be enormously asymmetric, and liquidity can vary from thousands of contracts to none. VIX options represent the extreme case. While the market was falling, current-month call volatilities hovered in the 200% range, and in-the-money puts traded for less than the amount by which they were in-the-money. These imbalances persisted for some time after the market stabilized in late March. On April 20, for example, when the VIX fell to 12.07, at-the-money calls traded for $1.45 (bid) / $1.65 (ask), while corresponding puts were worth only $0.45 and $0.50, respectively. Corresponding implied volatilities were 112% (bid) / 127% (ask) for the calls and 40% (bid) / 44% (ask) for the puts. The market supported this parity violation because it simply did not believe that the VIX could fall further. It was also evident that the market had a minimum value target for the index, because 10.00 strike price calls traded for $2.90 (bid) / $3.20 (ask). Corresponding implied volatilities were 144% and $173%. Adding together strike and option prices consistently predicted a VIX above 13 at expiration.

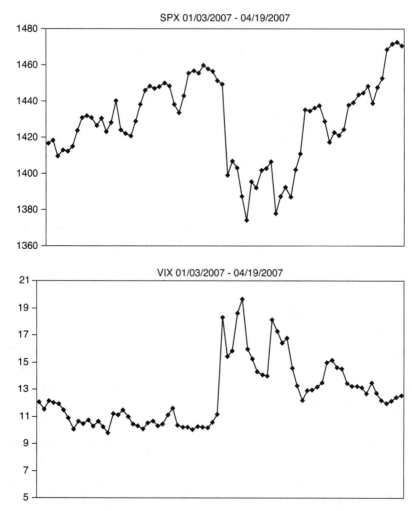

Figure 6.7   The S&P 500 (upper chart) and VIX (lower chart) during the
                   February 2007 market decline.

This behavior makes it difficult to trade VIX options as a stand-alone investment, and it is the reason that we are focused on their use as a hedge. For example, during the initial hours of the February 2007 drawdown, as the VIX climbed from 13 to 15, the price of 13.00 strike price puts did not lose value, because their volatility climbed dramatically as they moved out-of-the-money. An investor who sold these puts after correctly predicting the market decline and rise in the VIX would have been frustrated to discover that profit was limited by rising volatility. As the index continued rising, the 13.00 strike price puts eventually lost value.

This behavior, however, does not eliminate short deep in-the-money VIX puts as a hedge, because they tend to lose value in proportion to the rise of the index. Furthermore, such positions are more likely to deliver profit in minor drawdowns than far out-of-the-money calls, which may remain relatively worthless. In low VIX environments where the chance of a further decline of the index is limited, short deep in-the-money puts are an excellent hedge against minor market declines. In- or at-the-money calls are too expensive to use as a hedge, and far out-of-the-money calls can protect against only a very large move of the index. The selection of a hedge, therefore, depends on the investor's philosophy.

Finally, the value of VIX options as a hedge during a sudden but brief drawdown can be adversely affected by the fact that they are European-style contracts that can be exercised only at expiration. This fact normally does not impact the value of an option contract. However, the anticipation of a sharp decline in the index as the market regains stability after a sudden drop can create price distortions for options that cannot be exercised. Consider, for example, the thought process of an investor who is short calls that suddenly move in-the-money as the index rises during a market crash. Knowing that the VIX is likely to decline as the market stabilizes, and that implied volatilities of VIX options will fall, the investor is likely to hesitate before closing the position at a tremendous loss. This approach could not be taken if the calls were immediately exercisable. Unfortunately, because they are not, bid-ask spreads tend to widen by a surprising amount, and liquidity becomes an issue. These factors can limit the value of out-of-the-money VIX calls as a hedge against a market crash.

Summary

As is always the case, there is no such thing as a fully hedged, riskless, profitable trade that generates more than the risk-free interest rate. A common misconception among option traders is that such positions exist and that they can be found at the more complex end of the spectrum in large multipart trades. In this regard it is important to stress that these trades are designed to smooth out the return, limit risk, and cap both losses and gains. These are admirable goals. Most investors, regardless of their skill and knowledge, will realize larger gains if they carefully model the behavior of complex positions in advance and create a plan for making adjustments if necessary.

Complexity increases as we move from positions that span different strikes to positions that span both expirations and strikes. Ratios that use different quantities at different strike prices are next, and ratios that span expiration dates are even more complex. At the extreme end of the complexity spectrum are four-part trades that are long and short puts and calls with different expirations. These positions, because of their complex dynamics, offer tremendous opportunity, but the risks can be complex to model.

Some structures are designed to profit from time decay and/or falling volatility, and others from large price spikes and/or rising volatility. Equities for these trades should be selected based on their price change behavior. The reverse is also true: trades should be structured with a probabilistic view of the potential size and frequency of price spikes of the underlying. Some generalizations are appropriate:

- Stocks that exhibit predictable earnings spikes should not be included in positions that profit from time decay if the trade's time horizon crosses an earnings release.

- Options on stocks that exhibit predictable price spikes often experience increases in implied volatility as the triggering event approaches. These events can be used to time entry points for certain types of complex trades.

- Collateral requirements can be significant for short positions. Therefore, it is important to calculate the cost of risk-free interest on money that is set aside to collateralize positions.

- When a complex trade includes a hedge, it is important to model the decay of the hedge's effectiveness as expiration approaches. Far out-of-the-money hedges become insignificant in the final few days before expiration.

- Complex trades should not be closed in pieces unless the intent is to convert one type of trade into another. For example, it is rarely wise to close the long side of a ratio and let the short side decay unless new information would lead to the conclusion that a naked short position is desirable.

The most efficient use of any particular structure takes advantage of price distortions that arise from unusual market conditions. In some scenarios, implied volatility is predictably high, and investors are overcompensated for risk. In others it is relatively low. The latter is rare, because implied volatility can be too low only if the market is unaware of a potential risk factor.

Two very common events that affect implied volatility are earnings releases and options expiration. Each creates price distortions that can be profitably traded. The following chapters examine strategies for trading these distortions.

Further Reading

Brenner, M., and D. Galai, "New Financial Instruments for Hedging Changes in Volatility," *Financial Analysts Journal*, July–August 1989, pp. 61–65.

Chicago Board Options Exchange, "The New CBOE Volatility Index— VIX," white paper published on the CBOE website, Chicago Board Options Exchange, Inc., 09/18/2003.

Psychoyios, D., and G. Skiadopoulos, (2006), "Volatility Options: Hedging Effectiveness, Pricing, and Model Error," *Journal of Futures Markets*, 26:1, pp. 1–31.

Sornette, D., *Why Stock Markets Crash*, Princeton and Oxford: Princeton University Press, 2003.

Endnotes

[1] Note that the number of days remaining is calculated from the market close at 4:00 p.m. each day to 5:00 p.m. on expiration Saturday.

[2] Calculated at 18% volatility and a 5% risk-free rate of interest.

[3] A current-month option cannot reduce the collateral requirement for a distant month.

[4] The collateral requirement is reduced once the hedge has the same or further expiration date. The new calculation takes into account the spacing between long and short strike prices.

[5] The original VIX, now called VXO, was based on at-the-money S&P 100 index options. The two versions are closely correlated. The new VIX went into effect in 2003.

[6] Credit Suisse, "Can the VIX Signal Market Direction?", white paper published for Credit Suisse customers, 12/20/2006.

7

TRADING THE EARNINGS CYCLE

Quarterly earnings create tremendous opportunities for option traders. For stocks that have a history of large earnings-associated price spikes, the market tends to overprice options by setting implied volatility too high. The distortion is especially large when an earnings release coincides with options expiration. For these stocks, implied volatility rises sharply to offset the rapid time decay of the final few days of the expiration cycle.

A second distortion occurs just after earnings are announced and volatility collapses back to an appropriate level. The rate of collapse depends on the magnitude of the price spike. When the spike is much smaller than implied volatility would suggest, the collapse is very rapid—sometimes just a few minutes long. However, when implied volatility accurately anticipates the magnitude of the spike, the collapse occurs over an extended period of time that can last from hours to days. This effect is exaggerated in cases where the stock continues to move in the direction of the spike.

This chapter explores trading opportunities that arise from earnings-driven price distortions. We will focus on two specific categories:

- Trades that benefit from increasing volatility during the days that precede an earnings release
- Trades that benefit from post-earnings volatility collapse

The obvious third category would be trades that benefit from large earnings-associated price spikes that exceed the risk priced into option contracts. It is often the case that a surprise embedded in an earnings announcement generates a much larger price spike than the market anticipates. In this scenario, straddle and strangle sellers lose money because they are undercompensated for risk; buyers of these positions profit because one side of the trade was underpriced. After such a surprise, implied volatility sometimes stabilizes at a new level that is higher than before. The level can remain high for extended periods of time if the stock continues to be volatile. Sears exhibited this behavior on March 15, 2006 with an earnings price spike greater than 11 standard deviations. Before the earnings time frame, Sears at-the-money options traded with implied volatility of 18%. After the spike, both real and implied volatility stabilized around 24%. One year later, Sears options were still priced with 24% volatility.

There are certainly many other examples of extraordinarily large earnings-related price spikes that are not reflected in pre-announcement option prices. Unfortunately there is no reliable method for predicting such an event. The opposite case is much more common—pre-earnings option prices tend to exaggerate the risk by anticipating the largest possible spike. This dynamic certainly does not eliminate the possibility of generating an excellent return by purchasing underpriced options just before an earnings announcement. Markets are never perfectly efficient, and an earnings surprise can generate a price change that dwarfs the cost of a long straddle or strangle. One strategy involves placing a large number of very small bets by purchasing far out-of-the-money options on many stocks just before their quarterly earnings are announced. One very large price spike often generates enough profit to offset the many losses. Unfortunately, pre-earnings options prices generally reflect both publicly available data and confidential information held by insiders. Despite a broad range of laws that prohibit insider trading, it is not unusual for a severe upside or downside surprise to find its way into the prices of option contracts.

The remainder of this discussion focuses on opportunities that arise from rising volatility during the pre-earnings time frame or falling volatility immediately after.

Exploiting Earnings-Associated Rising Volatility

Scheduled earnings announcements are often accompanied by substantial increases in implied volatility. The magnitude of the increase depends on the size of the anticipated price spike. Some companies are notorious for their earnings surprises; options on these stocks often trade at surprisingly high prices just before an earnings release. Pricing dynamics for these events are unusual because they are driven by the risk parameters surrounding a single upcoming event.

Consider a stock that has exhibited 3 to 4 standard deviation price spikes with each of the past four quarterly earnings releases but is relatively nonvolatile the remainder of the time. If the stock trades for $100 per share, and normal volatility is 25%, at-the-money puts and calls must each trade for at least $6.30 to cover the risk of a 4 standard deviation spike (1 standard deviation would be $1.57 for this stock). Knowledgeable sellers will refuse to accept less, and buyers will try not to pay more.

The distortion is largest for at-the-money strikes and decreases as we move away from the stock price. Implied volatility remains unchanged at distant strikes that are unlikely to be affected. Time remaining before expiration is also important. The distortion increases dramatically for earnings announcements that occur close to expiration when out-of-the-money options normally lose most of their value. Some companies have a habit of announcing their quarterly earnings very close to options expiration—in the most extreme cases, just before the market opens on the final trading day. Such behavior creates extreme price swings because out-of-the-money options transition from being dramatically overpriced at the open to having virtually no implied volatility at the close.

Table 7.1 displays various scenarios for pricing call options to protect against a 4 standard deviation upward price spike for a $100 stock with historical volatility of 25% (1 standard deviation = $1.58). The data reveals tremendous discrepancies between implied volatilities for at-the-money and out-of-the-money options. The effect of close proximity to expiration is also apparent.

Table 7.1 Call pricing scenarios that anticipate a $6.32 (4 standard deviation) price spike for a $100 stock with 25% historical volatility.

Stock Price ($)	Strike	Days Remaining	Option Price ($)	Volatility
100.00	100	15	2.13	0.25
100.00	105	15	0.50	0.25
100.00	100	15	6.32	0.77
100.00	105	15	1.32	0.38
100.00	100	2	0.76	0.25
100.00	105	2	0.00	0.25
100.00	100	2	6.32	2.12
100.00	105	2	1.32	1.05

The top two sets of prices (above the gray bar) highlight the difference between calls priced with 25% volatility and protected calls that are priced to absorb a 4 standard deviation upward price spike. Dramatically elevated implied volatilities displayed below the gray bar illustrate the impact of moving an earnings announcement close to options expiration. In the second scenario, price protection can be obtained for at-the-money options only by raising the implied volatility to more than 200%. Only half this distortion is required to build appropriate protection for options that are $5.00 out-of-the-money. These numbers are somewhat conservative because the market usually anticipates a larger spike than price change history would suggest. The problem is also complicated by large variations in the size of previous earnings spikes. Many other factors can also contribute to the overall view.

Table 7.2 contains option pricing and implied volatility data for Google during the final ten days before the July 2006 earnings release. Earnings were announced with only one trading day left in the options expiration cycle.

Table 7.2 Google $420 call prices approaching the July 2006 earnings release.

Google Close ($)	Strike	Days Remaining	Call Price ($)	Volatility
424.56	420	11	15.95	0.45
417.25	420	10	11.95	0.47
408.83	420	9	8.10	0.49
403.50	420	8	6.25	0.52
407.89	420	7	7.40	0.64
403.05	420	4	5.95	0.73
399.00	420	3	5.60	0.91
387.12	420	2	4.40	1.30
390.11	420	1	0.00	0.01

The protective nature of rising volatility is evident in this table, which reveals a surprisingly high price for $30 out-of-the-money calls at the close on July 20 with just one trading day left before expiration. A $37 earnings price spike—4.8 standard deviations at 32% volatility—would not have placed these options further in-the-money than their cost. The next day, after earnings were released, Google stock closed virtually unchanged at $390.11.

Various trades that benefit from rising volatility gain an advantage during this time frame. Long straddles are the most straightforward example. Time decay normally eats away at the value of a long straddle, and the size of a price spike that is needed to generate profit increases with time. Owning a straddle or strangle near expiration is particularly dangerous because, as a percent of total value, time decay becomes much more significant. However, when an earnings release is commingled with expiration, the time decay cost of a straddle becomes negligible. This effect is illustrated in Table 7.3, which repeats the previous example with the stock price frozen at $400. Note that the price of the $420 strike price call remains nearly constant despite a very large and increasing theta.

Table 7.3 $420 call pricing using Google implied volatilities from Table 7.2 with the stock price frozen at $400.

Close ($)	Strike	Days Remaining	Call Price ($)	Volatility	Theta
400.00	420	11	5.35	0.45	−0.50
400.00	420	10	5.30	0.47	−0.54
400.00	420	9	5.20	0.49	−0.59
400.00	420	8	5.20	0.52	−0.66
400.00	420	7	4.85	0.64	−1.01
400.00	420	4	5.05	0.73	−1.29
400.00	420	3	5.90	0.91	−1.90
400.00	420	2	7.90	1.30	−3.45
400.00	420	1	0.00	0.01	0.00

The effect we are discussing involves a decoupling of option prices from the current behavior of the underlying security. This decoupling seems rational when you realize that options, like all securities, are priced by the aggressiveness of buyers and sellers. Many investors falsely believe that option prices are set according to the familiar mathematics of volatility and time. In fact, the opposite is true: prices are set by traders who buy and sell contracts using the mathematics as a guideline. Stock prices have their own mathematical guidelines such as price:earnings ratios. It is completely reasonable for the two to decouple, and that is often what happens when earnings are approaching.

We can continue analyzing the Google example by tracking the return of a near-term long strangle purchased before the volatility run-up. In Table 7.4, a wide strangle was purchased 19 days before expiration on Monday, July 3. This particular day was chosen because it avoided the time decay of the previous weekend but still preceded the impending sharp rise in implied volatility. That said, implied volatility had already risen slightly above the average of the preceding month, which was 28%. Each pair of entries in the table includes relevant data for a ten-contract far out-of-the-money long strangle that was initially delta-neutral.

Table 7.4 Return of $460/$390 strangle on Google stock during the final days before the July 2006 earnings release.

Google Close ($)	Option	Days Remaining	Option Price ($)	Volatility	Delta	Contract	Position Value ($)
423.20	460 call	19	2.20	0.32	0.143	10	
423.20	390 put	19	1.85	0.32	−0.117	10	4,050
424.56	460 call	11	2.85	0.45	0.167	10	
424.56	390 put	11	2.15	0.45	−0.126	10	5,000
417.25	460 call	10	1.80	0.47	0.116	10	
417.25	390 put	10	3.25	0.47	−0.178	10	5,050
408.83	460 call	9	0.95	0.49	0.070	10	
408.83	390 put	9	5.00	0.49	−0.253	10	5,950
403.50	460 call	8	0.65	0.52	0.050	10	
403.50	390 put	8	6.50	0.52	−0.311	10	7,150
407.89	460 call	5	0.80	0.64	0.060	10	
407.89	390 put	5	5.00	0.64	−0.260	10	5,800
403.05	460 call	4	0.60	0.73	0.047	10	
403.05	390 put	4	6.70	0.73	−0.318	10	7,300
399.00	460 call	3	0.65	0.91	0.048	10	
399.00	390 put	3	9.00	0.91	−0.374	10	9,650

Table 7.4   Continued

Google Close ($)	Option	Days Remaining	Option Price ($)	Volatility	Delta	Contract	Position Value ($)
387.12	460 call	2	0.65	1.30	0.042	10	
387.12	390 put	2	16.50	1.30	−0.510	10	17,150
390.11	460 call	1	0.00	0.01	0.000	10	
390.11	390 put	1	0.05	0.01	−0.213	10	50

The position, although purchased with only 19 days remaining before expiration, was remarkably resistant to the effects of time decay. Despite an initial theta of 19 cents on the call side and 15 cents on the put side, the trade gained 25% during the first eight days while the stock remained stationary. Because the long position cost nothing to own, it was essentially riskless.

We would have realized the largest profit by riding the implied volatility curve to the top and closing the trade just before earnings were announced. Had we pursued this strategy, we would have realized a profit of more than 300% as a result of both rising volatility and movement of the underlying stock. In the interest of completeness, it is important to understand the relative contribution of each. Over a period of 17 days, the stock fell $36.08. Using a starting volatility of 32%, we can calculate that the value of a 1 standard deviation change over 17 days for a $423 stock is $29.24:

365 calendar days / 17 = 21.47 time frames per calendar year

sqrt (21.47) = 4.634

starting volatility 0.32 / 4.634 = 0.0691

$423.20 × 0.0691 = $29.24 (1 standard deviation for this time frame)

The actual price change over 17 days was $36.08, or 1.23 standard deviations. Had volatility remained constant at 32% during this time frame, the price change alone would have raised the put price to $5.25, and the calls would have been worthless. The ten contract strangle would have been worth $5,250. However, as expiration approaches, implied volatility normally falls slightly. In the absence of a pending event, implied volatility for at-the-money options would have decreased to 24% at the open on the last day. At-the-money puts would have been worth $4.40–$4,400 for the ten contract strangle. Implied volatility behavior actually becomes quite complex during the final few days as overnight hours become a more significant portion of the remaining time. Volatility tends to fall each day near the close to adjust for overnight time decay, and it recovers at the market open the next day. The distortion becomes extreme on the last day, when virtually all remaining volatility vanishes during the 6.5 hours of trading. The number does not fall to zero, however, because extended-hours trading can have pronounced effects, and expiration is Saturday afternoon. These effects are most apparent in option prices for expensive equities such as Google, where several strikes remain significant until the very last day.

In our example, it is clear that rising implied volatility was the key driving force that generated most of the profit. Furthermore, the volatility run-up exaggerated the true risk. Table 7.5 contains the price spike history for the six earnings releases that preceded our example.

Table 7.5 Earnings-associated price spikes for Google.

Earnings Date	Associated Price Spike in Standard Deviations
04/20/2006	2.50
01/31/2006	−2.10
10/20/2005	−8.00
07/21/2005	−2.40
04/21/2005	3.40
02/01/2005	2.70

Most earnings-associated price spikes fell into a range of 2.5 to 3.5 standard deviations. The exception was the October 2005 spike that took the price from $303.20 at the close on 10/20 to $339.90 at the close on 10/21. Closing prices do not paint a complete picture of this event, because the stock actually traded for $345.80 at the open on 10/21 before reversing direction and falling $6.00. Traders who were short calls lost tremendous amounts of money at the open. This spike, super-imposed on all the others, set the trend that caused high levels of risk to be priced into future earnings releases.

Google is one of hundreds of stocks that exhibit this behavior. Sometimes the earnings effect is compounded by upcoming news events. One of the best examples was Apple Computer's (AAPL) January 2007 planned announcement of the iPhone and a new home entertainment product line. These announcements preceded earnings by only nine days; options expiration followed just two days later. Normally planned events drive higher implied volatilities, making it difficult for straddle buyers to profit. Such events often display the characteristics of an earnings release in the sense that after the announcement, volatility deflates. However, a flurry of analyst interpre-tations over the next few days continued the trend, which was exacer-bated by the approaching earnings announcement. Table 7.6 shows the results for a ten-contract long straddle.

Table 7.6 AAPL long strangle profit driven by announcement-related price changes coincident with earnings and options expiration. The gray bar marks the final close before earnings were announced.

AAPL Close ($)	Option	Days Remaining	Option Price ($)	Volatility	Delta	Contract	Position Value ($)
85.05	90.00	15	0.95	0.38	0.25	10	
85.05	80.00	15	0.75	0.38	−0.20	10	1,700
85.47	90.00	12	1.05	0.42	0.27	10	
85.47	80.00	12	0.65	0.42	−0.18	10	1,700
92.57	90.00	11	4.60	0.48	0.65	10	
92.57	80.00	11	0.10	0.48	−0.04	10	4,700

AAPL Close ($)	Option	Days Remaining	Option Price ($)	Volatility	Delta	Contract	Position Value ($)
97.00	90.00	10	8.10	0.55	0.81	10	
97.00	80.00	10	0.05	0.55	−0.01	10	8,150
95.80	90.00	9	7.20	0.60	0.76	10	
95.80	80.00	9	0.10	0.60	−0.02	10	7,300
94.62	90.00	8	6.65	0.70	0.71	10	
94.62	80.00	8	0.20	0.70	−0.05	10	6,850
97.10	90.00	4	8.20	0.90	0.80	10	
97.10	80.00	4	0.05	0.90	−0.02	10	8,250
94.95	90.00	3	6.35	0.98	0.74	10	
94.95	80.00	3	0.10	0.98	−0.02	10	6,450
89.07	90.00	2	0.70	0.40	0.37	10	
89.07	80.00	2	0.00	0.40	0.00	10	700
88.50	90.00	1	0.00	0.01	0.00	10	
88.50	80.00	1	0.00	0.01	0.00	10	0

The trade begins with a delta-neutral strangle purchased on the Friday preceding the product announcement. Monday morning, the day of the announcement, implied volatility rose enough to offset 14 cents of time decay experienced over the weekend. During the remaining days before earnings, the stock rose sharply, as did option-implied volatility. The gray bar marks the last close before earnings were announced. The profit was enormous—approximately 280%. Kept open through earnings and into expiration, the position would have turned into a 100% loss as volatility collapsed and the options expired worthless.

This example illustrates the importance of taking profit and closing the trade before earnings are announced. Surprisingly, had we made the mistake of keeping the position open, we still could have generated a significant profit by stopping out at the open on January 18 at a stock price of $92.10. At this price, with approximately 44 hours left before expiration, the calls were still worth $2.40. Despite the implied volatility collapse, we could have closed our trade for $2,400 and realized a 41% profit. Rapid execution in such situations is critical, because implied volatility falls very rapidly at the open. Although it is not possible to re-create the exact trading dynamics of the first few moments of January 18, it is clear that waiting for bid-ask spreads to shrink and option prices to stabilize would have been a mistake, because both the stock price and volatilities were falling.

In general terms, this trade is pervasive enough to form the basis of an investment strategy. It has some distinct advantages, because risk is limited to just a few weeks of time decay per quarter, and, as we have seen, rising volatility tends to offset this decay.

The next section examines a different opportunity that arises from overpriced risk. This opportunity, which has a much different risk:return profile, takes the form of trades that benefit from post-earnings implied volatility collapse.

Exploiting Post-Earnings Implied Volatility Collapse

Sometimes the implied volatility increase that accompanies an earnings announcement is so exaggerated that it makes sense to sell out-of-the-money puts and calls at the very peak before numbers are released. As we have seen, the distortion is greatest when earnings coincide with options expiration. In such cases the stock often closes the final session of the expiration cycle far from either strike price, and the options simply expire worthless.

In our previous Google example, an at-the-money short straddle would have been protected against spikes in the range of 4 standard deviations, and a $40 out-of-the-money strangle would have withstood price changes of more than 6 standard deviations. The reason for the difference is clear: a $390 straddle was worth $30.20, and a $430/$350 strangle was worth $5.60 when volatility peaked just before the announcement. Consequently, a $390 straddle would have effectively absorbed a $33 price change from $387 to $420, and the $430/$350 strangle could have absorbed a $48 spike to $435.60. These large distortions persist because, in some sense, the market remembers the 8 standard deviation spike of October 2005. Google, like other expensive stocks, provides a multiple strike price advantage that allows us to calibrate the risk of our trade. In our example, had we accepted some additional risk by selling at-the-money options, we would have realized a $30 profit ($390 puts and calls expired at-the-money).[1] Wider strike prices reduce both the risk and the gain. It is extremely unusual to lose money by selling the very widest strike prices that have value. In the Google example, we might have decided to structure a trade that was protected against the largest recent spike—8 standard deviations. A short $460/$330 strangle would have fit this description. The position would have been delta-neutral (0.042 call delta/–0.045 put delta) and worth approximately $1.40. Additionally, collateral requirements are reduced for out-of-the-money trades; approximately $130,000 would have been required as collateral for a 10 contract $390 straddle worth $30,000, but only $84,000 for the corresponding $460/$330 strangle. Purchasing a $500/$300 strangle as a hedge would have reduced the requirement to less than $30,000 while removing only 5 cents of profit from each side. Such trades, properly structured, have the potential to deliver outstanding profit with extremely limited market exposure.

Google is an excellent candidate for such trades. Fortunately many others exist; the number of candidates remains relatively high from quarter to quarter. Lower-priced stocks sometimes seem riskier when the trade is confined to very near strike prices. A detailed analysis, however, often reveals that this is not the case. Consider, for example, Schlumberger Limited (SLB). This stock normally exhibits relatively small earnings-associated spikes. Moreover, detailed analysis of the data reveals that the largest spikes in the group are greatly diminished when you measure close-open rather than close-close price changes. Table 7.7 contains relevant data for eight earnings announcements.

Table 7.7 Earnings-related price spikes for Schlumberger.

Earnings Date	Previous Close	Earn Open	Earn Close	C-O StdDev	C-C StdDev	Value of One StdDev ($)
01/19/2007	57.90	59.45	61.00	1.50	3.20	1.00
10/20/2006	62.70	63.31	60.10	−0.44	−1.80	1.40
07/21/2006	61.66	63.16	61.45	−0.83	−0.11	1.80
04/21/2006	68.07	69.40	68.51	1.00	0.33	1.30
01/20/2006	56.44	58.67	61.13	0.95	2.80	1.30
10/21/2005	40.29	39.75	40.01	−0.90	−0.40	0.80
07/22/2005	38.98	39.97	41.14	−1.65	−3.70	0.60
04/26/2005	35.85	35.59	35.01	−0.41	−1.30	0.63

This table displays opening and closing prices on earnings day as well as the previous day's close. The columns labeled "C-O StdDev" and "C-C StdDev" display the price changes (close-to-open and close-to-close) in standard deviations. Although earnings-related price spikes for SLB are generally moderate, implied volatility has repeatedly doubled to nearly 70%. This increase is large enough, in most cases, to protect against a 2.5 standard deviation price spike. Schlumberger has an unusual reporting strategy—each earnings announcement depicted in the table was just before the market open on the final trading day (Friday) of an expiration cycle.

Analyzing the history of earnings-related spikes can be difficult. The situation becomes very complex when a stock that normally conforms to the lognormal distribution exhibits repeated large and varying spikes around earnings. Yahoo! is an excellent example of this phenomenon. It exhibits lognormal behavior between earnings releases, yet the market has no accurate way of determining the risk associated with a quarterly announcement. Most of the time, risk is overpriced because the market has a low tolerance for uncertainty. Sometimes, however, extraordinary events can confound even the most conservative estimates. This problem is evident in Figure 7.1, which displays one year of price spikes for Yahoo!.

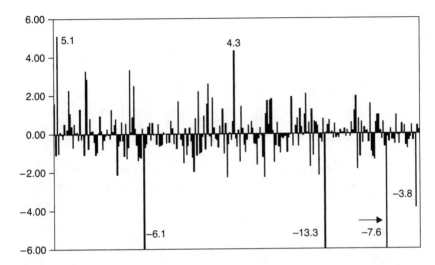

Figure 7.1   Yahoo! price spike history 10/17/2005–10/20/2006 in standard deviations. The value of each large spike is marked in standard deviations. Five of the six large spikes are earnings-related. The arrow marks a nonearnings spike (–7.6 standard deviations).

Note the third large downward spike from the right side of the chart. This price change, which occurred on July 19, 2006, is too large (–13.3 standard deviations) to display in the figure. A clearer picture can be obtained by rescaling the y-axis and charting absolute values for all the spikes, as shown in Figure 7.2.

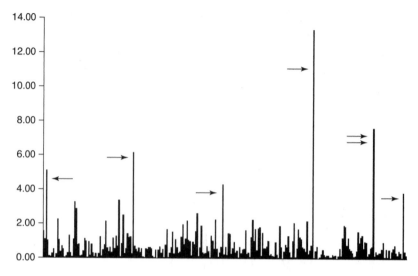

Figure 7.2   The data in Figure 7.1 displayed using absolute values (that is, all spikes are positive), with the y-axis rescaled to accommodate the magnitude of the largest spikes. The only nonearnings spike is marked with a double arrow.

This representation of the data makes it clear that earnings are highly significant events for Yahoo!. If we were planning to trade the October 17, 2006 event, we would need to frame the risks in the context of recent price changes. The 09/19 downward spike (double arrow) was caused by an earnings warning that preceded the actual release. In some sense it was a warning that reset expectations, lowered the stock price, and lessened the risk of a dramatic follow-on downward spike. However, at the close on 10/17, just before the announcement, at-the-money options still traded with implied volatility of 92%. Just a few moments before the close, the stock traded at $24.15, and a $25 long straddle traded for $2.00. A short position would have been protected against an upward spike of $2.85 or a downward spike of $1.15 ($27 / $23). Using the current 20-day volatility as a guide (20%), these numbers translate to 9.5 standard deviations on the call side and only 3.8 standard deviations on the put side. Therefore, the risk was far higher on the put side. The market was efficient enough to correctly discount some of the risk because of the previous large spike. The next day the stock opened slightly up at $24.57, and implied volatility immediately deflated to 32%, yielding a straddle price of $0.70. We would have closed the position immediately. By the close the stock had fallen to $22.99, a 3.8 standard deviation downward spike that exactly matched the value priced into the options. Two days later, the options expired $1.79 in-the-money.

Another way to think about the $23 floor priced into the put side is to measure the distance to the stock price just before the 09/19 downward spike in terms of standard deviations. On 09/18 the stock closed at $29 and 23% implied volatility. A $6 price decline over the following 22 trading days would have been equivalent to a 3 standard deviation change:

252 trading days per year / 22 trading days = 11.45

sqrt(11.45) = 3.38 (annualization factor for 22 trading days)

.23 volatility / 3.38 = 0.068

0.068 × $29 = $1.97 (1 standard deviation for this time frame)

$6.00 / $1.97 = 3.04 standard deviations

The options market, therefore, had priced in a total decline over 22 days of approximately 3 standard deviations and an instantaneous decline of about 3.8 standard deviations for the earnings event. This view is consistent with the magnitude and length of previous large declines for the stock. For example, between January 9 and February 13 of the same year (24 trading days), the stock fell $11.38 from $43.42 to $32.04. Using a starting volatility of 29% for this time frame, we can calculate that the magnitude of the fall was 3.4 standard deviations.

It is always difficult to assess risk for naked short trades. The Yahoo! example is no exception. At first glance you might believe that 92% implied volatility was excessive. Our analysis reveals that it was not. Furthermore, a surprise in the announcement could have generated a larger spike. Had we sold the call alone, we would have taken in only 60 cents, but we would have been protected against an upward spike to $25.60—4.8 standard deviations. This trade would have been much safer than either a short straddle or a naked put. This is because recent behavior of the stock, earnings warnings, and the recent large downward spike all hinted that a strong upward price change was unlikely. However, this pricing was also efficient because the two previous upward spikes evident in Figure 7.1 were of the same magnitude.

Finally, because we have reason to believe that, in broad terms, the pricing was rational and implied volatility was likely to fall, it might have made sense to structure a ratio put spread. Falling volatility tends to be destructive to the short side of such a trade. We would have purchased $25 strike price puts for $1.40 and sold $22.50 puts for $0.30. A ratio of 3:1 would have offset our cost by 90 cents. Two days later at expiration our position would have been long $1.80, and our profit would have been $1.30—$1,300 per ten contracts.

Throughout this discussion we have purposely avoided measuring price changes in percentages. Analyzing price changes in standard deviations has allowed us to compare time frames of different lengths spanning different prices and volatilities. Any other analysis would have failed to provide a balanced view. The market is very efficient, and pricing anomalies are difficult to find. When one is found, it is important to analyze as much historical data and news as possible and to factor this information into every trade.

Generally speaking, naked short trades are dangerous, and most investors realize greater gains from well structured long positions. Some of this risk can be offset by keeping positions small enough that they can be offset with long or short stock. In the event of a very large earnings surprise, stock can be bought or sold during one of the extended-hours sessions. Large positions would make this approach impossible to implement.

Summary

Option pricing distortions that accompany quarterly earnings announcements often provide excellent trading opportunities. Two major trends are evident: rising volatility during the days preceding an earnings announcement, and falling volatility immediately after earnings are released.

To take advantage of the first case, an investor might purchase a straddle during the final couple of weeks before earnings are announced and let rising volatility offset most of the time decay. At the implied volatility peak, just before earnings are released, the position would be closed.

The position might be closed early if a large price spike generates substantial profit ahead of the volatility peak. The second case involves opening a short position at the volatility peak, just before earnings are announced, and closing the position after the event, when implied volatility collapses. The rate of volatility collapse depends on the size of the distortion.

A perfectly reasonable investment strategy might be to avoid the everyday risks of the market, sit on the sidelines, and execute mathematically sound, carefully designed trades that take advantage of earnings-related price distortions. One advantage of this strategy is dramatically reduced market exposure. If long positions are the focus, market exposure is limited to a couple of weeks of time decay each quarter. Additionally, the risk is partly offset by rising volatility that tends to compensate for time decay when earnings and expiration occur in close proximity to each other.

Although short positions are riskier, it is often possible to limit the risk with a rational structure based on price change history. Such positions should be limited in size and, if a large price change occurs when earnings are announced, compensating trades can be placed in the before- or after-market sessions.

The next chapter focuses on another set of price distortions that are associated with options expiration. These situations, which also represent excellent trading opportunities, occur 12 times each year.

Endnote

1   Practically speaking, we would have closed both sides of the trade for 25 cents to avoid the risk of assignment following a surprise event after the close of the market.

8

TRADING THE EXPIRATION CYCLE

I n the preceding chapter, we explored trading opportunities that arise from earnings-related price distortions. Our analysis focused on implied volatility swings—the run-up that precedes most earnings announcements, and the collapse that follows. The dynamics are relatively complex because they depend on historical price change behavior, prevailing market conditions, and the stock's recent behavior.

This chapter focuses on a different set of price distortions that are rooted in the options expiration cycle. Most of these effects are a direct result of the interplay between the dynamics of trading and the mathematics of option pricing. For example, the amount of time that the market is closed each evening becomes increasingly significant as expiration approaches. The percentage of remaining time that elapses while the market is closed grows to 35% on the Thursday evening that precedes expiration. Market and technical distorting forces that come into play during the final few days include the following:

- Rapidly accelerating time decay during the final week

- Large daily implied volatility swings in the final few days

- Implied volatility collapse on the final trading day

- "Pinning" to a strike price caused by unwinding of complex positions and hedges

Each of these items is very important, because contemporary pricing models do not comprehend these effects. The fourth item, pinning to a strike price, has been the focus of an enormous number of academic research papers. The consensus is that this behavior is driven by delta hedging of a large number of long positions. Option contracts that exhibit high levels of open interest tend to cause the underlying stock to migrate toward the heavily traded strike price. Research has revealed that on expiration day, the returns of optionable stocks are altered by an average of at least 16.5 basis points, which translates into an aggregate market capitalization shift on the order of $9 billion.[1] Supporting evidence shows that the pinning effect is not evident in stocks that do not have listed options.

A trader who seeks an advantage in these distortions should have access to precise modeling tools. In this regard, this author has developed a customized set of statistical modeling and data mining tools for his own use. These tools are part of a much larger database infrastructure that is described in the final chapter.

The Final Trading Day

We begin with expiration Friday, the final trading day of the expiration cycle. This day is the most dynamic and complex of the cycle. It is characterized by two very significant forces: collapsing volatility and, for many stocks, rapid migration to a strike price. Table 8.1 contains summary data for the behavior of all optionable stocks over $50 across 22 expiration cycles.

Table 8.1 The number of stocks expiring within specific distances of a strike price ranked by number of occurrences.

Occurrences Across 22 Expirations	10 Cents	20 Cents	30 Cents	40 Cents	50 Cents
14				1	1
13					
12					
11			1		1
10				1	1
9			1	3	10
8		1	4	8	25
7		2	9	32	52
6	1	3	29	61	85
5	4	22	53	89	139
4	16	54	126	154	131
3	55	142	156	134	113
2	132	174	147	108	67
1	223	164	85	43	21

The population includes 654 stocks. For the distances to strikes listed across the top (10 cents, 20 cents...50 cents), the table displays the number of stocks at each occurrence level. For example, during the 22 expiration cycles tracked, 32 stocks ended an expiration time frame within 40 cents of a strike price seven times. Only one stock, Google, expired within 40 cents of a strike price 14 times. At the other extreme, 223 stocks closed expiration Friday within 10 cents of a strike price at least once. The data does not tell the whole story, because often a stock hovers within a few cents of a strike price for the final few hours before drifting away slightly at the close. This final movement of the stock occurs after most complex positions are unwound, hedges are closed, and large institutional traders move on to focus on the next month.

Very high trading levels cause the final settlements to continue for a minute or so after the market closes as entries in the queue are matched and recorded. The majority of these trades are not related to the market forces that drive migration to a strike price. Additionally, the stock reopens for trading a few minutes later in the final after-hours session of the expiration cycle. Large movements often occur during the final after-hours session as institutional investors create new positions for the following month. In this regard it is important to remember that traders generally are aware of the pinning effect, and many structure trades that anticipate an exaggerated move when the stock breaks free on the following Monday. The data, however, does not support this assertion. For example, FedEx stock, which regularly displays the pinning effect, averaged a 0.77 standard deviation price change the day following a nonpinned expiration and a 0.87 standard deviation change after pinning. Variability was large, with spikes ranging from 0.0 to 3.4 standard deviations after pinning and from 0.1 to 3.1 when the effect was absent.

Figure 8.1 shows a typical expiration day trading scenario for Google stock using minute-by-minute closing prices. Key points in the trading day are marked on the chart.

Figure 8.1   Minute-by-minute closing prices for Google on the final trading day of an expiration cycle (data of 03/17/2006).

In this example, the stock opened the trading day at $338.80. Over the next few minutes the price fell to $335.19 before beginning a rapid rise to $340. In most cases pinning occurs at the upper strike price. This behavior is thought to reflect differences in the dynamics of buying and shorting. Until July 2007, the uptick rule created an asymmetry that made it considerably easier to buy than to sell short.[2] At 11:40 the stock briefly crossed the strike price before falling back and stabilizing between $339 and $340, where it traded for the remainder of the day. Shortly after 3:00 the trading price rose to within 10 cents of the strike price, and trading activity slowed dramatically as the few remaining positions were unwound.

High options turnover is also characteristic of pinning behavior. Open interest normally is largest at the affected strike price. It is not uncommon for trading volumes to exceed twice the number of open contracts; that is, each contract trades more than once during the day. All of these factors—rapid rise toward a strike price, slight overshoot, stabilization near the strike, large open interest, and high options turnover—are diagnostic of pinning. One obvious trade involves selling at-the-money straddles that lose nearly all their value by the end of the day if the stock remains near the strike price.

Volatility collapse is the defining characteristic of this trade. Early in the day, when the stock still has 6.5 hours of normal trading time left and more than 31 hours before expiration, implied volatility is consistent with recent historical volatility. However, at the end of the normal trading session, one full day still remains before options expiration. If implied volatility remained relatively high, near and at-the-money options would have more value than the market would permit. The result is that volatility collapses to near zero as market forces reduce the prices of these options. In-the-money options are worth the amount by which they exceed the strike price. The volatility collapse is evident in minute-by-minute call and put prices. Figure 8.2 builds on our example with minute-by-minute implied volatilities of $340 strike price calls and puts.

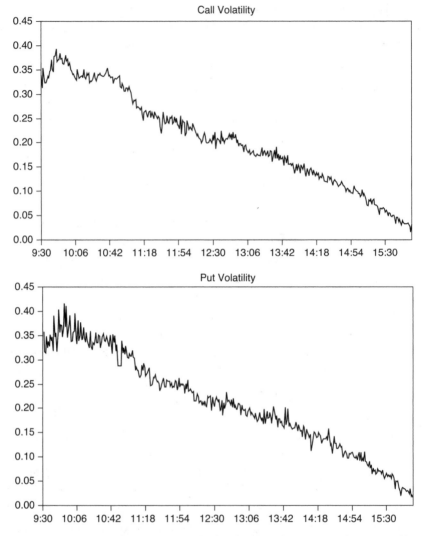

Figure 8.2 Minute-by-minute implied volatilities for $340 strike price calls and puts from Figure 8.1.

The initial rise in implied volatility during the first few minutes of trading reflected the rapid $3.60 drop in stock price. It also represented a reflation of values that were depressed before the previous day's close. One hour after the open, implied volatilities were approximately equal to their initial opening values. They began to fall just before 11:00 as the stock price climbed. When the stock stabilized near the strike price around 12:00, volatilities had already declined to 25%; approximately one-third of the value had already been lost. Waiting until this point before selling options is reasonable for conservative investors who do not want to experience excessive risk. However, many other strategies also are possible, including selling puts at the lower strike price ($330) and calls at the higher price ($340) immediately after the open when volatility is highest. In this scenario, the straddle is finally completed at the appropriate strike price as soon as the stock begins to move. Eventually the far out-of-the-money option can be closed for 5 cents. Figure 8.3 shows the minute-by-minute prices for the $340 straddle.

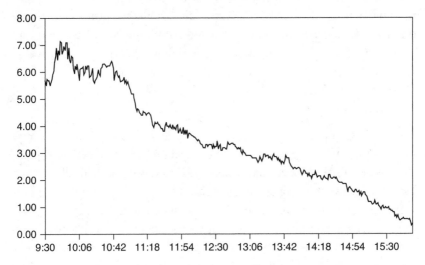

Figure 8.3   Minute-by-minute prices for the Google $340 straddle (03/17/2006).

The combined price peaked at 9:47, with the call trading for $1.35 and the put trading for $5.80. This would have been a dangerous time to enter the trade, because the stock had fallen to $335.23, and pinning behavior was not yet evident. Additionally, because the put delta was −0.74 while the call delta was only 0.28, the trade would have had a strong bullish bias. Had we pursued the second strategy, we would have sold the $330 put for $0.90 and the $340 call for $1.35 when the stock dropped at 9:47. Determining the entry point for the short $340 put depends more on risk tolerance than anything else. In the most conservative case we would have waited until the $340 strike price was reached, sold $340 puts for $2.00 to complement the short $340 call position, and left the far out-of-the-money $330 puts to decay (they were worth approximately 35 cents). Assuming that we closed the entire trade at 15:44 for 60 cents, we would have realized a profit of $3.65 ($0.90 for the $330 puts plus $3.35 for the $340 straddle minus $0.60 to close). It is important to mention that, despite a sharp rise in the underlying stock price, the $340 call price climbed to only $1.80 (delta 0.50) when the stock reached $340 at 11:36 and we sold $340 puts. The original straddle was still slightly profitable because the gain in the $340 call price was offset by a larger drop in the $330 put price.

We could also have simply waited until the stock began to exhibit pinning behavior and sold the $340 straddle. Our entry point, depending on risk tolerance, would have occurred sometime between 11:00 and 11:40. At 11:00, when the stock began rising, the straddle was worth $5.40. Between 11:36 and 11:51, as the stock was stabilizing around the $340 strike, the straddle price varied less than 20 cents between a low of $3.80 and a high of $4.00.

The universe of possible strategies is very large, and risk is limited because none of these positions will be taken home after the market closes; that is, there is absolutely no overnight exposure. However, it is critically important to stop out of losing positions without hesitation. This author always sets stop orders as soon as a position is launched, and the stops are tightened as option prices decay. Becoming overconfident and canceling a stop order is always a mistake, because the stock usually continues moving in the direction that activated the stop. Even if it returns, a superior position can usually be established by reselling the closed option for a higher price. When put and call deltas are similar, a reasonable stop for each side is equal to the current option price plus 50%.

Another excellent trade involves selling the pinned strike while purchasing in-the-money options that also expire the following day. An alternative involves a calendar spread where the same or more favorable strike is purchased with a later expiration date. The following examples contain structured trades built around these strategies. Delta neutral positions are preferable; however, the dynamics of rapid time decay and movement to the strike price can be complex to manage. Each trade is designed to benefit from an increase in the value of the long side while the short side rapidly decays. Table 8.2 illustrates three versions:

- 3:1 ratio—long current month $320 / short current month $340 calls

- 2:1 ratio—long next month $320 / short current month $340 calls

- 1:1 ratio—long next month $340 / short current month $340 calls

Each position was established at 11:00 when the stock began rising. 11:46 prices are also included because this time point represents the first crossing of the $340 strike. For simplicity we terminate all three positions at the market close.

Table 8.2   Three different strategies for trading the March 2006 Google expiration.

Time Price	Stock	Strike	Days Remaining	Price	Volatility	Delta	Contracts	Position Value
11:00	337.09	340	1.25	1.30	0.312	0.326	−30	
11:00	337.09	320	1.25	17.15	0.312	0.998	10	13,250
11:46	341.00	340	1.22	2.55	0.252	0.587	−30	
11:46	341.00	320	1.22	21.05	0.252	1.000	10	13,400
15:59	339.76	340	1.04	0.15	0.032	0.371	−30	
15:59	339.76	320	1.04	19.80	0.032	1.000	10	19,350
11:00	337.09	340	1.25	1.30	0.312	0.326	−20	
11:00	337.09	320	36.25	24.85	0.330	0.725	10	22,250
11:46	341.00	340	1.22	2.55	0.252	0.587	−20	
11:46	341.00	320	36.22	27.75	0.330	0.761	10	22,650

Table 8.2   Continued

Time Price	Stock	Strike	Days Remaining	Price	Volatility	Delta	Contracts	Position Value
15:59	339.76	340	1.04	0.15	0.032	0.371	−20	
15:59	339.76	320	36.04	26.80	0.330	0.750	10	26,500
11:00	337.09	340	1.25	1.30	0.312	0.326	−10	
11:00	337.09	340	36.25	13.35	0.330	0.506	10	12,050
11:46	341.00	340	1.22	2.55	0.252	0.587	−10	
11:46	341.00	340	36.22	15.40	0.330	0.550	10	12,850
15:59	339.76	340	1.04	0.15	0.032	0.371	−10	
15:59	339.76	340	36.04	14.70	0.330	0.536	10	14,550

The first trade is the most profitable because it is structured using a 3:1 ratio and a long option with a delta equivalent to stock. In this regard, deep in-the-money calls are superior to stock because they cost far less. To cover this trade we would have needed to purchase 1,000 shares of $337 stock for every 30 contracts sold—$337,000 per 30 short calls. Using deep in-the-money options reduced the cost of the long side to approximately $17,000.

The second trade is similar to the first, with the exception that the deep in-the-money long option expires in the next month. Maintaining delta neutrality reduces the ratio to 2:1. At expiration we would likely roll the short side forward by selling new options in the following month to create a same-month ratio. This trade provides advantages to investors who are bullish on the stock and who want to keep the long position open.

The third example is also long the following month, but at the same strike price. The ratio is reduced to 1:1 because long and short deltas are nearly the same at the start. Although this trade is nearly half the cost of the second, the profit is similar. As in the previous case, rolling the short side forward and creating a new trade in the next month will allow us to keep the position open if the view is bullish.

The first trade generated a 46% profit, the second 19%, and the third 21%. The first trade is most likely to fit the needs of day traders who have no desire to remain long or risk overnight exposure. Both sides should be closed by the end of the day. However, if the trade is left open after the market closes, the broker will automatically exercise the long side by calling the stock, while the short side expires worthless. That path is less efficient because the exercise involves additional trading costs. It is also riskier because the stock can move in the after and before market sessions that precede the open on Monday. Furthermore, a significant after-market news event or move of the stock could result in the short side being exercised. Although rare, such events have the potential to generate significant losses. The second and third scenarios allow the trader to focus on closing the short side because the long options can be kept open until the next expiration. The third trade has one special characteristic—it does not have a collateral requirement. Recall that owning the same or better strike price with a more distant expiration removes the collateral requirement normally associated with the short side of the trade. (None of the contracts are naked because both sides are comprised of the same number of contracts).

Pinning behavior is often prevented by a sudden large movement of the stock on the day that precedes expiration. Such was the case in the month that followed the preceding example. On April 20, Google announced earnings after the close, and the price rose sharply. The next day—expiration Friday—the stock opened nearly $34 higher at $448.90. The pinning effect failed during this trading session as the stock climbed past the $450 strike price, fell away, crossed the $440 strike, and ultimately closed at $437.10. The large upward earnings-related spike moved the stock into a new trading range where open interest was relatively small. Before the spike, investors were structuring positions using the $410 and $420 strikes; after earnings, on the final trading day of the expiration cycle, the key strikes were $440 and $450. It is not surprising that the pinning effect failed to materialize. Additionally, the move was considered an overreaction—over the following six days the stock price declined to $398.90. Figure 8.4 displays minute-by-minute trading prices for the stock on expiration Friday.

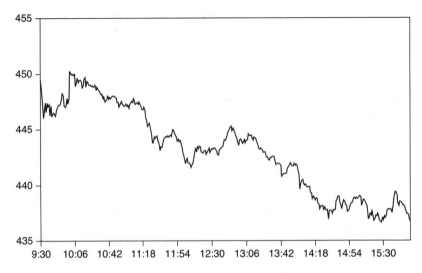

Figure 8.4 Google April 2006 expiration Friday—minute-by-minute prices.

The key events were as follows:

- 9:30: Stock opens at $448.90, up $34
- 10:02: Stock crosses $450 strike
- 10:37: Price falls below opening price
- 14:08: Stock crosses $440 strike
- 16:00: Stock closes $3.00 in-the-money on put side of $440 strike

It was clear that pinning to the $450 strike had failed at 10:02 when the stock fell below the opening price and continued heading toward the $440 strike. At this point, however, it would not have made sense to structure any trade around the $440 strike price that included short options, because there was no evidence that the price decline would end. The most logical choice was a simple long $440 put position. At 10:02, when the stock began to gravitate toward the lower strike, $440 puts were trading for $0.65. Just before the close they traded for $4.00—a 600% return.

As we have seen, expiration day provides some of the very best trading opportunities. The dynamics are complex, and sophisticated modeling tools provide an important advantage. The days that lead up to expiration also provide advantages to traders who want to focus on time-related volatility distortions.

The Days Preceding Expiration

Time decay is the overriding dynamic that characterizes the final days before expiration. As we have seen, the percentage of value that an option loses each day dramatically accelerates as expiration approaches. Because the options market is open for 6.5 hours each day and closed for 17.5 hours, the percentage of value lost each evening while the market is closed rapidly becomes a driving force that underlies option pricing.

Figure 8.5 displays the percentage of value lost each day while the market is open (the gray bar) and while the market is closed (the black bar) for the final five trading days leading up to expiration Friday. The chart begins on the Friday preceding the final weekend before expiration.

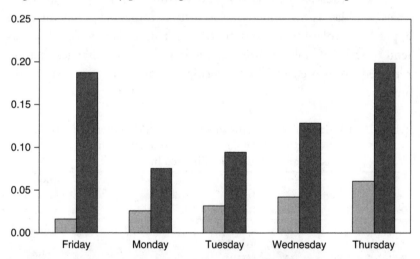

Figure 8.5   Percentage of value lost for an at-the-money straddle during the final six days before expiration. In each pair, the gray bar represents the percentage of value lost during trading hours, and the black bar represents the percentage lost between the market close and the next open. X-axis labels begin with the Friday that precedes expiration week. Expiration Friday is not shown because 100% of the remaining value decays during trading hours.

The data reveals that the time decay associated with the final weekend (the first set of bars) rivals the overnight loss of the penultimate trading day (the last set of bars). Each exceeds 19% of the total option value for at-the-money puts and calls. Expiration Friday would have distorted the chart with a gray bar equal to 100% and no black bar.

One might be tempted to sell a straddle near the close on Friday with eight days left before Saturday expiration. Paying strict attention to the theta component of standard pricing calculations would lead to the anticipation of a 19% price decline over the weekend, followed by a significant amount of decay during each of the remaining five days: Monday—10%, Tuesday—13%, Wednesday—17%, Thursday—26%, Friday—100%. Not surprisingly, the market also anticipates these price distortions and responds with a combination of implied volatility swings and widely varying bid-ask spreads. Buyers respond to escalating overnight time decay by lowering their bids, while sellers fight to keep prices high enough to compensate for overnight event exposure. Bid-ask spreads tend to narrow and volatility tends to rise after the open each day as the underlying security becomes active. As the close approaches, volatility and bid prices both tend to fall, while ask prices tend to stabilize. Table 8.3 reveals the large volatility changes that are required to protect against overnight time decay as expiration approaches.

Table 8.3 Closing volatility adjustments required to protect against overnight time decay for an at-the-money straddle. Adjusted volatilities are highlighted in gray.

Date	Security Price	Strike	Days Remaining	Straddle Price	Volatility	Theta	Position Value (10 Contract)
Fri 09:30	400	400	8.31	19.26	0.40	–0.55	19,260
Fri 16:00	400	400	8.04	15.40	0.33	–0.46	15,400
Mon 09:30	400	400	5.31	15.40	0.40	–0.70	15,400
Mon 16:00	400	400	5.04	13.87	0.37	–0.66	13,870

Date	Security Price	Strike	Days Remaining	Straddle Price	Volatility	Theta	Position Value (10 Contract)
Tues 09:30	400	400	4.31	13.87	0.40	−0.78	13,870
Tues 16:00	400	400	4.04	12.16	0.36	−0.73	12,160
Weds 09:30	400	400	3.31	12.16	0.40	−0.89	12,160
Weds 16:00	400	400	3.04	10.16	0.35	−0.81	10,160
Thurs 09:30	400	400	2.31	10.16	0.40	−1.07	10,160
Thurs 16:00	400	400	2.04	7.73	0.32	−0.91	7,730
Fri 09:30	400	400	1.31	7.73	0.40	−1.43	7,730
Fri 16:00	400	400	1.04	0.18	0.01	−0.02	180

This table is designed to parallel Figure 8.5. For clarity, we measure the value of an at-the-money straddle with the price frozen at $400 and implied volatility of 40%. Each day at the market close, implied volatility is adjusted so that the closing price reflects overnight (or weekend) time decay. As a result, each closing price is identical to the next trading day's opening price. In other words, the straddle does not suffer the effects of theta while the market is closed. Adjusting for the initial weekend's time decay requires that implied volatility be reduced from 40% to 33%. As shown in Figure 8.5, the distortion associated with the final weekend is as large as that of the final evening before expiration Friday. During expiration week, as the percentage of value lost each evening increases, the magnitude of the volatility offset grows. In our example, the magnitude of a 100% offset grows from 3% at the close on Monday to 8% on Thursday. The rightmost column in the table displays the value of a 10 contract straddle for each day and time. It is important to emphasize that market prices normally embody some level of compromise in the sense that each day's closing price represents a blend of anticipated overnight time decay and the risk of an unforeseen event. As a result, option prices tend to fall slightly at the close and rise slightly at the open.

A successful expiration week trading strategy should comprehend the effects of accelerated time decay and potential swings in implied volatility. There are many plausible strategies. One obvious choice involves selling a straddle or strangle just after the open on Friday before the final weekend (the first line of Table 8.3). It is often possible to close this trade the same day for a profit. An investor might also choose to capitalize on the accelerating time decay of the final week by keeping the position open through the weekend. It is important to calculate and track option prices to determine the level of pricing efficiency and make trading decisions. For example, if you had reason to believe that a stock might be affected by overnight news, and it was determined that most or all of the overnight time decay had been discounted, a long straddle would be an excellent choice. The goal would be to close the trade the next morning on rising volatility and a move of the underlying.

As we have seen, expiration week pricing is affected by many factors, the most prominent being the interplay between event risk and accelerating time decay. These dynamics can be used to help select entry and exit points for long and short positions. Various authors have commented that long positions benefit from long expiration time frames and short positions the reverse. Generally speaking, market pricing mechanisms are too efficient to allow such an obvious statistical arbitrage to persist. It is for these reasons that we have chosen to focus on more subtle distortions that are inescapable characteristics of option pricing models. Well understood and carefully tracked, these characteristics can form the basis of a successful expiration week trading strategy.

Summary

Expiration week is characterized by a variety of price distortions that are caused by accelerating time decay and swings in implied volatility. These effects are so pronounced that the Chicago Board Options

Exchange shifts its VIX calculation forward by one month each time the final eight days of an expiration cycle are reached.[3] The final day represents the largest opportunity, because at-the-money and out-of-the-money options must lose all their remaining value before the end of the regular trading session.

On expiration Friday many stocks experience an effect known as "pinning." The effect is driven by a variety of forces, including the unwinding of large hedged positions that involve both stock and options. Large open interest, high levels of liquidity, proximity to a strike price, and relatively stable behavior in the days leading up to expiration are all contributing factors. It is possible to structure trades that take advantage of the combined effects of pinning and rapid volatility collapse on expiration day. Such positions often generate very large returns with only brief market exposure.

Significant tradeable distortions begin to appear on the Friday that precedes expiration week. This weekend is very significant because 34% of the time remaining before expiration elapses between the close on Friday and the open on Monday. Option buyers respond by reducing their bids to compensate for weekend time decay, while sellers try to stabilize asking prices to protect against unforeseen events that can occur while the market is closed. As you might expect, bid-ask spreads tend to widen in response to these dynamics. Additionally, the percentage of value lost to overnight time decay rises sharply during the final few days before expiration, with Thursday's loss being larger than the previous weekend.

Finally, closing prices tend to blend the effects of overnight time decay and event-related risks. A detailed understanding of these effects in combination with careful tracking of implied volatilities is essential to successful trading during expiration week. The goal is to capitalize on distortions that result from the interplay between market schedules and the time decay of option contracts.

Further Reading

Avellaneda, M. and M. Lipkin, "A market induced mechanism for stock pinning," *Quantitative Finance*, vol 3 (Sept. 2003), 417–425.

Daniels, M. G., J. D. Farmer, L. Gillemot, G. Iori, and E. Smith, "Quantitative model of price diffusion and market friction based on trading as a mechanistic random process," *Physical Review Letters*, vol 90, no 10 (Mar. 2003), 108102(1–4).

Frey, R. and A. Stremme (1997), "Market Volatility and Feedback Effects from Dynamic Hedging," *Mathematical Finance*, vol 7, no 4 (Oct. 1997), 351–374.

Jeannin, M., G. Iori, and D. Samuel, "Modeling Stock Pinning," City University of London Department of Economics, Discussion Paper Series No. 06/04, May 30, 2006 (www.city.ac.uk/economics/dps/discussion_papers/0604.pdf).

Krishnan, H. and I. Nelken, "The effect of stock pinning upon option prices," *RISK* (Dec. 2001), S17–S20.

Endnotes

[1] Ni, S. X., N. D. Pearson, and A. M. Poteshmana, "Stock Price Clustering on Option Expiration Dates," Journal of Financial Economics, vol 78, no 1 (May 2005), 49–87.

[2] The 70-year-old uptick rule which restricted selling in a declining market was rescinded by the SEC effective July 6, 2007.

[3] Chicago Board Options Exchange, "The New CBOE Volatility Index—VIX," technical white paper appearing on the CBOE website, 09/18/2003.

9

BUILDING A TOOLSET

The investment community has developed thousands of trading systems. The best are proprietary and generally not available to the investing public. Many have proven themselves by generating excellent profits across a broad range of conditions that sometimes persist for extended periods of time. However, markets are complex, and conditions change. The past 20 years have seen periods of high and low inflation, rising and falling market volatility, normal and inverted yield curves, rapidly rising and falling oil prices, commodity shortages, currency devaluations, and a dramatic increase in worldwide liquidity. Despite claims to the contrary, no trading system can perform well across such widely varying conditions. Although favorable circumstances can persist for extended periods of time, all systems eventually fail.

An investor who expects to consistently outperform the market over extended periods of time must have a technical edge that does not depend on trading triggers that are linked to specific market conditions. A software infrastructure that includes data mining and visualization tools for studying the price change behavior of individual securities can provide such an edge. The design should focus on tools for identifying subtle distortions and statistical arbitrages that are not immediately apparent to the market. It should also be extensible and include facilities for incorporating a variety of external data sources.

Many private investors believe that they can gain an advantage by using commercially available tools to discover unique combinations of indicators that can be used as trade triggers. They often spend many months analyzing charts to fine-tune the parameters for their indicators and establish trading rules. Although such tools are undeniably important, it is unlikely that a freely available off-the-shelf software package can become the core component of a system that consistently beats the market over extended periods of time. The most effective approach builds on commercially available charting and data analysis tools with customized software that can be used to mine large datasets for answers to complex questions. The ultimate goal is to have the power and flexibility to develop trading strategies that can be modified or replaced as needed.

The infrastructure we are discussing contains two distinct classes of tools. The first includes commercially available charting and data analysis software of the sort just mentioned. In recent years online brokers and data vendors have created packages of these tools as differentiators of their services. Typical components include the following:

- Real-time charting software and data feeds that contain prices for various securities and related derivatives

- A package of indicators with appropriate back testing facilities

- Access to newswires, with a system of filters and alerts

- Customizable option pricing screens that include the Greeks

- Methods for setting triggers and alerts

Many of the packages also include a macro language that can be used for automated strategy testing. Generally speaking, these are the tools that an option trader uses throughout the trading day.

The second class of tools, which includes data infrastructure and management software, is the focus of this chapter. An investor uses these tools to analyze historical data and plan new trades. First and foremost are facilities for downloading and managing large amounts of historical pricing data. Because the quality of this data is critical to your success, it is important that the system include data cleansing programs that can flag anomalies. The toolset's analytical components should include software for data mining and visualization, statistical analysis, and position modeling. Each of these categories is both broad and complex. Recognizing that these tools are a key success factor has motivated investment banks and hedge funds to maintain large technical teams who continually test new approaches and develop new software.

The trend has become dramatic. Between 2000 and 2006, algorithmic trading in U.S. equities grew from 5% to 27% of the total volume.[1] During the same time frame, Banc of America Securities slashed its trader population by almost half while increasing its equity trading volume by 160%. Today, the majority of its trades are generated algorithmically.[2] Wall Street has evolved into a large, sophisticated software developer, and it is the quality of this software that separates winners from losers.

The goal of this chapter is to establish a set of guidelines that both private and institutional investors can use to develop a software infrastructure for option trading.

Some Notes on Data Visualization Tools

Data visualization tools display large amounts of quantitative data in a readily comprehensible form. Throughout this book we have referred to charts that depict underlying price changes in terms of standard deviation measured against a moving volatility window. These charts are helpful because they normalize price changes in a way that facilitates the direct comparison of many securities. They also provide a consolidated view that can span time frames as short as a few minutes or as long as several decades.

One of the advantages of a flexible data infrastructure is that you can easily create new display modes that efficiently summarize large amounts of information. The price spike charts you have seen represent one of many visualization strategies used by the author. We can, for example, transform this data to create a more visually appealing chart that highlights volatility changes. Such a chart can be used to quickly evaluate securities for different types of option trades.

Figures 9.1 and 9.2 display transformed price change data for two different types of stocks. The first is a poorly behaved stock in which price spike frequency and size fit poorly with the normal distribution. The second is a well-behaved stock.

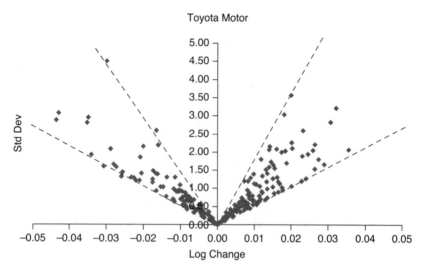

Figure 9.1   Log of the price change versus standard deviations for Toyota
Motor—a poorly-behaved stock. Each point measures the log of
a daily price change in terms of standard deviations based on
the most recent 20-day volatility window.

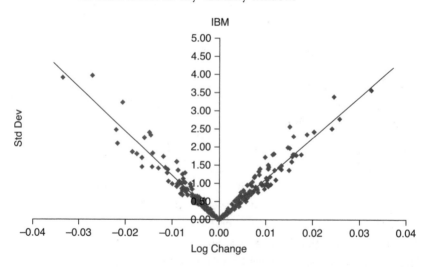

Figure 9.2   Log of the price change versus standard deviations for IBM—a
well-behaved stock. Each point measures the log of a daily price
change in terms of standard deviations based on the most
recent 20-day volatility window.

In both figures, the log of each daily price change (x-axis) is plotted against the number of standard deviations represented by that change (y-axis). The dashed lines in Figure 9.1 reveal the variability of this measure when historical volatility spans a broad range. The distribution of points is scattered because active and calm periods alternate to drive volatility swings. As a result, the number of standard deviations that corresponds to a change of a particular magnitude varies widely over time. Conversely, stocks that exhibit few large spikes and slowly varying volatility have daily price change profiles that are tightly clustered around a straight line. Such behavior is evident in Figure 9.2. The ratio between the size of a price change and the number of standard deviations represented by that change remains relatively constant across a broad range from 0 to 4 standard deviations. Large spikes fall near the line because they do not occur with enough frequency to distort the distribution.

Highly volatile stocks can be well-behaved, and stocks with low volatility can be poorly-behaved. At the time of this writing, options on both IBM and Toyota Motor traded with 20% implied volatility. It is often the case that options on stocks exhibiting the profile evident in Figure 9.1 exhibit unusually wide bid-ask spreads. This discrepancy represents individual traders' fears that they are either overpaying or undercompensated for risk. Options on stocks that we have been referring to as "well-behaved" tend to have narrow bid-ask spreads and relatively large open interest. Their smooth price change behavior allows traders to agree more closely on risk.

The software infrastructure described in the following sections is designed to facilitate the rapid generation of useful data and charts. Figures 9.1 and 9.2 are typical examples. It is easy to see that you can rapidly scan a large number of such charts for stocks that are candidates for particular types of trades. It is also possible to automate the screening process using custom filters that sort stocks according to the variability of their price change behavior. The author's personal design automates the generation of hundreds of charts using different length volatility windows, multiple day composite data points, and varying date ranges.

Database Infrastructure Overview

A database infrastructure for option trading must be designed so that new statistical analysis and data-mining programs can be added with minimal modifications to the original structure. The information presented in this chapter is based on the design currently implemented by the author, but many designs are possible. The following core components are likely to fit any implementation:

- Download facility with associated data cleansing programs

- Calendar integrity database with decimal/system/calendar date conversion

- Data import facility

- Data export facility

- Parameter tables that store settings for data-mining and statistical programs

- Templates for output tables

- Backup facility

The download facility is particularly important because it feeds the remainder of the system. All data feeds are subject to errors, so it is particularly important to screen every record for anomalies. It is not uncommon, for example, for a price or volume number to be corrupted. Some errors can be surprisingly subtle. The most common errors of this type are associated with stock splits or merger and acquisition activity. If we assume a download of 500 days of price history for 5,000 stocks (2.5 million stock days), and each record contains open, high, low, close, and volume information, we need to check the integrity of 12.5 million pieces of information. We must also check the date sequence to ensure that the records are contiguous. Alignment with nontrading dates should also be checked. Any missed dates that do not correspond to a market holiday or weekend must be dealt with separately. (In very rare circumstances, trading may have been halted due to an order imbalance.) One solution to the corrupt or blank record problem is to insert a duplicate entry as a placeholder.

The calendar integrity database supports a variety of date arithmetic calculations. It also facilitates free exchange of dates between the database and the operating system. It is important that any database used for option trading provide the capability to add and subtract date and time information, because option prices normally are calculated using the number of seconds until expiration. The database's date structure must facilitate information exchange with the underlying operating system and associated programs. Microsoft systems store dates as sequential numbers that are referred to as serial numbers. By default, January 1, 1900 is serial number 1. Counting forward yields the serial number 40148 for December 1, 2009. Decimal fractions are added to count time as a portion of a day. December 1, 2009 at 1:00 p.m. is 40148.5417.

Accurate decimal dates also allow the construction of proportionally correct stock price charts. Most stock charts are distorted by weekends and holidays because they incorrectly portray the data points as being equally spaced. Proportionally correct stock charts can be created using hybrid dates that have a recognizable year followed by a precisely correct decimal portion of a year. Dates that are formatted this way can be instantly converted to system dates for any operating environment. The hybrid date format for December 1, 2009 is 2009.9169. Because date conversion calculations can be time-consuming when millions of records are being processed, it makes sense to generate a single reference table containing all appropriate dates in the formats that are needed. The table used by this author includes the operating system date, data source date, weekday, day of year, hybrid decimal date, and a notation indicating the number of days remaining before options expiration for each record. The table is built around a 25-year calendar beginning in 1985 and ending in 2010. Virtually every program in the system references this table; modeling tools extend the dates with time information so that seconds until expiration can be calculated when needed. As you saw in Chapter 8, "Trading the Expiration Cycle," precise time-of-day information becomes important in the final days and hours before expiration.

Finally, calendar information is used by many statistical programs that correlate specific types of price change behavior with the date. A simple example is a program that measures the correlation between the number of days remaining before expiration and the average price spike size. An even simpler example is the correlation between the magnitude of each price change and the day of the week. The possibilities are essentially limitless, but each depends on having a software facility for managing date information.

Parameter tables serve an important function, because they facilitate the creation of automated work flows. Sophisticated systems are most efficient when they are composed of a large number of small modules, each having a very specific function. Assembled in various configurations, the modules can be used to create highly functional work flows. If the various modules each access a parameter table, execution can be automated, and the need for user input is eliminated. The parameter table is extended with new fields to accommodate modules that are added to the system.

Figure 9.3 shows the basic components of a working database system that can be used to generate price change history for a large number of stocks. The work flow is a reflection of the table structure outlined in the figure. It begins with a selective download containing historical pricing data for a particular class of optionable stocks and proceeds as follows: Each record is checked for integrity; a variety of calculations are executed to format and extend the contents of the dataset with basic numerical relationships and date information; new tables are created that contain detailed volatility and price change data; summary tables are populated with statistical information; and finally, key results are exported for use with other programs.

The database structure outlined in the figure is only a small portion of a much larger design that includes a variety of analytical and trading tools. Furthermore, each of the three facilities mentioned at the bottom of the figure—statistical analysis, trade modeling, and data mining— has its own complex infrastructure of tables and programs. The data-mining facility is particularly complex, and new capabilities are added on a regular basis. Not surprisingly, the capabilities conferred by a complex set of data-mining tools have the greatest potential as a differentiator, because they can be used to discover complex relationships between securities. The tools can also be used to discover correlations that exist between particular types of economic news and market behavior. In the options world these correlations extend to changes in implied volatility and, on a broad scale, to the closely watched VIX.

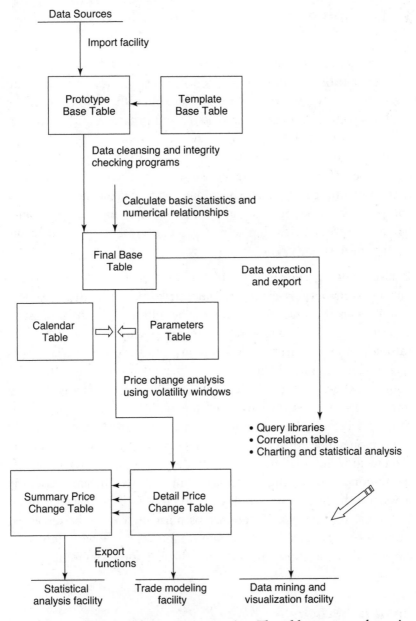

Figure 9.3 Database infrastructure overview. The table structure shown in the figure is designed to facilitate various analytical methods, including historical price change analysis.

Data Mining

Well-constructed data-mining experiments have the potential to reveal subtle relationships that are unknown to the market. Some take the form of statistically significant links between securities, and others are more abstract. Among the most important but difficult to quantify are the links between economic news items and price change behavior of specific equities. This type of analysis depends on a variety of sophisticated algorithms that can extract and classify events from textual data, such as news feeds. One of the more difficult underlying tasks involves decorating time series data with various events to create heterogeneous composite information. This heterogeneous data must then be analyzed to discover price change patterns that are not apparent in the absence of the events.

Data-mining experiments were used to discover stocks that exhibit the link between options expiration and strike price pinning that was described in the preceding chapter. The author has also used such experiments to study effects related to end-of-month, end-of-quarter, earnings announcements, long weekends, and various financial events such as interest rate changes. Many different pieces of relevant economic news are also released each week. Each represents a potentially important event that can drive both the market and individual stocks. Examples include, but are not limited to, employment data, supply chain money flow, business inventories and spending, gross domestic product growth, inflation data, and trade imbalances. Different securities respond to each of these items in different ways. In some cases the news and the market's reaction combine to affect the behavior of an individual security. Such relationships normally cannot be discerned without context-sensitive data-mining tools. The following functions are central to a software infrastructure that supports data mining.

Event Extraction

Events must be extracted and classified from textual data such as news feeds. One of the most difficult technical challenges involves building a data dictionary that can be used to extract specific categories from semistructured data. For example, the category "missed earnings" might not be apparent in the statement "Analysts were disappointed today when XYZ Corporation reported earnings that were 2 cents below expectation." Other categories are more obvious in their original context: "Oil prices rose 2% today"; "The chairman of XYZ stepped down"; "Consumer confidence set a new record." Each of these statements includes words that can be classified and stored in a data dictionary.

Context Discovery

Traditional technical analysis is context-free; the market is not. For example, if consumer confidence were to rise unexpectedly, the market might be expected to react positively. However, in an inflationary environment where monetary tightening is having a negative effect on the market, high levels of consumer confidence might be considered to be negative news. Context discovery is complex and requires the development of software for parsing and semantically analyzing phrases. Many examples of such software exist in the bioinformatics and medical informatics world, where researchers routinely search large text databases.

Time Series Correlation

It is important to capture price changes in the form of a time series and to measure the effects of specific events as distortions in the series. One strategy is to sort a repeating time series into two groups—one that contains a potentially distorting event for each series, and one that does not. Neural network and pattern discovery software can be used to create weighting functions that can distinguish between the two groups. In this regard, it is important that the key event be consistently aligned in each time series.

Figure 9.4 displays the results of a comparative data-mining experiment. The goal was to identify triggers for entering and exiting option positions on the Philadelphia Gold/Silver Index (ticker: XAU) and corresponding positions in gold through investments in the streetTRACKS Gold Trust (ticker: GLD)—an exchange-traded fund that tracks the price of gold. The chart compares the value of XAU to the GLD/XAU ratio. Certain time frames are characterized by a well-defined relationship in which the GLD/XAU ratio has a specific value for any particular value of the index (upper chart). Other time frames do not support a trend (lower chart).

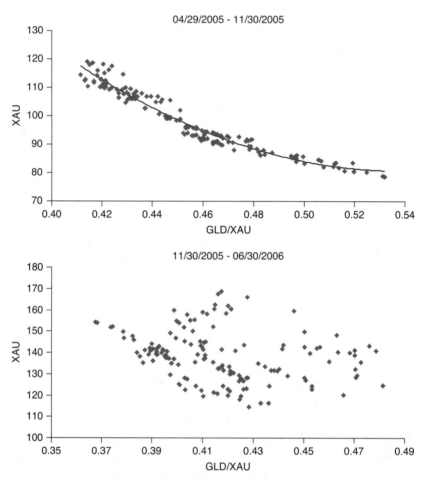

Figure 9.4   The relationship between XAU and the GLD/XAU ratio for two
different time frames. The upper chart reflects a seven-month
time frame that was characterized by a well-defined relationship
between GLD and XAU (a precise GLD/XAU ratio for each
value of XAU). The relationship disappeared over the next
seven-month time frame, as shown in the lower chart.

During the time frame of the upper chart, intraday entry points for option trades could be identified as subtle deviations from the trend line. Variations were sometimes large enough to be considered statistical arbitrages, with points above the line representing high gold/low XAU and points below the line representing low gold/high XAU. The two time frames were also characterized by different market conditions. The upper chart represents a time when oil prices were somewhat stable, as were the U.S. dollar and gold, which rose from $434 to $491. During the time frame of the lower chart, gold rose at a much faster rate ($491 to $612), and oil climbed nearly 40%.

This example is not unique, because data-mining experiments tend to have a strong statistical component. However, unlike simple statistical analyses, data-mining experiments can involve open-ended searches for new correlations. In this example we discovered both the existence of a correlation and the time frame for which it was valid. Using variable-length sliding windows and refining the analysis allows the construction of a library containing many time series with valid correlations. Library entries can then be compared with news events and market data to discover the most favorable conditions. Eventually a set of favorable conditions can be assembled and tested against future occurrences.

An active data-mining program is important because links and relationships between the behavior of equities, commodities, and other tradeable assets tend to form and dissolve rapidly. You have just seen that a tightly coherent link between the price change behavior of gold and gold stocks can rapidly disappear. The reverse occurred during February 2007, when many commodities, stocks, and other securities began to behave in a coherent fashion. Figure 9.5 reveals the relationships that existed between the performance of the overall equities market, gold, and the Japanese yen between late February and mid-March 2007. The upper chart reveals daily closing prices for Standard & Poor's (S&P) Depositary Receipts (SPDRs) (ticker: SPY) and streetTRACKS Gold (ticker: GLD). The lower chart tracks closing prices for the CurrencyShares Japanese Yen Trust (ticker: FXY).[3]

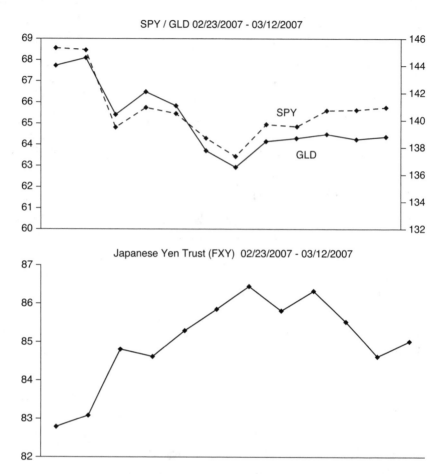

Figure 9.5   The relationship between the S&P 500, gold, and the Japanese
yen between late February and mid-March 2007. The upper
chart contains closing prices for Standard & Poor's Depositary
Receipts (SPY) and streetTRACKS Gold Trust (GLD). The lower
chart reveals price changes for the CurrencyShares Japanese Yen
Trust (FXY) during the same time frame.

This time frame was very important because it was characterized by a
very large 5.5% market drawdown that began on February 27 and continued through March 5. High levels of market volatility persisted
through March 14, when a new rally began and prices rose above their
pre-2/27 levels. Market drawdowns are most likely when behavior
becomes coherent across a number of asset classes and overall volatility

is low. In this case partial unwinding of the yen carry trade was the culprit. Investors around the world for many years had been borrowing yen at very low interest rates—effectively shorting the weak Japanese currency—and investing in other asset classes. On February 27, a 2% rally of the yen caused these investors to close positions in gold, oil, and stocks and repay loans denominated in yen. With each strengthening tick of the yen, other markets fell. When the Japanese currency finally weakened, the carry trade returned, and markets stabilized.

During this time frame many gold investors were surprised to see the precious metal lose its "safe haven" status. Most had invested in gold because they expected it to serve as a hedge against the possibility of a significant market drawdown. Worse still, because they were unable to discover the statistical correlations between the yen and other markets, they were unsure how to react. Some kept their long gold positions open, assuming that the initial sell-off represented a single wave of profit-taking because gold had rallied 8.4% in just over four months.

For an option trader, the realization that gold and equities were moving in a coherent fashion, with the yen moving in the opposite direction, represented a significant trading opportunity. Properly structured trades during this time frame could realize the advantages of a statistical arbitrage between implied volatilities of options on the S&P 500 and gold futures. Combined with the statistical knowledge accumulated from data-mining experiments, these trades had the potential to deliver significant profits. Monitoring price coherence would have allowed an investor to identify an exit point when the correlation was no longer valid.

In the options trading world, identifying a set of conditions that are tightly linked to a volatility trend or a correlation between the price changes of different tradeable assets can be critically important. As the experiment's sophistication increases, the likelihood that the market will discover the trend or relationship decreases. This inverse relationship is very important, because most interpretations of financial news provided by market analysts are relatively primitive. Data-mining tools allow an investor to leapfrog those interpretations by discovering subtle correlations that are much more predictive.

Statistical Analysis Facility

The option pricing methodologies we reviewed in Chapter 2, "Fundamentals of Option Pricing," were designed to statistically approximate the behavior of a stock or index. Recognizing the limitations of these models has driven institutional investors to pursue more sophisticated approaches. The goal is always to use improvements in statistical accuracy to spot mispriced option contracts. In this regard, it is important to have a software infrastructure and processes for analyzing and summarizing historical price change information.

Statistical inference can be applied on a broad basis to understand market dynamics or at the level of individual securities. Sometimes the two views can be combined to gain an edge. For example, the overall stock market varies slightly with regard to the size of a typical price change that is experienced for each trading day of the week. Surprisingly, Monday's close tends to embody a smaller spike than each of the other days despite the 72-hour gap from the previous close on Friday. Some stocks, however, exhibit their largest price spikes on Monday because they are affected by worldwide events that transpire while the U.S. equity markets are closed. It is sometimes possible to spot subtle distortions in the implied volatilities of options on such stocks. Figure 9.6 shows average daily price change data for the S&P 500 tabulated over 1,000 trading days.

With the appropriate infrastructure of databases and software in place, you can build a library of such charts. You can tabulate price change magnitudes by day, week, month, quarter, and any other time frame that makes sense. Securities can be grouped according to a variety of criteria—industry group, trading price, historical volatility, trading volume, market capitalization, short interest. A flexible design should store computed datasets that can be accessed through a query tool. This sort of efficient design lets you assemble virtually any summary chart with minimal effort.

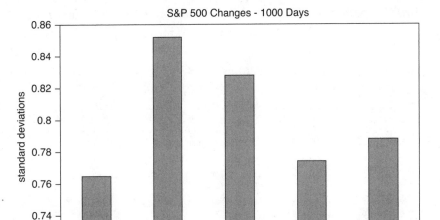

Figure 9.6   Average price spike by day for the S&P 500. Changes are measured in standard deviations against a 20-day sliding volatility
window and are tabulated across 1,000 trading days.

You can expand the scope of your library to include a wide variety of
statistical parameters. For each stock, index, or commodity, the library
should contain a summary of the number of price changes in various
size categories measured against different-length volatility windows. The
library should also include summary price change data for different
time frames, such as the number of 2, 3, and 4 standard deviation spikes
spanning three trading days. To facilitate price change calculations that
span multiple days, a new base table is constructed that contains a single
composite entry for each set of days. For example, to analyze three-day
composites, each entry will contain the opening price on day 1, the closing price on day 3, and high/low values spanning all three days. A 20-day
sliding window will contain 20 composites (60 trading days). The annualization factor for volatility calculations is adjusted appropriately to
reflect 84 time frames per year rather than the normal 252. (Note that
sqrt(84) = 9.165.) Using very large composites becomes problematic
because a statistically significant number of entries would span an
extended period of time and, therefore, different market environments.
The practical limit for most purposes is three days.

The ultimate goal of this work is to create a set of filters that can be used to identify candidates for specific trading strategies. The first step is to define a simple work flow that describes the construction of a library. Figure 9.7 shows a sample work flow that utilizes our original infrastructure diagram.

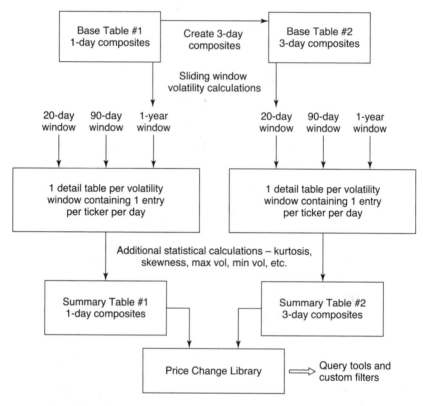

Figure 9.7   Basic work flow for price change library construction. The example creates summary data for single-day and three-day composite entries.

The price change library is part of a larger database infrastructure that contains links to news items and financial metrics. It is updated each day after market close by repeating the computational work flow with new data. Table 9.1 is a sample extract of the 04/16/2007 library.

Table 9.1 04/16/2007 price change library extract for four securities.

	IBM	ISRG	SPY	GLD
Count (days)	300	300	300	300
Last close ($)	96.18	125.49	146.70	68.40
1 standard deviation ($)	0.64	1.46	0.83	0.45
Final spike (StdDev)	2.17	0.51	1.62	1.24
Skewness	−0.15	1.11	−0.74	−0.79
Kurtosis	1.33	12.02	4.69	2.48
Series volatility	0.14	0.47	0.11	0.23
90-day volatility	0.15	0.37	0.12	0.17
20-day volatility	0.11	0.18	0.09	0.10
Intraday volatility	0.12	0.29	0.12	0.10
High volatility	0.19	0.87	0.21	0.19
Low volatility	0.09	0.17	0.06	0.09
Spikes > 1 StdDev	88	75	88	81
Spikes > 2 StdDev	20	22	17	23
Spikes > 3 StdDev	6	7	5	5
Spikes > 4 StdDev	1	4	1	0
Spikes > 5 StdDev	0	3	1	0
3-day composites (100)				
Spikes > 1 StdDev	30	22	31	31
Spikes > 2 StdDev	6	5	5	7
Spikes > 3 StdDev	2	3	2	1
Spikes > 4 StdDev	0	2	1	0
Spikes > 5 StdDev	0	1	1	0

The table spans 300 individual trading days (100 × three-day composites). This length was selected to be long enough to support the statistical significance of calculations surrounding the three-day composite dataset. Longer time frames, as previously mentioned, can distort results for securities that have undergone significant adjustments to their price change behavior. As protection against this phenomenon, the complete library also contains information about long-term volatility trends for each ticker. Some of the values reflect a final calculation for the time frame. Included in this category are the final spike, 20-day, 90-day, and intraday volatilities, and the value of a 1 standard deviation price change. "Series volatility" refers to a single calculation spanning the entire time frame.

For purposes of brevity, this table is somewhat abbreviated; library entries are actually more complex than depicted. The complete data structure has a finer level of granularity with regard to price spike size; two-day composites normally are included, along with calculations that reveal ratios between one-, two-, and three-day statistics. Additional volatility windows are calculated for each composite. The complete structure also includes correlation coefficients that measure the relatedness of various groups of securities as well as the fit between individual securities and other members of the same group. A complete entry, therefore, is significantly larger than the example shown in Table 9.1. It is also important to note that a comprehensive library should contain many summary tables spanning different time frames and terminating on different dates.

As soon as the library is complete, customized query tools and statistical filters are used to build lists of trading candidates. Each candidate is further analyzed using price change data from the detail database in addition to standard charting tools. Although a detailed description of various filters and their links to specific trading strategies is beyond the scope of this book, the flexibility implied by such a system is evident in the complexity of the infrastructure. One of the advantages of such a system is the ability to build a profile based on a high or low frequency of price spikes in a specific size range. Incorporating a fine level of granularity into the screening criteria is important, because it allows an investor to derive different profiles that are diagnostic of different types of behavior. For example, stocks that exhibit a small number of very large spikes clustered around news events can be distinguished from those that have a large number of randomly occurring moderately sized spikes. Simple statistical methods, volatility assessments, and most charting techniques would not reveal the same differences.

This level of granularity is achieved by using a combination of volatility windows of varying lengths, different length composites (one-day, two-day, three-day), and screening criteria that exclude certain size price changes. It is also important to combine this information with other statistical and fundamental parameters. Overall, the best approaches involve screening against a set of statistical and fundamental criteria that include, but are not limited to, the following:

- Magnitude and distribution of price changes (with the variations just described)
- Volatility trends
- Basic statistical parameters such as kurtosis and skewness
- Correlation thresholds with financial news and market trends
- Short interest
- Trading volumes
- PE ratios
- Repeating chart patterns

A library of statistical summary tables can be a valuable resource. However, the power depends on the quality of the tools that are used to search and analyze the data. This author has found tremendous value in a toolset that includes pattern discovery and other artificial intelligence software. A general approach involves creating lists of library entries that meet certain trading criteria and using discovery algorithms to select the most significant data items. These data items then become the focus of development for statistical filters. Basic neural network programs have proven invaluable for these efforts. More-complex unbounded pattern discovery programs have been used to discover repeating but subtle chart patterns. The power of the overall system scales in direct proportion to the library's complexity and the sophistication of associated software tools.

Trade Modeling Facility

Trade modeling tools are indispensable to an option trader. Many excellent commercially available packages can be used to model the effects of changes in any of the key pricing parameters—volatility, price of the underlying, time left before expiration, and risk-free interest rates. As we have seen, collateral requirements can be significant for positions that contain a naked short component. These requirements can also limit the size or number of trades that can be executed. Therefore, it is important to use a tool that incorporates collateral requirements into trading scenarios.

Generally speaking, the most important characteristic is ease of use. Highly functional modeling software must facilitate rapid construction of a trading scenario and allow the user to step through incremental price and/or volatility changes. It is also important that the modeling facility be integrated with other parts of the software infrastructure that we have been describing. Such integration allows what-if experiments to be performed on large datasets containing historical prices. These experiments are particularly valuable because they allow an investor to build hedging models that protect against adverse market moves. In this regard, a modeling facility must be flexible enough to comprehend volatility trends and different pricing models. As discussed in Chapter 2, the most refined pricing models embody customized three-dimensional maps, sometimes referred to as volatility surfaces, that relate calendar information and underlying price to volatility. A realistic trade-modeling exercise must incorporate such maps so that moves in the underlying and approaching financial events are comprehended in option price calculations.

Table 9.2 contains a set of scenarios similar to those that appear throughout this book. The chart was prepared using modeling software set to calculate prices using standard Black-Scholes methodology. All calculations for this scenario were based on a 5% risk-free rate of interest. The goal was to model a complex four-part trade spanning two expiration dates. We are long the far expiration and short the current month. As always, volatility falls to near zero on the final trading day. The scenarios are separated by gray bars. The first set is the starting point.

The example begins with a delta-neutral position on the short side and a 46/39 call/put delta ratio on the long side. The custom tool used to generate the example calculates the delta-neutral point automatically and sets the starting point. If we had chosen to begin with the long side set at the delta-neutral point, the initial stock price would have been $85.86.

Table 9.2 Scenario modeling for a complex four-part trade spanning two expiration dates.

Type	Stock Price	Strike	Days Remaining	Option Price	Volatility	Delta
Call	87.07	90	10.04	1.41	0.44	0.35
Put	87.07	85	10.04	1.56	0.44	−0.35
Call	87.07	90	45.04	4.21	0.43	0.46
Put	87.07	85	45.04	3.97	0.43	−0.39
Call	88.00	90	1.04	0.00	0.02	0.00
Put	88.00	85	1.04	0.00	0.02	0.00
Call	88.00	90	36.04	4.04	0.43	0.48
Put	88.00	85	36.04	3.14	0.43	−0.36
Call	90.00	90	1.04	0.05	0.02	0.55
Put	90.00	85	1.04	0.00	0.02	0.00
Call	90.00	90	36.04	5.06	0.43	0.54
Put	90.00	85	36.04	2.48	0.43	−0.30
Call	92.00	90	1.04	2.01	0.02	1.00
Put	92.00	85	1.04	0.00	0.02	0.00
Call	92.00	90	36.04	6.21	0.43	0.61
Put	92.00	85	36.04	1.94	0.43	−0.25

Gamma	Vega	Theta	Rho	Contracts	Option Value	Position Value	Total
0.06	0.05	−0.12	0.01	−10	−1410		
0.06	0.05	−0.11	−0.01	−10	−1560	−2970	
0.03	0.12	−0.06	0.04	10	4210		
0.03	0.12	−0.05	−0.05	10	3970	8180	5210
0.00	0.00	0.00	0.00	−10	0		
0.00	0.00	0.00	0.00	−10	0	0	
0.03	0.11	−0.07	0.04	10	4040		
0.03	0.10	−0.06	−0.03	10	3140	7180	7180
4.11	0.02	−0.03	0.00	−10	−50		
0.00	0.00	0.00	0.00	−10	0	−50	
0.03	0.11	−0.07	0.04	10	5060		
0.03	0.10	−0.05	−0.03	10	2480	7540	7490
0.00	0.00	−0.01	0.00	−10	−2010		
0.00	0.00	0.00	0.00	−10	0	−2010	
0.03	0.11	−0.07	0.05	10	6210		
0.03	0.09	−0.05	−0.02	10	1940	8150	6140

Position modeling is a dynamic exercise that is relatively difficult to represent on paper. This example is built around the $85/$90 strike price combination. You would likely build models around other strike price combinations, more dramatic price changes, and different combinations of expiration dates. The possibilities are virtually endless, and some scenarios are more complex to model than others. For example, simulating a series of price changes over a longer time frame would have worked best if we incorporated a more detailed volatility model.

Summary

Fully functional online trading systems have been available to public customers for several years. When they were introduced, a relatively powerful toolset consisted of web-based trading software and commercially available analytical tools. The window has closed, and it is no longer possible to gain an advantage using commercially available online trading and analytical tools. To discover subtle pricing relationships and statistical arbitrages, you need a data infrastructure with associated data-mining and analytical tools that are more sophisticated than those in the public domain.

With these goals in mind, this author has developed a data infrastructure for his own use. This approach is possible because the cost of computing horsepower and storage has declined drastically. In today's environment, a system that would have been described as "high-performance" just a couple of years ago is easily within the reach of a private investor. Large databases, multiprocessing, and clustered systems are all within the reach of private individuals. The playing field is finally close to level. A private investor with some programming skills can gain the kind of analytical advantage that was once the exclusive domain of institutions.

The data infrastructure should be carefully planned so that it can be extended with new analytical capabilities. A complete design typically includes facilities for data mining, statistical analysis, trade modeling, and data visualization. Market data and financial news events are ultimately merged with calculated statistical parameters at the individual security level. This data is assembled into a summary library that can be searched with customized query tools and statistical filters for candidates that fit specific trading strategies. A well-designed system can become a differentiator and a true source of value creation.

Endnotes

1   Reported by Tower Group, Needham, Mass.

2   Mara Der Hovanesian, "Cracking the Street's New Math," *BusinessWeek,* April 18, 2005.

3   CurrencyShares Japanese Yen Trust is a grantor trust that issues Japanese yen shares that represent units of fractional undivided beneficial interest in, and ownership of, the Trust.

INDEX

C

calculations
   Black-Scholes, 82
   Bollinger Bands, 65-67
   historical volatility, 50-60
   intraday volatility, 110-111
   option volatility, 86
   price spike, 63
   VIX, 195-201
   volatility, 17, 50
calendars
   integrity databases, 248-249
   ratio calls, 176
   spreads, 152-162
calls
   covered, 137-143
   diagonal spreads pricing, 153-156
   options, 12
   ratio
      backspread, 167
      calendar spreads, 176
      trades, 164
   reverse calendar spreads, 159
   single-sided put and call
      positions, 100, 103-118
   straddles, 118-136
   strangles, 118-136
CBOE (Chicago Board Options
   Exchange), 5, 23
CBOT (Chicago Board of Trade), 5
Cephalon (CEPH), 62
Chairman of the U.S. Federal
   Reserve, influence of, 3
chaos, operation of price discovery,
   7-9
charts
   data visualization tools, 245-247
   database infrastructure, 248-251

price spike for Apple (APPL), 104
   technical limitations of, 9-12
Chicago Board of Trade (CBOT), 5
Chicago Board Options Exchange
   (CBOE), 5, 23
Chicago Board Options Exchange
   Volatility Index (VIX), 38
closing price, standard deviation
   of, 65
collapse (volatility)
   exploiting, 216-222
   final trading day, 229
collateral requirements, 187
   long/short contracts, 81
combinations, strangles, 118-136
complex positions
   calendar and diagonal spreads,
      152-162
   hedging with the VIX, 195-201
   managing, 151
   multipart trades, 182
      butterfly spreads, 183-186
      condors, 187-195
   multiple expiration dates,
      175-182
   ratio trades, 162-175
condor trades, 187-195
   bid-ask spreads, 79-82
context discovery, 253
continuous stream of transactions,
   creation of market liquidity, 6
contracts
   binomial trees, 42-44
   Bollinger Bands, measuring
      volatility, 65-67
   collateral requirements, 81
   liquidity, affect on, 91-94
covered calls and puts, 137-143
Cox, John, 42